digits™

Homework Helper

Grade 8 Volume 2

Boston, Massachusetts • Chandler, Arizona • Glenview, Illinois • Upper Saddle River, New Jersey

Acknowledgments for Illustrations:
Rory Hensley, David Jackson, Jim Mariano, Rich McMahon, Lorie Park, and Ted Smykal

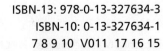

ISBN-13: 978-0-13-327634-3
ISBN-10: 0-13-327634-1
7 8 9 10 V011 17 16 15

Contents

Unit E: Geometry

Authors and Advisors

Francis (Skip) Fennell
digits Author

Approaches to mathematics content and curriculum, educational policy, and support for intervention

Dr. Francis (Skip) Fennell is Professor of Education at McDaniel College, and a senior author with Pearson. He is a past president of the National Council of Teachers of Mathematics (NCTM) and a member of the writing team for the Curriculum Focal Points from the NCTM, which influenced the work of the Common Core Standards Initiative. Skip was also one of the writers of the Principles and Standards for School Mathematics.

Art Johnson
digits Author

Approaches to mathematical content and support for English Language Learners

Art Johnson is a Professor of Mathematics at Boston University who taught in public school for over 30 years. He is part of the author team for Pearson's high school mathematics series. Art is the author of numerous books, including Teaching Mathematics to Culturally and Linguistically Diverse Students published by Allyn & Bacon, Teaching Today's Mathematics in the Middle Grades published by Allyn & Bacon, and Guiding Children's Learning of Mathematics, K–6 published by Wadsworth.

Helene Sherman
digits Author

Teacher education and support for struggling students

Helene Sherman is Associate Dean for Undergraduate Education and Professor of Education in the College of Education at the University of Missouri in St. Louis, MO. Helene is the author of Teaching Learners Who Struggle with Mathematics, published by Merrill.

Stuart J. Murphy
digits Author

Visual learning and student engagement

Stuart J. Murphy is a visual learning specialist and the author of the MathStart series. He contributed to the development of the Visual Learning Bridge in enVisionMATH™ as well as many visual elements of the Prentice Hall Algebra 1, Geometry, and Algebra 2 high school program.

Janie Schielack
digits Author

Approaches to mathematical content, building problem solvers,and support for intervention

Janie Schielack is Professor of Mathematics and Associate Dean for Assessment and PreK–12 Education at Texas A&M University. She chaired the writing committee for the NCTM Curriculum Focal Points and was part of the nine-member NCTM feedback and advisory team that responded to and met with CCSSCO and NGA representatives during the development of various drafts of the Common Core State Standards.

Eric Milou
digits Author

Approaches to mathematical content and the use of technology in middle grades classrooms

Eric Milou is Professor in the Department of Mathematics at Rowan University in Glassboro, NJ. Eric teaches pre-service teachers and works with in-service teachers, and is primarily interested in balancing concept development with skill proficiency. He was part of the nine-member NCTM feedback/advisory team that responded to and met with Council of Chief State School Officers (CCSSCO) and National Governors Association (NGA) representatives during the development of various drafts of the Common Core State Standards. Eric is the author of Teaching Mathematics to Middle School Students, published by Allyn & Bacon.

William F. Tate
digits Author

Approaches to intervention, and use of efficacy and research

William Tate is the Edward Mallinckrodt Distinguished University Professor in Arts & Sciences at Washington University in St. Louis, MO. He is a past president of the American Educational Research Association. His research focuses on the social and psychological determinants of mathematics achievement and attainment as well as the political economy of schooling.

Randall I. Charles
digits Advisor

Dr. Randall I. Charles is Professor Emeritus in the Department of Mathematics at San Jose State University in San Jose, CA, and a senior author with Pearson. Randall served on the writing team for the Curriculum Focal Points from NCTM. The NCTM Curriculum Focal Points served as a key inspiration to the writers of the Common Core Standards in bringing focus, depth, and coherence to the curriculum.

> *Pearson tapped leaders in mathematics education to develop* **digits**. *This esteemed author team—from diverse areas of expertise including mathematical content, Understanding by Design, and Technology Engagement—came together to construct a highly interactive and personalized learning experience.*

Jim Cummins
digits Advisor

Supporting English Language Learners

Dr. Jim Cummins is Professor and Canada Research Chair in the Centre for Educational Research on Languages and Literacies at the University of Toronto. His research focuses on literacy development in multilingual school contexts as well as on the potential roles of technology in promoting language and literacy development.

Grant Wiggins
digits Consulting Author

Understanding by Design

Grant Wiggins is a cross-curricular Pearson consulting author specializing in curricular change. He is the author of Understanding by Design published by ASCD, and the President of Authentic Education in Hopewell, NJ. Over the past 20 years, he has worked on some of the most influential reform initiatives in the country, including Vermont's portfolio system and Ted Sizer's Coalition of Essential Schools.

Jacquie Moen
digits Advisor

Digital Technology

Jacquie Moen is a consultant specializing in how consumers interact with and use digital technologies. Jacquie worked for AOL for 10 years, and most recently was VP & General Manager for AOL's kids and teen online services, reaching over seven million kids every month. Jacquie has worked with a wide range of organizations to develop interactive content and strategies to reach families and children, including National Geographic, PBS, Pearson Education, National Wildlife Foundation, and the National Children's Museum.

Welcome to digits™

Using the Homework Helper

digits is designed to help you master mathematics skills and concepts in a way that's relevant to you. As the title ***digits*** suggests, this program takes a digital approach. ***digits*** is digital, but sometimes you may not be able to access digital resources. When that happens, you can use the Homework Helper because you can refer back to the daily lesson and see all your homework questions right in the book.

Your Homework Helper supports your work on ***digits*** in so many ways!

The lesson pages capture important elements of the digital lesson that you need to know in order to do your homework.

9-1 | Translations

Vocabulary
image, rigid motion, transformation, translation

CCSS: 8.G.A.1, 8.G.A.1a, 8.G.A.1b, 8.G.A.1c, 8.G.A.3

Key Concept

A **transformation** is a change in the position, shape, or size of a figure. The blue triangle is larger and is in a different position than the black triangle.

A **rigid motion** is a transformation that changes only the position of the figure. The blue triangle has the same shape and size as the black triangle, but a different position.

An **image** is the result of a transformation of a figure. To identify the image of a point, use prime notation. The image of point A is A' (read "A prime").

Part 1

Intro

A **translation**, or slide, is a rigid motion that moves every point of a figure the same distance and in the same direction.

Every point of the black triangle moves 5 units to the right and 5 units down.

Example Recognizing and Describing Translations

Find the transformation that is a translation. Describe in words the translation that maps △ABC to its image △A'B'C'.

continued on next page >

Part 1

Example continued

Point A moves 3 units left and 1 unit down.

Point B moves 3 units left and 1 unit down.

Point C moves 3 units left and 1 unit down.

s the image of △ABC after a translation of 3 units left down.

e image of △ABC after a translation of and 3 units down. rrow notation to show how each vertex s to its image after the translation.
(−2, −2)
, 0)
, −3)

aphing Translations of Figures
ABC are A(1, 4), B(−1, 2), and C(3, −2). Graph △ABC and e after a translation of 5 units left and 1 unit down. Then n to show how each vertex of △ABC maps to its image.

continued on next page >

Every lesson in your Homework Helper also includes two pages of homework. The combination of homework exercises includes problems that focus on reasoning, multiple representations, mental math, writing, and error analysis. They vary in difficulty level from thinking about a plan to challenging. The problems come in different formats, like multiple choice, short answer, and open response, to help you prepare for tests.

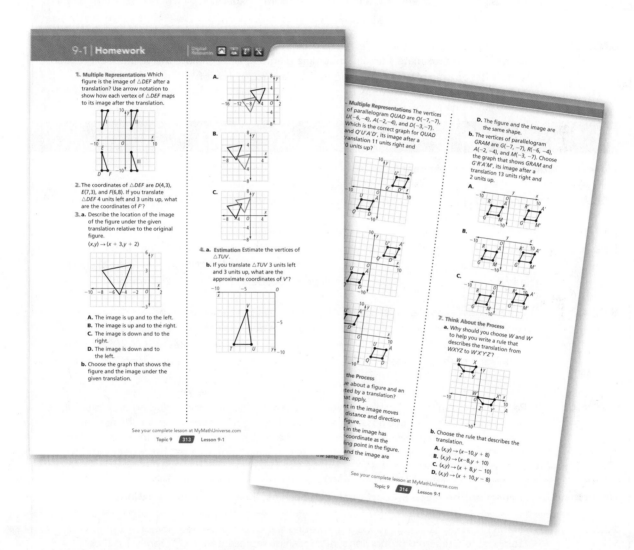

Grade 8 | Common Core State Standards

Number	Standard for Mathematical Content

8.NS   The Number System

Know that there are numbers that are not rational, and approximate them by rational numbers.

8.NS.A.1	Know that numbers that are not rational are called irrational. Understand informally that every number has a decimal expansion; for rational numbers show that the decimal expansion repeats eventually, and convert a decimal expansion which repeats eventually into a rational number.
8.NS.A.2	Use rational approximations of irrational numbers to compare the size of irrational numbers, locate them approximately on a number line diagram, and estimate the value of expressions (e.g., π^2). For example, by truncating the decimal expansion of $\sqrt{2}$, show that $\sqrt{2}$ is between 1 and 2, then between 1.4 and 1.5, and explain how to continue on to get better approximations.

8.EE   Expressions and Equations

Work with radicals and integer exponents.

8.EE.A.1	Know and apply the properties of integer exponents to generate equivalent numerical expressions. For example, $3^2 \times 3^{(-5)} = 3^{(-3)} = \frac{1}{(3^3)} = \frac{1}{27}$.
8.EE.A.2	Use square root and cube root symbols to represent solutions to equations of the form $x^2 = p$ and $x^3 = p$, where p is a positive rational number. Evaluate square roots of small perfect squares and cube roots of small perfect cubes. Know that $\sqrt{2}$ is irrational.
8.EE.A.3	Use numbers expressed in the form of a single digit times an integer power of 10 to estimate very large or very small quantities, and to express how many times as much one is than the other. For example, estimate the population of the United States as 3×10^8 and the population of the world as 7×10^9, and determine that the world population is more than 20 times larger.
8.EE.A.4	Perform operations with numbers expressed in scientific notation, including problems where both decimal and scientific notation are used. Use scientific notation and choose units of appropriate size for measurements of very large or very small quantities (e.g., use millimeters per year for seafloor spreading). Interpret scientific notation that has been generated by technology.

Understand the connections between proportional relationships, lines, and linear equations.

8.EE.B.5	Graph proportional relationships, interpreting the unit rate as the slope of the graph. Compare two different proportional relationships represented in different ways. For example, compare a distance-time graph to a distance-time equation to determine which of two moving objects has greater speed.
8.EE.B.6	Use similar triangles to explain why the slope m is the same between any two distinct points on a non-vertical line in the coordinate plane; derive the equation $y = mx$ for a line through the origin and the equation $y = mx + b$ for a line intercepting the vertical axis at b.

Number	Standard for Mathematical Content

8.EE   Expressions and Equations (continued)

Analyze and solve linear equations and pairs of simultaneous linear equations.

8.EE.C.7	Solve linear equations in one variable.
8.EE.C.7a	Give examples of linear equations in one variable with one solution, infinitely many solutions, or no solutions. Show which of these possibilities is the case by successively transforming the given equation into simpler forms, until an equivalent equation of the form $x = a$, $a = a$, or $a = b$ results (where a and b are different numbers).
8.EE.C.7b	Solve linear equations with rational number coefficients, including equations whose solutions require expanding expressions using the distributive property and collecting like terms.
8.EE.C.8	Analyze and solve pairs of simultaneous linear equations.
8.EE.C.8a	Understand that solutions to a system of two linear equations in two variables correspond to points of intersection of their graphs, because points of intersection satisfy both equations simultaneously.
8.EE.C.8b	Solve systems of two linear equations in two variables algebraically, and estimate solutions by graphing the equations. Solve simple cases by inspection. For example, $3x + 2y = 5$ and $3x + 2y = 6$ have no solution because $3x + 2y$ cannot simultaneously be 5 and 6.
8.EE.C.8c	Solve real-world and mathematical problems leading to two linear equations in two variables. For example, given coordinates for two pairs of points, determine whether the line through the first pair of points intersects the line through the second pair.

8.F   Functions

Define, evaluate, and compare functions.

8.F.A.1	Understand that a function is a rule that assigns to each input exactly one output. The graph of a function is the set of ordered pairs consisting of an input and the corresponding output.
8.F.A.2	Compare properties of two functions each represented in a different way (algebraically, graphically, numerically in tables, or by verbal descriptions). For example, given a linear function represented by a table of values and a linear function represented by an algebraic expression, determine which function has the greater rate of change.
8.F.A.3	Interpret the equation $y = mx + b$ as defining a linear function, whose graph is a straight line; give examples of functions that are not linear. For example, the function $A = s^2$ giving the area of a square as a function of its side length is not linear because its graph contains the points (1,1), (2,4) and (3,9), which are not on a straight line.

Use functions to model relationships between quantities.

8.F.B.4	Construct a function to model a linear relationship between two quantities. Determine the rate of change and initial value of the function from a description of a relationship or from two (x, y) values, including reading these from a table or from a graph. Interpret the rate of change and initial value of a linear function in terms of the situation it models, and in terms of its graph or a table of values.
8.F.B.5	Describe qualitatively the functional relationship between two quantities by analyzing a graph (e.g., where the function is increasing or decreasing, linear or nonlinear). Sketch a graph that exhibits the qualitative features of a function that has been described verbally.

Grade 8 Common Core State Standards *continued*

Number	Standard for Mathematical Content
8.G Geometry	
Understand congruence and similarity using physical models, transparencies, or geometry software.	
8.G.A.1	Verify experimentally the properties of rotations, reflections, and translations:
8.G.A.1a	Verify experimentally the properties of rotations, reflections, and translations: Lines are taken to lines, and line segments to line segments of the same length.
8.G.A.1b	Verify experimentally the properties of rotations, reflections, and translations: Angles are taken to angles of the same measure.
8.G.A.1c	Verify experimentally the properties of rotations, reflections, and translations: Parallel lines are taken to parallel lines.
8.G.A.2	Understand that a two-dimensional figure is congruent to another if the second can be obtained from the first by a sequence of rotations, reflections, and translations; given two congruent figures, describe a sequence that exhibits the congruence between them.
8.G.A.3	Describe the effect of dilations, translations, rotations, and reflections on two-dimensional figures using coordinates.
8.G.A.4	Understand that a two-dimensional figure is similar to another if the second can be obtained from the first by a sequence of rotations, reflections, translations, and dilations; given two similar two- dimensional figures, describe a sequence that exhibits the similarity between them.
8.G.A.5	Use informal arguments to establish facts about the angle sum and exterior angle of triangles, about the angles created when parallel lines are cut by a transversal, and the angle-angle criterion for similarity of triangles.
Understand and apply the Pythagorean Theorem.	
8.G.B.6	Explain a proof of the Pythagorean Theorem and its converse.
8.G.B.7	Apply the Pythagorean Theorem to determine unknown side lengths in right triangles in real-world and mathematical problems in two and three dimensions.
8.G.B.8	Apply the Pythagorean Theorem to find the distance between two points in a coordinate system.
Solve real-world and mathematical problems involving volume of cylinders, cones, and spheres.	
8.G.C.9	Know the formulas for the volumes of cones, cylinders, and spheres and use them to solve real-world and mathematical problems.

Number	Standard for Mathematical Content

8.SP Statistics and Probability

Investigate patterns of association in bivariate data.

Number	
8.SP.A.1	Construct and interpret scatter plots for bivariate measurement data to investigate patterns of association between two quantities. Describe patterns such as clustering, outliers, positive or negative association, linear association, and nonlinear association.
8.SP.A.2	Know that straight lines are widely used to model relationships between two quantitative variables. For scatter plots that suggest a linear association, informally fit a straight line, and informally assess the model fit by judging the closeness of the data points to the line.
8.SP.A.3	Use the equation of a linear model to solve problems in the context of bivariate measurement data, interpreting the slope and intercept.
8.SP.A.4	Understand that patterns of association can also be seen in bivariate categorical data by displaying frequencies and relative frequencies in a two-way table. Construct and interpret a two-way table summarizing data on two categorical variables collected from the same subjects. Use relative frequencies calculated for rows or columns to describe possible association between the two variables.

Number	Standard for Mathematical Practice
MP1	Make sense of problems and persevere in solving them.
MP2	Reason abstractly and quantitatively.
MP3	Construct viable arguments and critique the reasoning of others.
MP4	Model with mathematics.
MP5	Use appropriate tools strategically.
MP6	Attend to precision.
MP7	Look for and make use of structure.
MP8	Look for and express regularity in repeated reasoning.

| **Translations**

Vocabulary
image, rigid motion, transformation, translation

CCSS: 8.G.A.1, 8.G.A.1a, 8.G.A.1b, 8.G.A.1c, 8.G.A.3

Key Concept

A **transformation** is a change in the position, shape, or size of a figure. The blue triangle is larger and is in a different position than the black triangle.

A **rigid motion** is a transformation that changes only the position of the figure. The blue triangle has the same shape and size as the black triangle, but a different position.

An **image** is the result of a transformation of a figure. To identify the image of a point, use prime notation. The image of point A is A' (read "A prime").

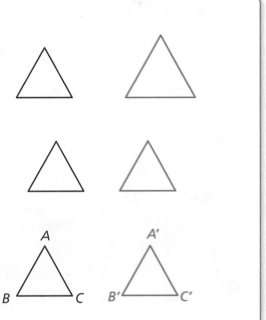

Part 1

Intro

A **translation**, or slide, is a rigid motion that moves every point of a figure the same distance and in the same direction.

Every point of the black triangle moves 5 units to the right and 5 units down.

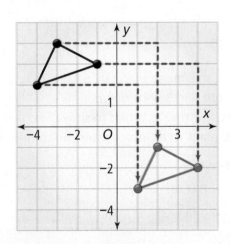

Example Recognizing and Describing Translations

Find the transformation that is a translation. Describe in words the translation that maps △ABC to its image △A'B'C'.

continued on next page >

Example continued

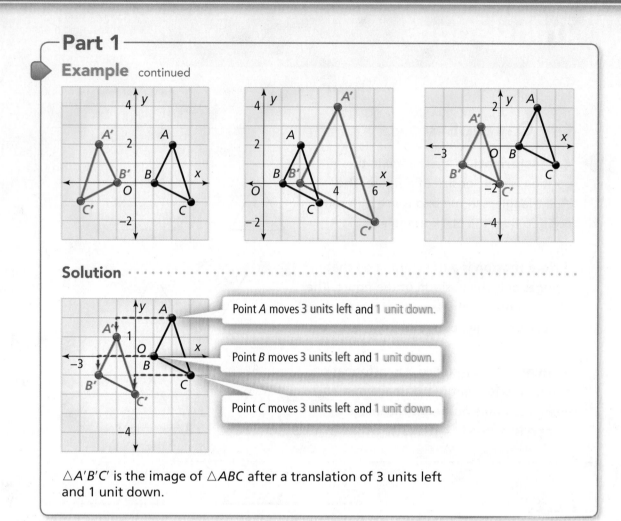

Solution

Point A moves 3 units left and 1 unit down.

Point B moves 3 units left and 1 unit down.

Point C moves 3 units left and 1 unit down.

△A'B'C' is the image of △ABC after a translation of 3 units left and 1 unit down.

Part 2

Intro

△A'B'C' is the image of △ABC after a translation of 2 units right and 3 units down.

You can use arrow notation to show how each vertex of △ABC maps to its image after the translation.

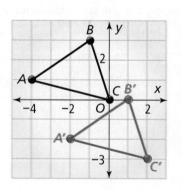

$A(-4, 1) \rightarrow A'(-2, -2)$

$B(-1, 3) \rightarrow B'(1, 0)$

$C(0, 0) \rightarrow C'(2, -3)$

Example Graphing Translations of Figures

The vertices of △ABC are A(1, 4), B(−1, 2), and C(3, −2). Graph △ABC and △A'B'C', its image after a translation of 5 units left and 1 unit down. Then use arrow notation to show how each vertex of △ABC maps to its image.

continued on next page >

Part 2

Example continued

Solution ·

Step 1 Graph △ABC. Plot each point. Then connect the points.

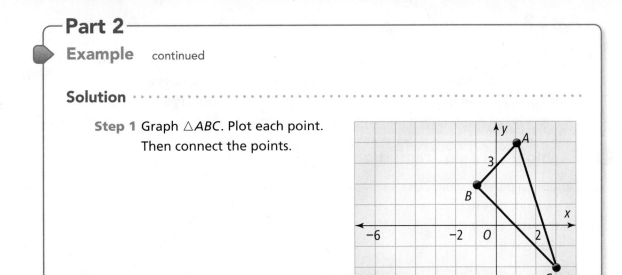

Step 2 Translate each vertex 5 units left and 1 unit down.

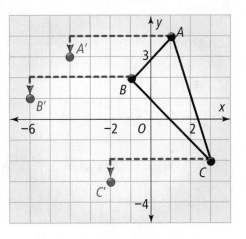

Step 3 Draw △A′B′C′.

$A(1, 4) \rightarrow A'(-4, -3)$

$B(-1, 2) \rightarrow B'(-6, 1)$

$C(3, -2) \rightarrow C'(-2, -3)$

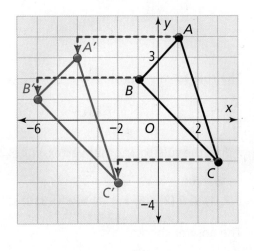

Part 3

Intro

You can also use arrow notation to write a general rule that describes a translation. For example, $(x, y) \rightarrow (x + 4, y - 2)$ shows the ordered pair (x, y) and describes a translation 4 units right and 2 units down.

Example Writing Translation Rules Using Arrow Notation

ABCD is a parallelogram. Use arrow notation to write a rule that describes the translation of *ABCD* to *A'B'C'D'*.

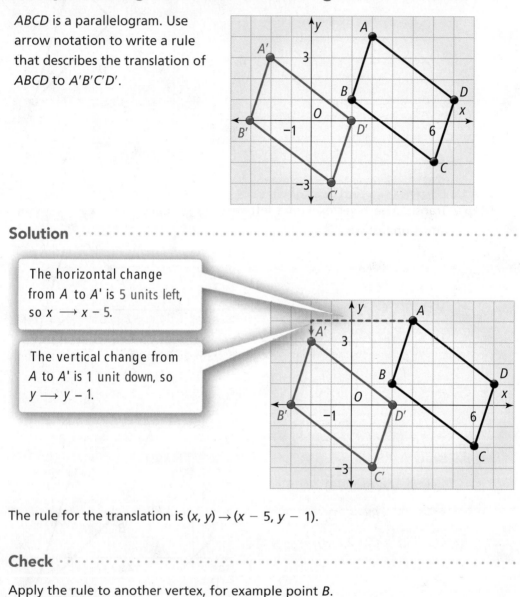

Solution

The horizontal change from *A* to *A'* is 5 units left, so $x \longrightarrow x - 5$.

The vertical change from *A* to *A'* is 1 unit down, so $y \longrightarrow y - 1$.

The rule for the translation is $(x, y) \rightarrow (x - 5, y - 1)$.

Check

Apply the rule to another vertex, for example point *B*.

$(x, y) \rightarrow (x - 5, y - 1)$
$B(2, 1) \rightarrow B'(2 - 5, 1 - 1) = B'(-3, 0)$ ✔

The answer checks.

1. **Multiple Representations** Which figure is the image of △DEF after a translation? Use arrow notation to show how each vertex of △DEF maps to its image after the translation.

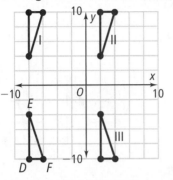

2. The coordinates of △DEF are D(4,3), E(7,3), and F(6,8). If you translate △DEF 4 units left and 3 units up, what are the coordinates of F'?

3. **a.** Describe the location of the image of the figure under the given translation relative to the original figure.

$(x,y) \rightarrow (x + 3, y + 2)$

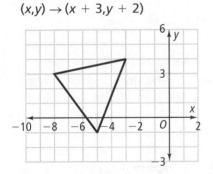

   A. The image is up and to the left.

   B. The image is up and to the right.

   C. The image is down and to the right.

   D. The image is down and to the left.

   b. Choose the graph that shows the figure and the image under the given translation.

A.

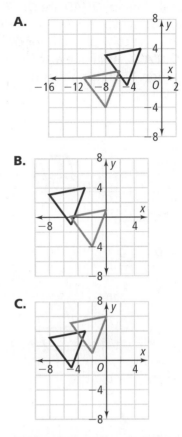

B.

C.

4. **a.** **Estimation** Estimate the vertices of △TUV.

   b. If you translate △TUV 3 units left and 3 units up, what are the approximate coordinates of V'?

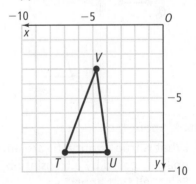

5. Multiple Representations The vertices of parallelogram *QUAD* are *Q*(−7,−7), *U*(−6,−4), *A*(−2,−4), and *D*(−3,−7). Which is the correct graph for *QUAD* and *Q′U′A′D′*, its image after a translation 11 units right and 10 units up?

A.

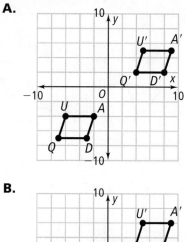

B.

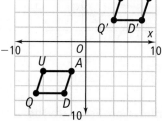

C.

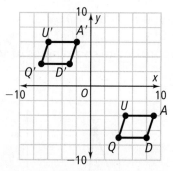

6. Think About the Process

a. What is true about a figure and an image created by a translation? Select all that apply.

A. Each point in the image moves the same distance and direction from the figure.

B. Each point in the image has the same *x*-coordinate as the corresponding point in the figure.

C. The figure and the image are the same size.

D. The figure and the image are the same shape.

b. The vertices of parallelogram *GRAM* are *G*(−7, −7), *R*(−6, −4), *A*(−2, −4), and *M*(−3, −7). Choose the graph that shows *GRAM* and *G′R′A′M′*, its image after a translation 13 units right and 2 units up.

A.

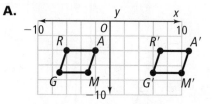

B.

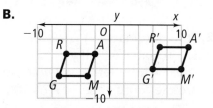

C.

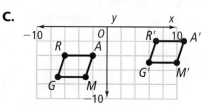

7. Think About the Process

a. Why should you choose *W* and *W′* to help you write a rule that describes the translation from *WXYZ* to *W′X′Y′Z′*?

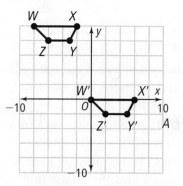

b. Choose the rule that describes the translation.

A. $(x,y) \rightarrow (x-10, y + 8)$

B. $(x,y) \rightarrow (x-8, y + 10)$

C. $(x,y) \rightarrow (x + 8, y - 10)$

D. $(x,y) \rightarrow (x + 10, y - 8)$

Reflections

Vocabulary
line of reflection, reflection

CCSS: 8.G.A.1, 8.G.A.1a, 8.G.A.1b, 8.G.A.1c, 8.G.A.3

Key Concept

A **reflection**, or flip, is a rigid motion that flips a figure over a line called the **line of reflection.**

If a point A is on the line of reflection, then its image A' is itself (A' = A).

If a point B is not on the line of reflection, then B and B' are on opposite sides of the line of reflection. They are on a line perpendicular to the line of reflection, and are the same distance from the line of reflection.

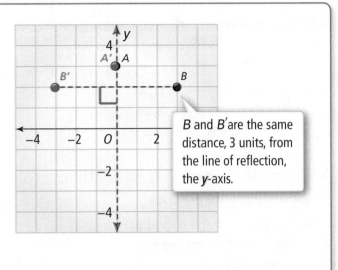

B and B' are the same distance, 3 units, from the line of reflection, the y-axis.

Part 1

Example Recognizing Reflections

Determine which transformation is a reflection.

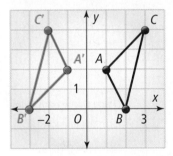 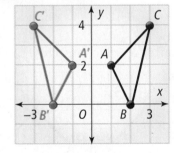 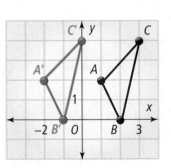

Solution

The second transformation is a reflection across the y-axis.

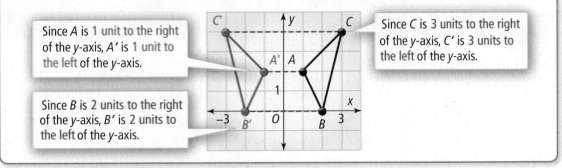

Since A is 1 unit to the right of the y-axis, A' is 1 unit to the left of the y-axis.

Since B is 2 units to the right of the y-axis, B' is 2 units to the left of the y-axis.

Since C is 3 units to the right of the y-axis, C' is 3 units to the left of the y-axis.

See your complete lesson at MyMathUniverse.com

Part 2

Intro

△$A'B'C'$ is the image of △ABC after a reflection across the y-axis.

You can use arrow notation to show how each vertex of △ABC maps to its image after the reflection.

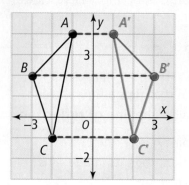

$$A(-1, 4) \longrightarrow A'(1, 4)$$
$$B(-3, 2) \longrightarrow B'(3, 2)$$
$$C(-2, -1) \longrightarrow C'(2, -1)$$

Example   Describing Reflections

$PQRS$ is a rectangle. Describe in words how to map $PQRS$ to its image $P'Q'R'S'$. Then use arrow notation to show how each vertex of $PQRS$ maps to its image.

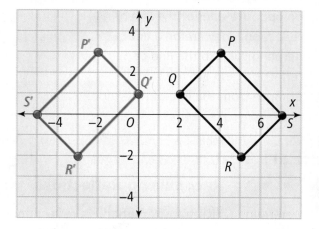

Solution

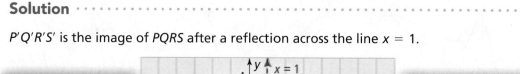

$P'Q'R'S'$ is the image of $PQRS$ after a reflection across the line $x = 1$.

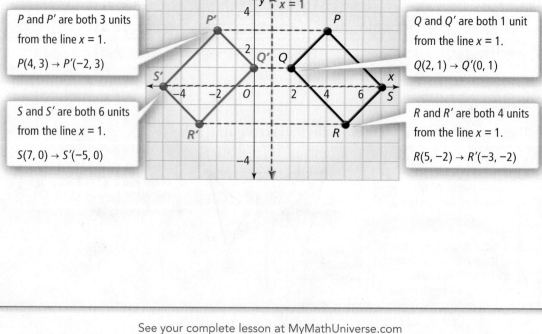

P and P' are both 3 units from the line $x = 1$.

$P(4, 3) \rightarrow P'(-2, 3)$

Q and Q' are both 1 unit from the line $x = 1$.

$Q(2, 1) \rightarrow Q'(0, 1)$

S and S' are both 6 units from the line $x = 1$.

$S(7, 0) \rightarrow S'(-5, 0)$

R and R' are both 4 units from the line $x = 1$.

$R(5, -2) \rightarrow R'(-3, -2)$

Part 3

Example Graphing Reflections

The vertices of △*ABC* are *A*(1, 3), *B*(−2, 4), and *C*(−1, 1). Graph △*ABC* and △*A'B'C'*, its image after a reflection across the *x*-axis.

Solution ·

Step 1 Graph △*ABC*. Show the *x*-axis as the line of reflection.

A(1, 3)
B(−2, 4)
C(−1, 1)

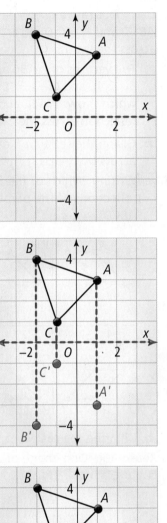

Step 2 Find the image points *A'*, *B'*, and *C'*.

Since *A* is 3 units above the *x*-axis, *A'* is 3 units below the *x*-axis.

Since *B* is 4 units above the *x*-axis, *B'* is 4 units below the *x*-axis.

Since *C* is 1 unit above the *x*-axis, *C'* is 1 unit below the *x*-axis.

Step 3 Draw △*A'B'C'*.

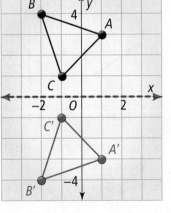

1. The vertices of △ABC are A(−5,4), B(−2,4), and C(−4,2). If △ABC is reflected across the y-axis to produce the image △A′B′C′, find the coordinates of the vertex C′.

2. The vertices of trapezoid ABCD are A(2,−2), B(6,−2), C(8,−7), and D(1,−7). Draw a graph which shows ABCD and A′B′C′D′ after a reflection across the y-axis.

3. **a.** The vertices of △ABC are A(−5,5), B(−2,4), and C(−2,3). Draw a graph which shows △ABC and its reflection across the x-axis, △A′B′C′.

   b. Graph the reflection of △A′B′C′ across the y-axis.

4. **a. Writing** Which of the figures are reflections of the parallelogram ABCD?

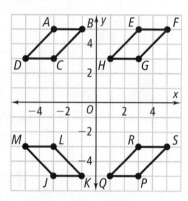

   b. Describe the reflections in words.

5. **Reasoning** One image of △ABC is A′B′C′.

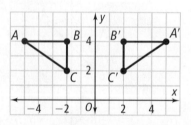

   a. How do the x-coordinates of the vertices change?

   b. How do the y-coordinates of the vertices change?

   c. What type of reflection is the image △A′B′C′?

6. **Think About the Process**

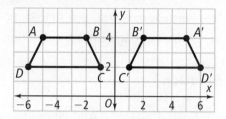

   a. What is true about a figure and an image created by a reflection? Select all that apply.

   A. They are the same size.

   B. The figure and the image are the same shape.

   C. Each point on the image has the same x-coordinate as the corresponding point in the figure.

   D. Each point on the image moves the same distance and direction from the figure.

   b. One image of ABCD is A′B′C′D′. What type of reflection is the image A′B′C′D′?

7. **Error Analysis** Your friend incorrectly says that the reflection of △EFG to its image △E′F′G′ is a reflection across the x-axis.

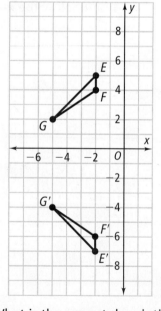

   a. What is the correct description of the reflection?

   b. What is your friend's mistake?

8. Think About the Process

   a. Given points $J(4,5)$, $A(6,4)$, and $R(5,2)$, graph $\triangle JAR$ and its image after a reflection across the line $x = 1$.

   b. What effect does a reflection have on a figure?

9. Kite Making You fold a large piece of cardboard in half to make a kite. The vertices of $\triangle ABC$ are $A(0,5)$, $B(6,-1)$, and $C(0,-4)$. Draw a graph which shows $\triangle ABC$ and $\triangle A'B'C'$ after a reflection across the y-axis.

10. Mental Math The rectangle $ABCD$ is reflected across the y-axis. What are the coordinates of the vertex D'?

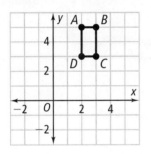

11. Show how each vertex of $\triangle EFG$ maps to its image.

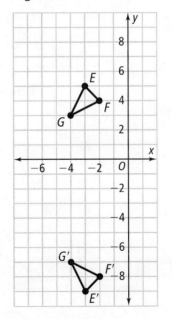

a. Complete the table with the coordinates of the image points E', F', and G'.

△EFG		△E'F'G'	
E	$(-3, 5)$	E'	
F	$(-2, 4)$	F'	
G	$(-4, 3)$	G'	

b. Write a statement which describes the reflection?

12. The vertices of $\triangle ABC$ are $A(-5,5)$, $B(-2,5)$, and $C(-2,3)$. If $\triangle ABC$ is reflected across the line $y = -1$ to produces the image $\triangle A'B'C'$, find the coordinates of the vertex C'.

13. a. Challenge What reflection of the parallelogram $ABCD$ results in the image $A'B'C'D'$?

   b. Is the image unique using only one reflection? Is the image unique using one reflection and one translation?

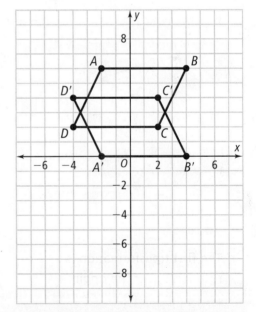

14. Challenge The vertices of $\triangle ABC$ are $A(-5,5)$, $B(-2,4)$, and $C(-4,2)$. $\triangle ABC$ is reflected across the y-axis and then reflected across the x-axis to produce the image $\triangle A''B''C''$. What is a graph that shows $\triangle ABC$ and $\triangle A''B''C''$?

Vocabulary
angle of rotation,
center of rotation,
rotation

CCSS: 8.G.A.1, 8.G.A.1a, 8.G.A.1b, 8.G.A.1c, 8.G.A.3

Key Concept

A **rotation** is a rigid motion that turns a figure about a fixed point called the **center of rotation**. The **angle of rotation** is the number of degrees the figure rotates. A positive angle of rotation turns the figure counterclockwise.

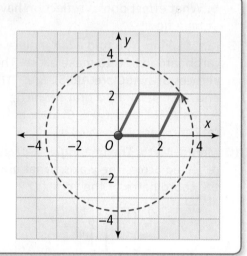

Part 1

Example Recognizing Rotations

Identify which transformation is a rotation.

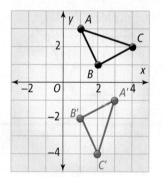 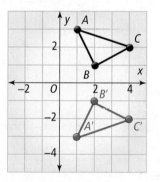 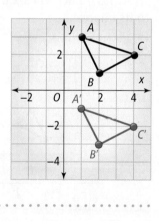

Solution

The first transformation is a rotation about the origin.

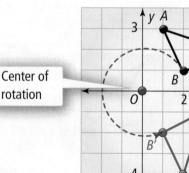

Center of rotation

Part 2

Intro

You can use a protractor to find an angle of rotation.

Suppose you have point *P*. You rotate point *P* about a center of rotation *O*.

The angle of rotation is 135°.

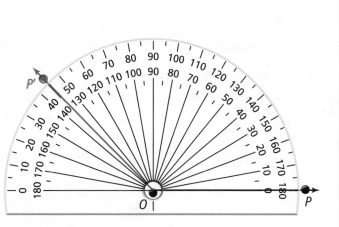

Example Finding Angles of Rotation

What is the angle of rotation about the origin that maps △*ABC* to △*A'B'C'*?

Solution

Draw and measure ∠*AOA'*.

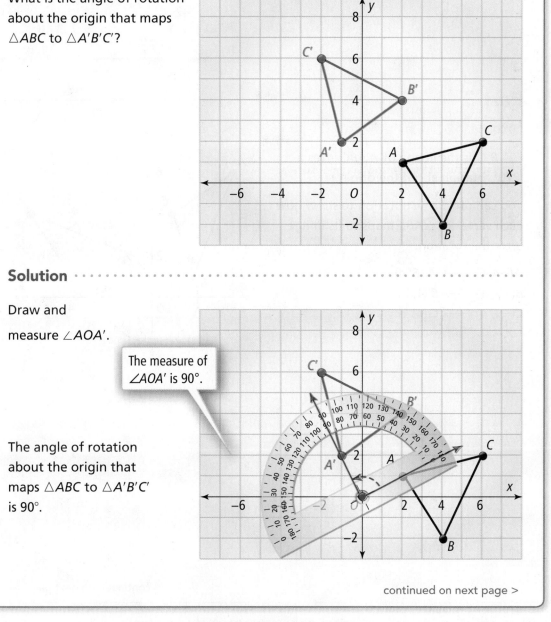

The measure of ∠*AOA'* is 90°.

The angle of rotation about the origin that maps △*ABC* to △*A'B'C'* is 90°.

continued on next page >

Part 2

Solution continued

Draw and measure ∠BOB'.

The measure of ∠BOB' equals the measure of ∠AOA'.

The answer checks. ✔

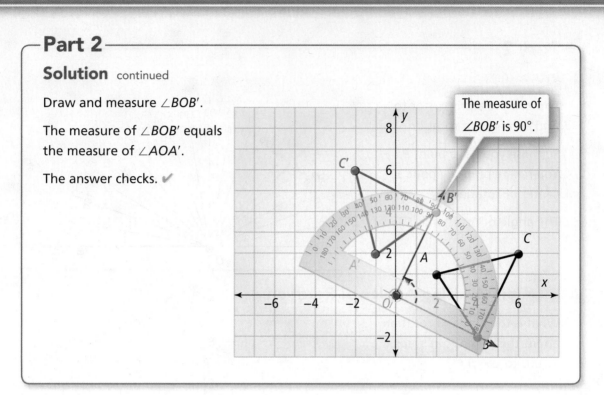

The measure of ∠BOB' is 90°.

Part 3

Intro

△A'B'C' is the image of △ABC after a 270° rotation about the origin.

You can use arrow notation to show how each vertex of △ABC maps to its image after the rotation.

A(−4, 6) ⟶ A'(6, 4)
B(−2, 1) ⟶ B'(1, 2)
C(−1, 4) ⟶ C'(4, 1)

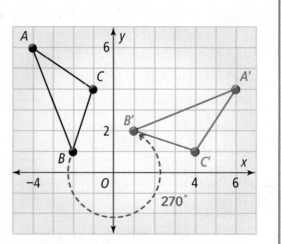

continued on next page >

Part 3

Example Graphing Rotations

Rectangle *ABCD* has coordinates *A*(1, 2), *B*(1, 0), *C*(5, 0), and *D*(5, 2).

- Show the image of *ABCD* after a rotation of 90° about the origin.
- Label the vertices of the image.
- Use arrow notation to show how each vertex of *ABCD* maps to its image.

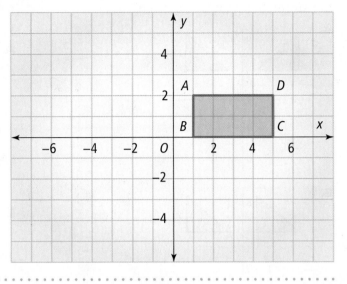

Solution

The blue rectangle *A'B'C'D'* is the image of *ABCD* after a rotation of 90° about the origin.

$A(1, 2) \longrightarrow A'(-2, 1)$
$B(1, 0) \longrightarrow B'(0, 1)$
$C(5, 0) \longrightarrow C'(0, 5)$
$D(5, 2) \longrightarrow D'(-2, 5)$

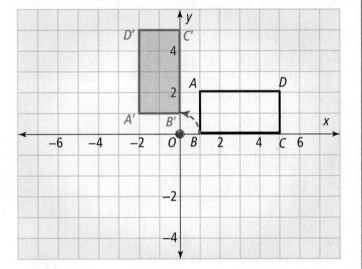

1. Which of these graphs shows a
   transformation that is a rotation?

   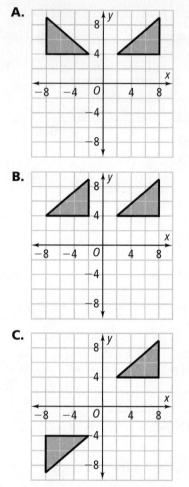

   A.

   B.

   C.

2. Point *P* has coordinates (2,6). If you
   rotate *P* 90° about the origin, (0,0),
   what are the coordinates of *P'*?

   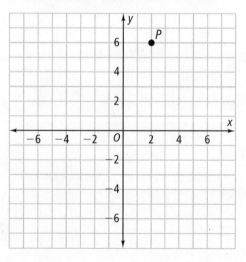

3. **a.** Which of these graphs shows a
   rotation of △*PQR* about the origin,
   (0,0)?

   A.

   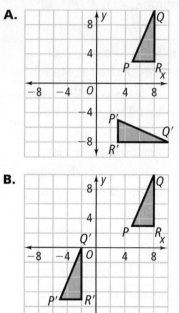

   B.

   C.

   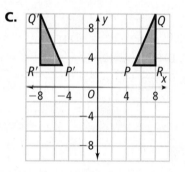

   b. For each graph that does not show
   a rotation of △*PQR* about the
   origin, (0,0), describe what
   transformation the graph does
   show.

4. a. Reasoning What is the angle of rotation about the origin, (0,0), that maps △*TRI* to △*T'R'I'*?

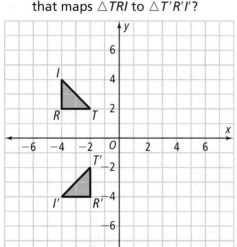

A. 90°   **B.** 180°

C. 360°   **D.** 270°

b. Explain why any rotation can be described by an angle between 0° and 360°.

5. Windmill An architect is designing a new windmill with four sails. In her sketch, the sails' center of rotation is the origin, (0,0), and the tip of one of the sails, point *Q*, has coordinates (2,−3). She wants to make another sketch that shows the windmill after the sails have rotated 270° about their center of rotation. What would be the coordinates of *Q'*?

6. Rotate rectangle *KLMN* 270° about the origin, (0,0), where the vertices of rectangle *KLMN* are *K*(−3,2), *L*(−5,2), *M*(−5,4), and *N*(−3,4).

7. a. Point *Q* has coordinates (4,6). If you rotate *Q* 90° about the origin, (0,0), what are the coordinates of *Q'*?

b. How could you rotate *Q'* to get back to *Q*?

c. Give two other ways to rotate *Q* to get to *Q'*.

8. Think About the Process You want to find the angle of rotation about the origin, (0,0), that maps △*TRI* to △*T'R'I'*.

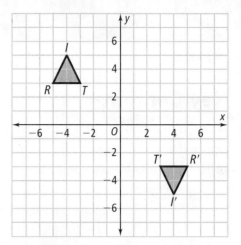

a. Draw a graph which shows an angle you could measure to find the angle of rotation about the origin, (0,0).

b. What is the angle of rotation about the origin, (0,0)?

A. 90°   **B.** 360°

C. 270°   **D.** 180°

9. a. Challenge Select each angle of rotation about the origin, (0,0), that maps *WXYZ* to *W'X'Y'Z'*.

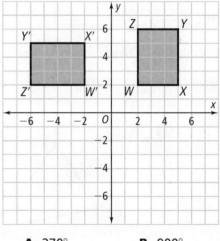

A. 270°   **B.** 900°

C. 360°   **D.** 1,080°

E. 630°   **F.** 180°

G. 90°   **H.** 720°

I. 810°   **J.** 540°

K. 450°   **L.** 990°

b. Does a negative angle of rotation make sense? If so, find three negative angles of rotation about the origin, (0,0), that map *WXYZ* to *W'X'Y'Z'*. If not, explain why not.

CCSS: 8.G.A.2

Key Concept

A two-dimensional figure is **congruent** to another two-dimensional figure if you can map one figure to the other by a sequence of rotations, reflections, and translations. The symbol ≅ means "is congruent to."

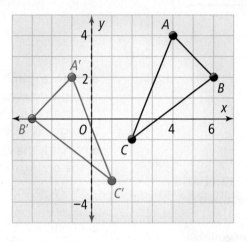

Part 1

Example Describing Sequences of Translations

Given △ABC ≅ △A'B'C', describe a sequence of rigid motions that maps △ABC to △A'B'C'.

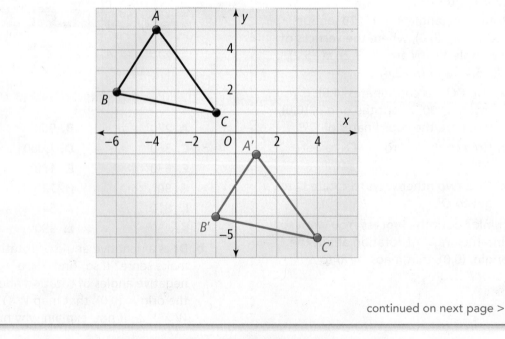

continued on next page >

See your complete lesson at MyMathUniverse.com

Part 1

Example continued

Solution

Method 1 Use a sequence of two translations. First, translate △ABC to the right 5 units. Then translate the triangle down 6 units. A translation of 5 units right followed by a translation of 6 units down maps △ABC to △A'B'C'.

Method 2 Use a single translation. A single translation of 5 units right and 6 units down maps △ABC to △A'B'C'.

Part 2

Example Describing Sequences of Rigid Motions

ABCD is a rectangle. Given ABCD ≅ A'B'C'D', describe a sequence of rigid motions that maps ABCD to A'B'C'D'.

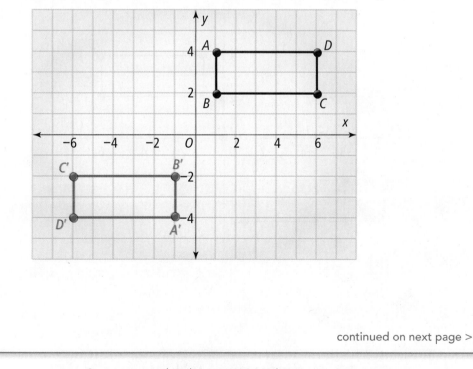

continued on next page >

Solution ·

Method 1 Use two reflections.

First, reflect *ABCD* across the *y*-axis. Then reflect the image across the *x*-axis.

A reflection across the *y*-axis followed by a reflection across the *x*-axis maps *ABCD* to *A'B'C'D'*.

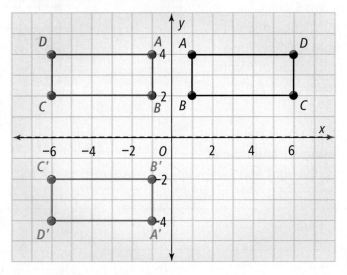

Method 2 Use a single rotation.

A single rotation of 180° about the origin maps *ABCD* to *A'B'C'D'*.

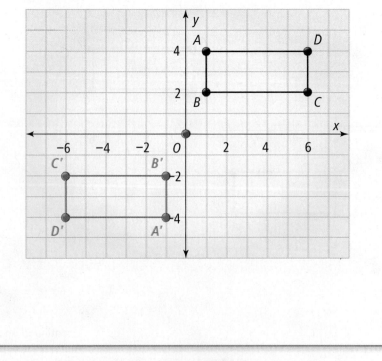

Part 3

Intro

Trapezoid $ABCD \cong$ Trapezoid $EFGH$

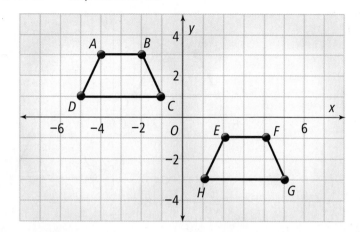

Effects on Line Segments Line segments are taken to line segments of the same length.

$\overline{AB} \to \overline{EF}$, so $\overline{AB} \cong \overline{EF}$

$\overline{BC} \to \overline{FG}$, so $\overline{BC} \cong \overline{FG}$

$\overline{DC} \to \overline{HG}$, so $\overline{DC} \cong \overline{HG}$

$\overline{AD} \to \overline{EH}$, so $\overline{AD} \cong \overline{EH}$

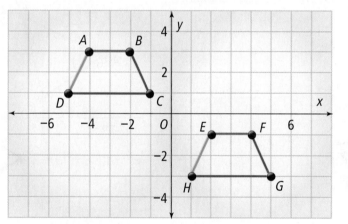

Effects on Angles Angles are taken to angles of the same measure.

$\angle A \to \angle E$, so $\angle A \cong \angle E$

$\angle B \to \angle F$, so $\angle B \cong \angle F$

$\angle C \to \angle G$, so $\angle C \cong \angle G$

$\angle D \to \angle H$, so $\angle D \cong \angle H$

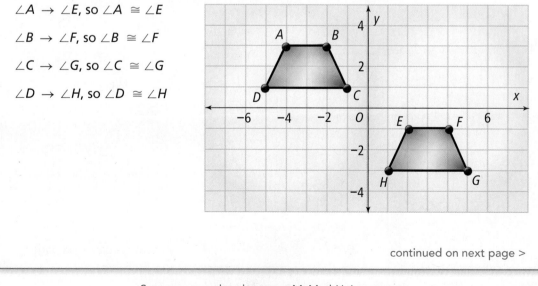

continued on next page >

Part 3

Intro continued

Effects on Parallel Lines Parallel lines are taken to parallel lines.

$AB \parallel CD \rightarrow EF \parallel HG$

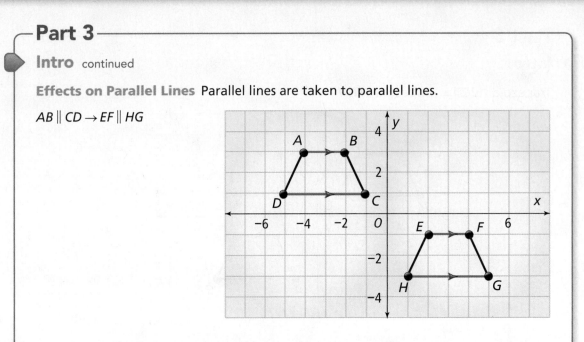

Example Determining If Figures are Congruent

Is $\triangle JAR \cong \triangle LID$? Explain.

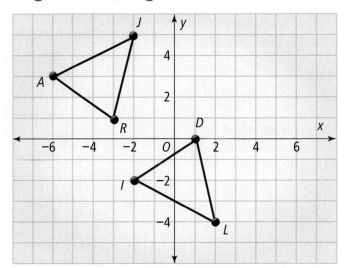

continued on next page >

Example continued

Solution ·

First, translate △*JAR* right
4 units and down 1 unit.

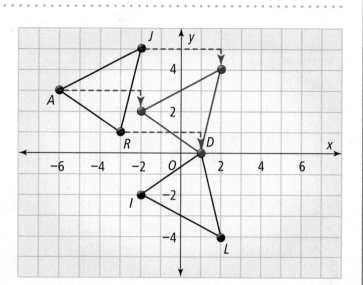

Next, reflect the image across
the *x*-axis.

A translation of 4 units to
the right and 1 unit down,
followed by a reflection
across the *x*-axis, maps △*JAR*
to △*LID*. So △*JAR* is congruent
to △*LID*.

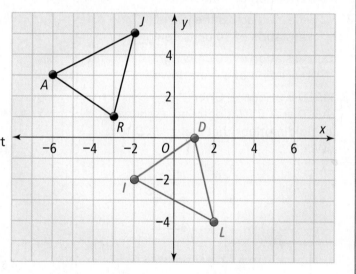

1. Given △QRS ≅ △Q'R'S', describe a pair of rigid motions that maps △QRS to △Q'R'S'.

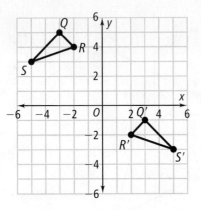

A. reflection across the y-axis, translation of 6 units down

B. rotation of 90° about the origin, translation of 6 units up

C. reflection across the y-axis, translation of 10 units down

D. translation of 10 units right, translation of 6 units down

2. ABCD is a square. Given ABCD ≅ A'B'C'D', describe a sequence of rigid motions that maps ΛBCD to A'B'C'D'.

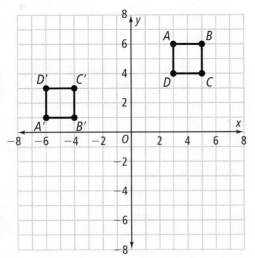

3. Is △DEF ≅ △D'E'F'? Explain.

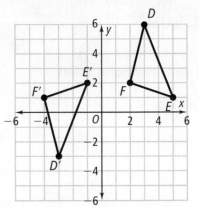

4. Which two triangles are congruent?

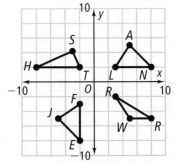

5. a. Writing Given △DEF ≅ △D'E'F', describe a pair of rigid motions that maps △DEF to △D'E'F'.

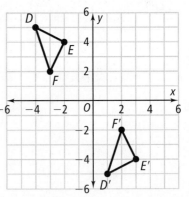

b. Describe a way you can show that △DEF is identical to △D'E'F'

6. Triangle Flags You are making two triangle flags for a project and need the flags to be the same shape and size. △XYZ and △X'Y'Z' are the same flags you have drawn. Are the flags the same shape and size?

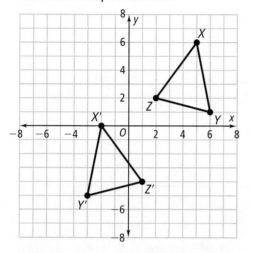

7. Multiple Representations Describe a sequence of rigid motions that maps △XYZ to △X'Y'Z', given △XYZ ≅ △X'Y'Z'.

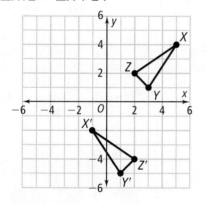

8. Open-Ended

   a. Given △DEF ≅ △D'E'F', describe a pair of rigid motions that maps △DEF to △D'E'F'.

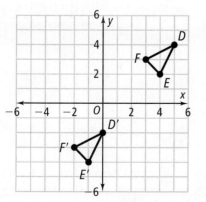

b. Describe a pair of rigid motions that maps △D'E'F' to △DEF.

9. Think About the Process ABCD is a rectangle and ABCD ≅ △A'B'C'D'.

   a. How can you tell that using only translations will not map ABCD to △A'B'C'D'?

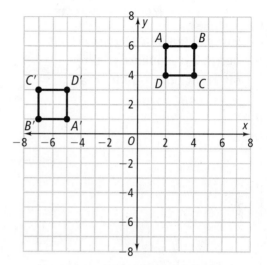

b. Describe a sequence of rigid motions that maps ABCD to A'B'C'D'.

10. Think About the Process

   a. How can you decide if △DEF ≅ △D'E'F'

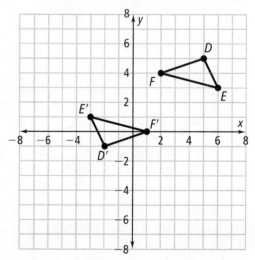

b. Is △DEF ≅ △D'E'F'? Explain.

| **Problem Solving**

CCSS: 8.G.A.2

Part 1

Example Describing Sequences of Three Rigid Motions

Given △ABC ≅ △DEF, describe a sequence of three different rigid motions that map △ABC to △DEF.

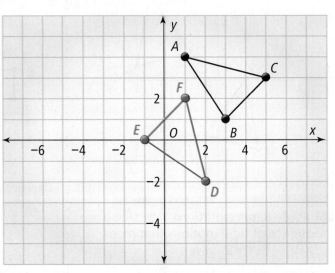

Solution

First, translate △ABC left 3 units and down 2 units.

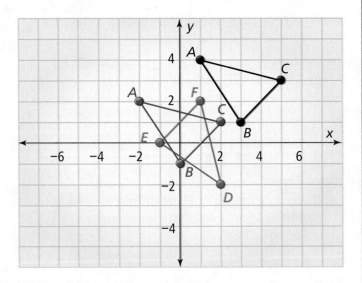

continued on next page >

See your complete lesson at MyMathUniverse.com

Solution continued

Next, rotate △ABC 90°
about the origin.

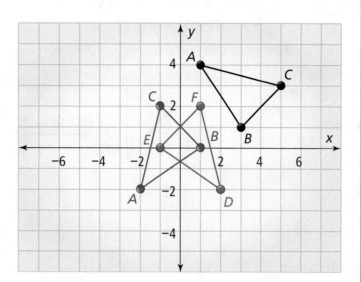

Then reflect △ABC across
the y-axis.

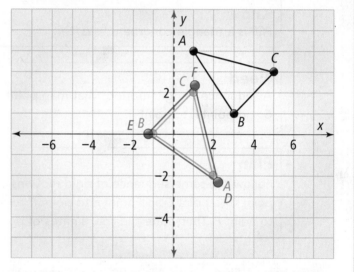

A translation 3 units to the
left and 2 units down,
followed by a rotation of
90° about the origin, followed
by a reflection across the
y-axis, maps △ABC to △DEF.

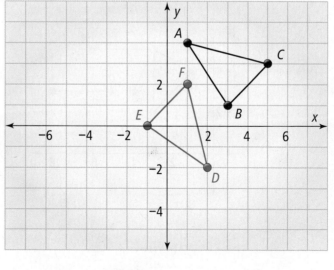

Part 2

Example Finding Missing Vertices of Congruent Figures

Given △FGH ≅ △PQR, find possible coordinates for point F.

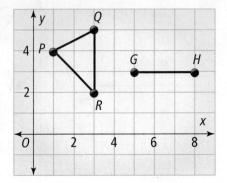

Solution

Know
FGH is a triangle congruent to △PQR.

Need
A sequence of rigid motions that map point Q to point G and point R to point H.

Plan
Follow the same sequence of rigid motions that map point Q to point G and point R to point H to map point P to point F. Then state the coordinates of point F.

Method 1 First, rotate △PQR 90° about point Q.

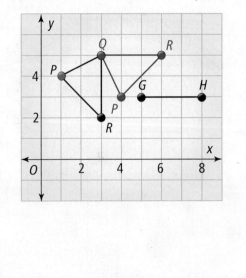

continued on next page >

Then translate △*PQR* to the right 2 units and down 2 units.

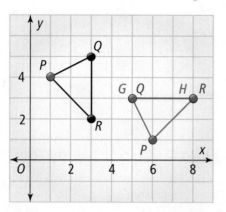

One possible set of coordinates for point *F* is (6, 1).

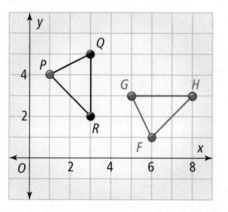

Method 2 Follow the sequence of rigid motions from Method 1.

Then reflect △*PQR* across the line *y* = 3.

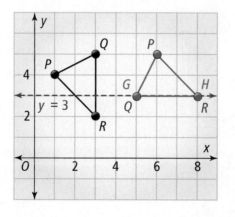

continued on next page >

Solution continued

Another possible set of coordinates for point *F* is (6, 5).

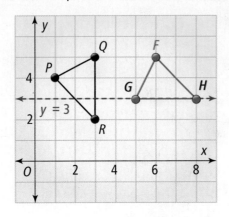

1. There are two triangles, △QRS and △ABC. The coordinates of △QRS are Q(−3,3), R(−6,3), and S(−3,8). The coordinates of △ABC are A(0, −3), B(0, −6), and C(5, −3).

Which of the following is a description of rigid motions which map △QRS to △ABC?

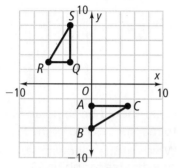

A. A rotation of 90° about the origin, followed by a translation 3 units to the left and then a reflection across the y-axis

B. A rotation of 90° about the origin, followed by a translation 4 units to the right and then a reflection across the x-axis

C. A rotation of 90° about the origin, followed by a translation 3 units to the right and then a reflection across the y-axis

2. △EFG and △HIJ are congruent triangles. The coordinates of △EFG are E(5,4), F(7,4), and G(7,8). The coordinates of HI are H(0,0), and I(0,2).

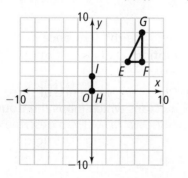

a. What are possible coordinates of point J?

   A. (−3,2)   **B.** (−5,2)

   C. (−4,2)   **D.** (−6,2)

b. Explain why there can be different possibilities for the coordinates for point J.

3. On a math test Nikol needs to describe the motions which map △EFG to △MNO. The coordinates of △EFG are E(4,5), F(6,5), and G(4,10). The coordinates of △MNO are M(0,0), N(−2,0), and O(0,5). She says there is a translation 4 units to the left and 5 units down, followed by a reflection across the x-axis.

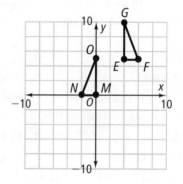

a. Write a description of the rigid motions which maps △EFG to △MNO.

b. What is Nikol's likely error?

4. The coordinates of the figure ABCD are A(6,2), B(8,2), C(8,6), and D(6,6). The coordinates of the figure HIJK are H(−1,0), I(−1,−2), J(−5,−2), and K(−5,0).

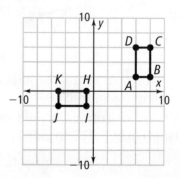

a. Write a description of rigid motions used.

b. Describe a different sequence of rigid motions that will still map ABCD to HIJK.

See your complete lesson at MyMathUniverse.com

5. The coordinates of $\overline{QR}$ are Q(5,1), R(8,1). The coordinates of △TUV are T(0,1), U(−3,1), and V(−1,6).

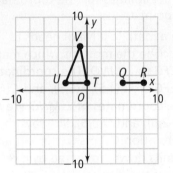

a. If △QRS and △TUV are congruent, what are possible coordinates for point S?

A. (6,5)   **B.** (6,7)

C. (6,6)   **D.** (5,6)

b. What is the distance between point R and its corresponding point?

A. 13 units   **B.** 10 units

C. 11 units   **D.** 12 units

6. Think About the Process The coordinates of △ABC are A(3, −4), B(7, −5), and C(6, −9). The coordinates of △EFG are E(0,0), F(4,1), and G(3,5).

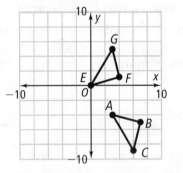

a. What would be the best first step to map △ABC to △EFG?

b. Write a description of rigid motions which map △ABC to △EFG.

7. Think About the Process There are two congruent triangles, △QRS and △TUV.

The coordinates of $\overline{QR}$ are Q(4,3), R(9,3). The coordinates of △TUV are T(−1, −2), U(−6, −2), and V(−3, 2).

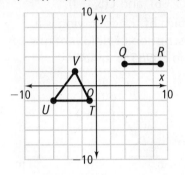

a. What should be the plan in order to map point V to point S?

b. Which of the following are possible coordinates for point S?

A. (6,6)   **B.** (6,8)

C. (6,7)   **D.** (4,7)

8. Challenge The coordinates of the figure ABCD are A(2,2), B(5,3), C(5,4), and D(2,4). The coordinates of the figure HIJK are H(−2,−4), I(1,−5), J(1,−6), and K(−2,−6).

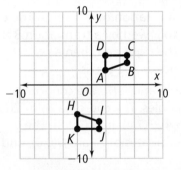

a. Describe the sequence of rigid motions that maps figure ABCD to HIJK.

b. Describe a sequence of three rigid motions which maps the figure ABCD to HIJK. Then describe a sequence using four rigid motions.

CCSS: 8.G.A.3

VOCABULARY

dilation,
enlargement,
reduction, scale
factor

Key Concept

A **dilation** is a transformation that moves each point along the ray through the point starting from a fixed center, and multiplies distances from the center by a common scale factor.

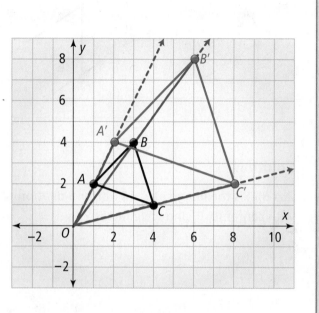

If a vertex of a figure is the center of dilation, then the vertex and its image after the dilation are the same point.

The **scale factor** is the ratio of a length in the image to the corresponding length in the original figure.

scale factor = $\frac{6}{3}$, or 2

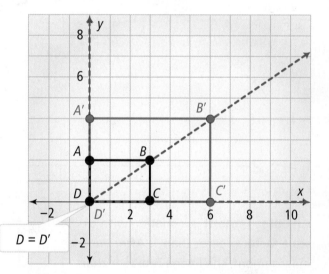

$D = D'$

See your complete lesson at MyMathUniverse.com

Part 1

Example Recognizing Dilations

Choose the transformation that is a dilation.

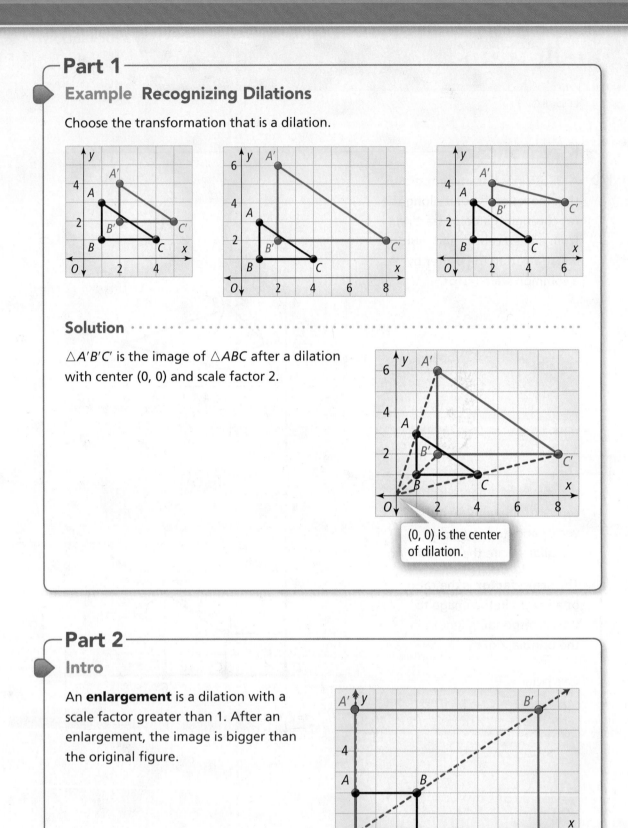

Solution

△A′B′C′ is the image of △ABC after a dilation with center (0, 0) and scale factor 2.

(0, 0) is the center of dilation.

Intro

An **enlargement** is a dilation with a scale factor greater than 1. After an enlargement, the image is bigger than the original figure.

Scale factor = 3

continued on next page >

Part 2

Intro continued

A reduction is a dilation with a scale factor less than 1. After a reduction, the image is smaller than the original figure.

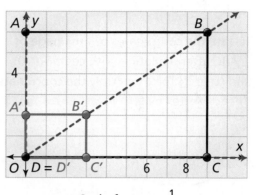

Scale factor $= \frac{1}{3}$

Example Finding Scale Factors of Dilations

For the given dilation, find the scale factor. Then decide whether the dilation is an enlargement or a reduction.

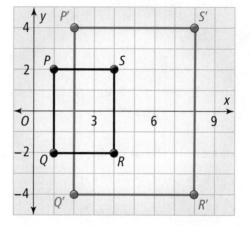

Solution

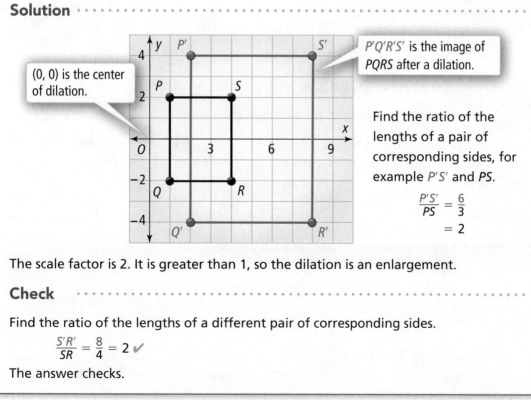

(0, 0) is the center of dilation.

P'Q'R'S' is the image of PQRS after a dilation.

Find the ratio of the lengths of a pair of corresponding sides, for example P'S' and PS.

$$\frac{P'S'}{PS} = \frac{6}{3}$$
$$= 2$$

The scale factor is 2. It is greater than 1, so the dilation is an enlargement.

Check

Find the ratio of the lengths of a different pair of corresponding sides.

$$\frac{S'R'}{SR} = \frac{8}{4} = 2 ✔$$

The answer checks.

Intro

To find the coordinates of the image of △ABC after a dilation with center (0, 0) and scale factor $\frac{2}{3}$, multiply the coordinates of each vertex by $\frac{2}{3}$.

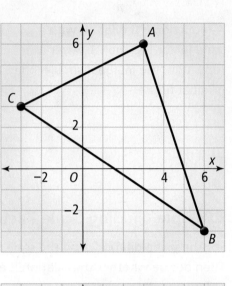

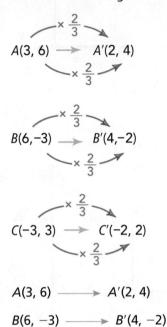

$A(3, 6) \longrightarrow A'(2, 4)$

$B(6, -3) \longrightarrow B'(4, -2)$

$C(-3, 3) \longrightarrow C'(-2, 2)$

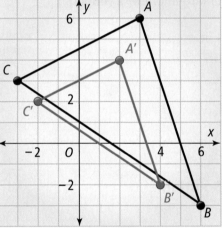

Example Graphing Dilations

The vertices of △ABC are A(1, 2), B(−2, 1), and C(−1, −1).

Use arrow notation to find the coordinates of △A′B′C′, the image of △ABC after a dilation with center (0, 0) and a scale factor of 3. Then graph △ABC and △A′B′C′.

Solution ·

> **Step 1** Multiply the coordinates of each vertex of △ABC by 3.
>
> $A(1, 2) \longrightarrow A'(3, 6)$
>
> $B(-2, 1) \longrightarrow B'(-6, 3)$
>
> $C(-1, -1) \longrightarrow C'(-3, -3)$

continued on next page >

Solution continued

Step 2 Graph △ABC and △A'B'C'.

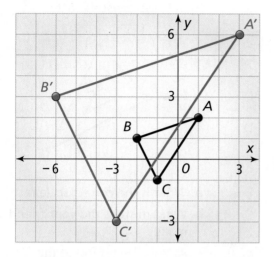

1. What is the scale factor for the dilation shown?

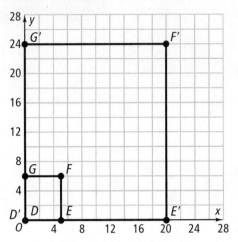

2. △RST has vertices R(0,0), S(4,2), and T(2,−2). △R'S'T' is the image of △RST after a dilation with center (0,0) and scale factor $\frac{1}{2}$. What are the coordinates of point S'?

3. The coordinates of △LMN are L(1,3), M(5,6), and N(6,5). Draw a graph showing △LMN and the image of △LMN for the dilation with center (0,0) and scale factor 2.

4. Writing △KLM has vertices K(1,3), L(5,7), and M(5,5). Draw a graph showing △KLM and △K'L'M', its image after a dilation with center K and scale factor 2.

5. a. Reasoning Draw a graph showing △D'E'F', the image of △DEF after a dilation.

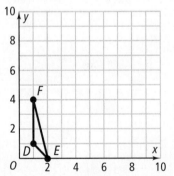

b. What types of transformations are shown in the other graphs? Explain.

6. Error Analysis For the dilation with center (0,0) shown on the graph, your friend says the scale factor is $\frac{7}{2}$.

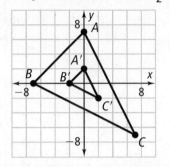

a. What is the correct scale factor?

b. What mistake did your friend likely make?

A. Your friend found the ratio between two sides of the original triangle.

B. Your friend found the ratio between two sides of the image triangle.

C. Your friend found the scale factor that enlarges △A'B'C' to △ABC.

D. Your friend found the ratio between non-corresponding sides.

7. Photography A photographer uses a computer program to enlarge a photograph. When laid on a grid, the original photograph has coordinates P(0,0), H(9,0), O(9,6), and T(0,6). Draw a graph showing rectangles PHOT and P'H'O'T', its image after a dilation with center at the origin and scale factor $\frac{7}{3}$.

8. Rectangle QUAD has coordinates Q(5,4), U(5,8), A(10,8), and D(10,4). Q'U'A'D' is the image of QUAD after a dilation with center (0,0) and scale factor 2. What are the coordinates of point D'?

9. Estimation

a. Without doing calculations, use side *DE* and side *D'E'* to estimate the scale factor for the dilation shown.

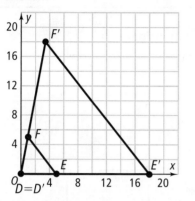

b. Use two corresponding sides to find the scale factor.

10. Think About the Process The graph shows △*JKL* and △*J'K'L'*, its image after a dilation.

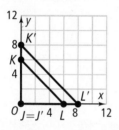

a. Is the dilation an enlargement or a reduction?

Explain.

A. An enlargement, because the image figure is larger than the original figure.

B. An enlargement, because the image figure is smaller than the original figure.

C. A reduction, because the image figure is smaller than the original figure.

D. A reduction, because the image figure is larger than the original figure.

b. Find the scale factor of the dilation.

11.

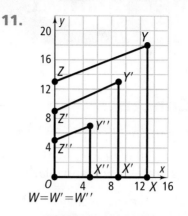

a. **Challenge** Find the scale factor for the dilation from *WXYZ* to *W'X'Y'Z'*.

b. Find the scale factor for the dilation from *W'X'Y'Z'* to *W"X"Y"Z"*.

12. Think About the Process Quadrilateral *EFGH* has vertices *E*(3,3), *F*(9,3), *G*(9,12), and *H*(3,12).

a. Using a scale factor of $\frac{4}{3}$, how can you find the coordinates of point *G'*, the image of point *G*?

A. Multiply the coordinates of *G* by $\frac{4}{3}$.

B. Add $\frac{4}{3}$ to the coordinates of *G*.

C. Multiply the coordinates of *G* by 3.

D. Multiply the coordinates of *G* by 4.

b. Graph rectangles *EFGH* and *E'F'G'H'*, its image after a dilation with center at *E*(3,3) and scale factor $\frac{4}{3}$.

13. Challenge The coordinates of △*PQR* are *P*(1,−3), *Q*(1,5), and *R*(4,−3). Draw a graph showing △*PQR* and △*P'Q'R'*, its image after a dilation with center (0,0) and scale factor 3.

| **Similar Figures**

CCSS: 8.G.A.3, 8.G.A.4

Key Concept

A two-dimensional figure is similar to another two-dimensional figure if you can map one figure to the other by a sequence of rotations, reflections, translations, and dilations.

The symbol ~ means "is similar to."

Suppose you start with rectangle *ABCD* and translate it 6 units to the left and 1 unit up.

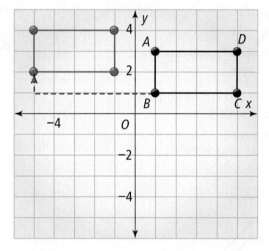

Rotate it 90 degrees about the origin.

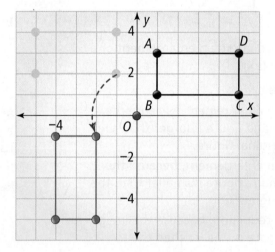

continued on next page >

continued

Then, reflect it across the *y*-axis.

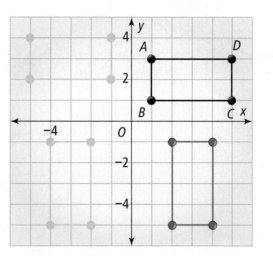

And, finally, dilate it by a scale factor of $\frac{1}{2}$.

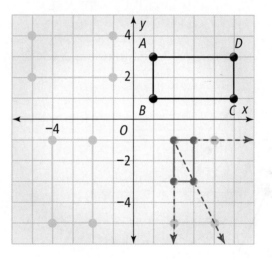

The final image is still similar to rectangle *ABCD*.

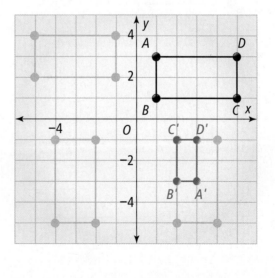

Part 1

Example Describing Sequences of Translations and Dilations

Given △ABC ~ △NOP, describe a
sequence of a rigid motion followed by
a dilation with center (0, 0) that maps
△ABC to △NOP.

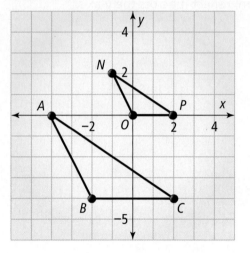

Solution

To map △ABC to △NOP, first translate △ABC 2 units right and 4 units up.

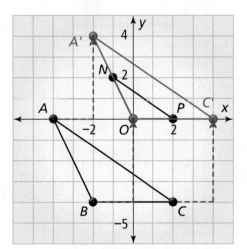

continued on next page >

Part 1

Solution continued

Now, find the scale factor that relates the two triangles.

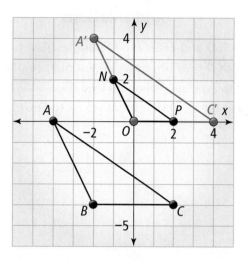

Multiply by the scale factor $\frac{1}{2}$.

$$A'(-2, 4) \rightarrow \left(-2 \cdot \frac{1}{2}, 4 \cdot \frac{1}{2}\right) = N(-1, 2)$$

A scale factor of $\frac{1}{2}$ relates the triangles.

A sequence of a translation 2 units right and 4 units up, followed by a dilation with center (0, 0) and scale factor $\frac{1}{2}$ maps $\triangle ABC$ to $\triangle NOP$.

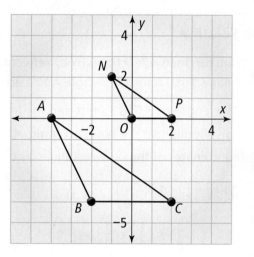

Part 2

Example Describing Sequences of Reflections and Dilations

ABCD and *EFGH* are rectangles. Given *ABCD* ~ *EFGH*, describe a sequence of a rigid motion followed by a dilation with center (0, 0) that maps *ABCD* to *EFGH*.

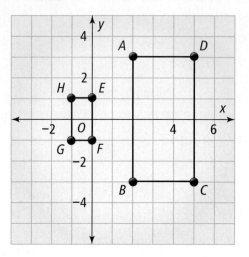

Solution

You can map *ABCD* to *EFGH* by reflecting *ABCD* and then dilating that image. First, reflect rectangle ABCD across the line, $x = 1$.

The length of *B'C'* is 3 units and the length of *GF* is 1 unit. So, a scale factor of $\frac{1}{3}$ should map the blue rectangle, *A'B'C'D'* to rectangle *EFGH*. Multiply the coordinates of the blue rectangle by the scale factor, $\frac{1}{3}$.

$(0, 3) \rightarrow \left(0 \cdot \frac{1}{3}, 3 \cdot \frac{1}{3}\right) = (0, 1)$

$(-3, 3) \rightarrow \left(-3 \cdot \frac{1}{3}, 3 \cdot \frac{1}{3}\right) = (-1, 1)$

$(-3, -3) \rightarrow \left(-3 \cdot \frac{1}{3}, -3 \cdot \frac{1}{3}\right) = (-1, -1)$

$(0, -3) \rightarrow \left(0 \cdot \frac{1}{3}, -3 \cdot \frac{1}{3}\right) = (0, -1)$

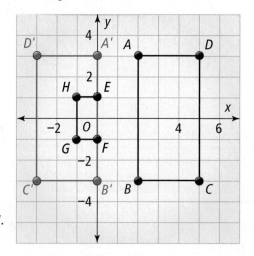

A sequence of a reflection across the line $x = 1$, followed by a dilation with center (0, 0) and scale factor $\frac{1}{3}$ maps *ABCD* to *EFGH*.

Part 3

Intro

△ADE is the image △ABC after a dilation with center (0, 0) and scale factor 2, so △ABC ~ △ADE.

Effects on Angles Angles are taken to angles of the same measure.

$$\triangle ABC \quad : \quad \triangle ADE$$
$$\angle A \to \angle A \text{ so } \angle A \cong \angle A$$
$$\angle B \to \angle D \text{ so } \angle B \cong \angle D$$
$$\angle C \to \angle E \text{ so } \angle C \cong \angle E$$

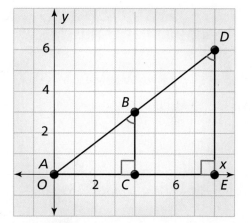

Effects on Line Segments Line segments are taken to line segments so that the ratio of the length in the image to the corresponding length in the original figure is equal to the scale factor.

$$ABC \sim ADE$$
$$\overline{AB} \to \overline{AD}, \text{ so } \frac{AD}{AB} = \frac{2}{1}$$
$$\overline{BC} \to \overline{DE}, \text{ so } \frac{DE}{BC} = \frac{2}{1}$$
$$\overline{AC} \to \overline{AE}, \text{ so } \frac{AE}{AC} = \frac{2}{1}$$

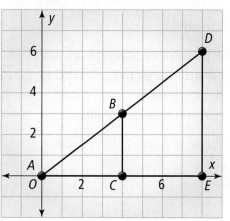

Example Determining If Figures are Similar

Is △MNO ~ △PQO? Explain.

Solution

Look for a series of rigid motions and dilations that maps △MNO to △PQO. If there is one, then the two triangles are similar.

First, rotate △MNO 180° about the origin.

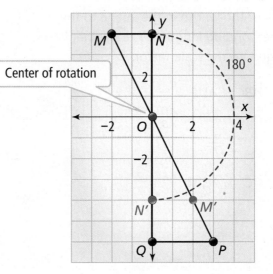

Center of rotation

continued on next page >

Part 3

Solution continued

Then, dilate $\triangle M'N'O'$ with center $(0, 0)$ and scale factor $\frac{3}{2}$.

$$M'(2, -4) \rightarrow \left(2 \cdot \frac{3}{2}, -4 \cdot \frac{3}{2}\right) = P(3, -6)$$

A rotation of 180° about the origin followed by a dilation with center $(0, 0)$ and scale factor $\frac{3}{2}$ maps $\triangle MNO$ to $\triangle PQO$.

So, $\triangle MNO \sim \triangle PQO$.

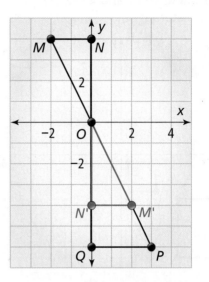

1. Reasoning *RSTU* and *VXYZ* are quadrilaterals.

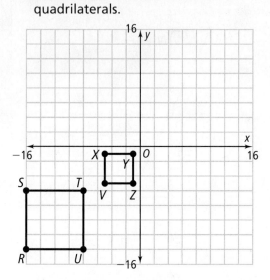

a. Given *RSTU* ~ *VXYZ*, which answer describes a sequence of transformations that maps *RSTU* to *VXYZ*?

   A. translation 6 units right and 4 units up, dilation with center (0,0) and scale factor $\frac{1}{2}$

   B. translation 4 units left and 6 units down, dilation with center (0,0) and scale factor $\frac{1}{2}$

   C. translation 11 units right and 9 units up, dilation with center (0,0) and scale factor 2

   D. translation 11 units left and 9 units down, dilation with center (0,0) and scale factor 2

b. Does a translation followed by a dilation always map a figure to the same image as that same dilation followed by that same translation? Explain your reasoning.

2. Given △*ABC* ~ △*DEF*, describe a sequence of rigid motions followed by a dilation with center (0,0) that maps △*ABC* to △*DEF*.

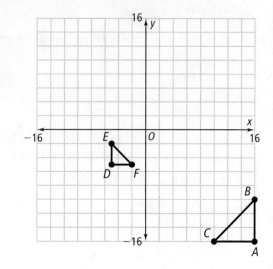

A. Reflection across the *x*-axis, translation 11 units left and 11 units down, dilation with center (0,0) and scale factor 2

B. Reflection across the *x*-axis, translation 6 units right and 6 units up, dilation with center (0,0) and scale factor 2

C. Reflection across the *y*-axis, translation 6 units right and 6 units up, dilation with center (0,0) and scale factor $\frac{1}{2}$

D. Reflection across the *y*-axis, translation 11 units right and 11 units up, dilation with center (0,0) and scale factor $\frac{1}{2}$

3. a. Multiple Representations Is △*PQR* similar to △*XYZ*?

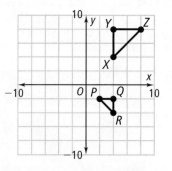

b. If the triangles are similar, give two sequences of rigid motions and dilations that map △*PQR* to △*XYZ*. If the triangles are not similar, give two sequences of rigid motions that map point *P* to point *X*.

4. Open-Ended

a. Given △NOP ~ △QRS, describe a sequence of a rigid motions followed by a dilation with center (0,0) that maps △NOP to △QRS. Write the answer to complete your choice.

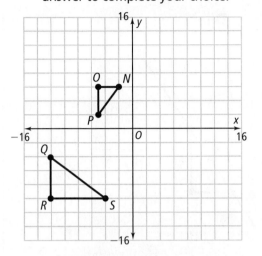

A. Rotation of 90° about (0,0), dilation with center (0,0) and scale factor ▦

B. Rotation of 270° about (0,0), dilation with center (0,0) and scale factor ▦

C. Rotation of 180° about (0,0), dilation with center (0,0) and scale factor ▦

b. Describe a dilation followed by a sequence of rigid motions that maps △NOP to △QRS and compare it to the first sequence.

5. Think About the Process ABCD ~ EFGH. ABCD can be mapped to EFGH using a sequence of a reflection, a translation, and a dilation with center (0,0).

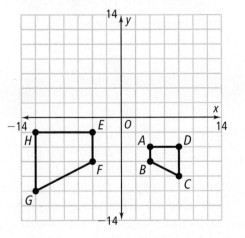

a. What aspect of *EFGH* should you use to decide what kind of reflection should be used?

   A. The coordinates of its vertices

   B. The lengths of its sides

   C. Its orientation

   D. Its area

b. Describe the sequence. Write the answer to complete your choice.

   A. Reflection across the y-axis, translation ▦ unit(s) right and ▦ unit(s) up, dilation with center (0,0) and scale factor ▦

   B. Reflection across the y-axis, translation ▦ unit(s) left and ▦ unit(s) down, dilation with center (0,0) and scale factor ▦

   C. Reflection across the x-axis, translation ▦ unit(s) right and ▦ unit(s) up, dilation with center (0,0) and scale factor ▦

6. Think About the Process

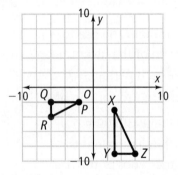

a. If △PQR were similar to △XYZ, what angle would correspond to ∠Q?

b. Is △PQR similar to △XYZ?

See your complete lesson at MyMathUniverse.com

Relating Similar Triangles and Slope

CCSS: 8.G.A.3, 8.G.A.4, 8.EE.B.6

Part 1

Example Comparing Triangles to Their Dilations

Draw the triangle that is the image of the given triangle after a dilation with center $(0, -2)$ and a scale factor of 2. Look at the ratio of the rise to the run of each triangle. How do the ratios compare? Explain.

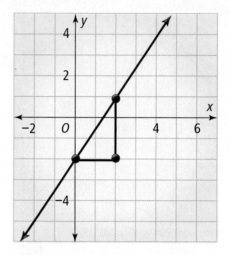

Solution

The ratio of the rise to the run of the given triangle is $\frac{3}{2}$. The ratio of the rise to the run of the image triangle is $\frac{6}{4}$, which is equivalent to $\frac{3}{2}$. So, the ratios of the rise to the run of the two triangles are the same.

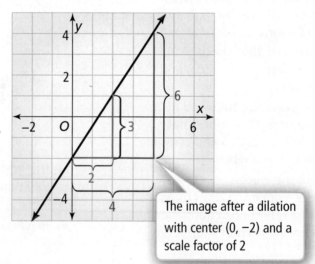

The image after a dilation with center $(0, -2)$ and a scale factor of 2

Part 2

Intro

For any two distinct points on a non-vertical line in the coordinate plane, you can draw a slope triangle for the line. You can draw slope triangle above or below the line.

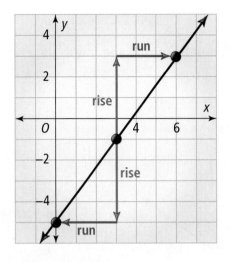

Example Identifying Appropriate Slope Triangles

Decide whether you could use each of the slope triangles to find the slope of the line with equation $y = \frac{3}{5}x + 5$.

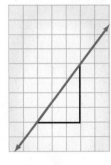 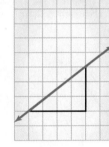 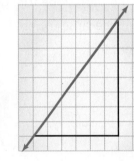 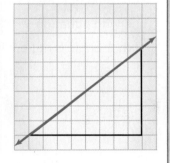

continued on next page >

Part 2

Solution ···

You could use the second and fourth slope triangles to find the slope of the line with equation $y = \frac{3}{4}x + 5$ because the ratio of the rise to the run of each triangle is equivalent to $\frac{3}{4}$.

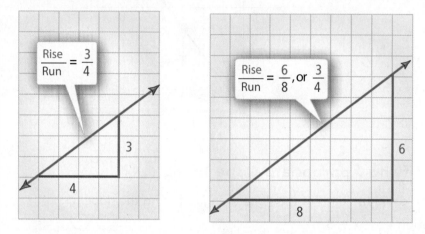

You could not use the first and third slope triangles to find the slope of the line with equation $y = \frac{3}{4}x + 5$ because the ratio of the rise to the run of each triangle is not equivalent to $\frac{3}{4}$.

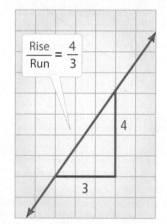 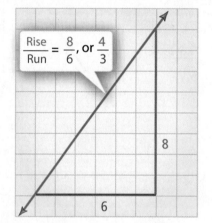

Key Concept

You can use similar triangles to explain why the slope m is the same between any two distinct points on a non-vertical line in the coordinate plane.

If you begin with a line passing through the origin and the point (a, b), the ratio of the rise to the run of the triangle is

$$\frac{\text{rise}}{\text{run}} = \frac{b}{a}$$

Now dilate the triangle by scale factor k with center at the origin. The ratio of the rise to the run for the dilation is

$$\frac{\text{rise}}{\text{run}} = \frac{\cancel{k}b}{\cancel{k}a}$$
$$= \frac{b}{a}$$

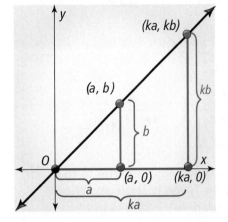

The ratio is the same as for the original triangle.

You can also show that the ratio of the rise to the run is the same as the slope of the line through the point (a, b) and (ka, kb). Use the slope formula.

$$\frac{\text{rise}}{\text{run}} = \frac{b}{a}$$

$$\text{Slope } m = \frac{\text{change in } y}{\text{change in } x}$$
$$= \frac{kb - b}{ka - a}$$
$$= \frac{b\cancel{(k - 1)}}{a\cancel{(k - 1)}}$$
$$= \frac{b}{a}$$

This also works for a non-vertical line that does not pass through the origin. A translation up results in triangles that are congruent to those formed by the line passing through the origin. So the ratio of the rise to the run between any two points on this new line is still b to a.

$$\frac{\text{rise}}{\text{run}} = \frac{b}{a}$$

1. a. Draw a triangle which is the image of the given triangle after dilation with center (0, −5) and a scale factor of 3?

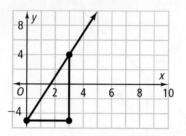

b. What is the ratio of the rise to the run of the given triangle and the image triangle?

c. How do the ratios compare?

A. The ratios of the rise to the run of the two triangles are the same.

B. The ratio of the rise to the run of the image triangle is 3 times the ratio of the given triangle.

C. The ratio of the rise to the run of the given triangle is 3 times the ratio of the image triangle.

2. The slope of the given line is $\frac{1}{5}$. One slope triangle is shown. Another slope triangle with a ratio of the rise to the run of $\frac{1}{5}$ has vertices at (0,0) and (5,0). Find the coordinates of the third vertex.

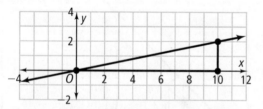

3. a. Draw a triangle that is the image of the given triangle after dilation with center (−1,0) and a scale factor of 2.

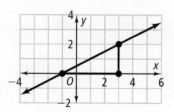

b. Look at the ratio of the rise to the run of each triangle. How do the ratios compare?

c. Draw a triangle with the same ratio of the rise to the run with center (0,0).

4. a. Writing Draw a triangle which is the image of the given triangle after dilation with center (2,1) and a scale factor of 3?

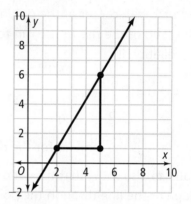

b. What is the ratio of the rise to the run of the given triangle and the image triangle?

5. Error Analysis Your friend incorrectly says that the image of the given triangle after a dilation with center (0,0) and a scale factor of $\frac{1}{2}$ has a ratio of the rise to the run of 2.

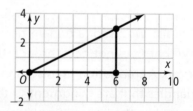

a. Draw a graph which shows the image of the given triangle?

b. What is the correct ratio of the rise to the run?

c. What mistake did your friend make?

See your complete lesson at MyMathUniverse.com

6. Ceramics A friend is helping you cut mosaic tiles. Your friend brings you four tiles. The tiles need to have the same slope as the equation $y = \frac{2}{5}x$. Select each tile you can use.

Tile Q

Tile R

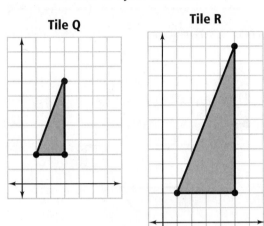

Tile S

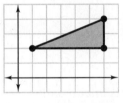

Tile T

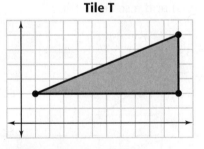

7. Multiple Representations

a. Identify the slope triangle that can be used to find the slope of the line with the equation $y = \frac{1}{2}x + 7$.

Slope Triangle Q

Slope Triangle R

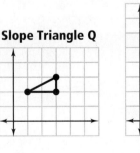

Slope Triangle S

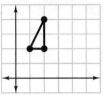

b. Draw two other triangles that can be used to find the slope of the line.

8. Think About the Process

a. What is the first step to find the ratio of the rise to the run of the given triangle?

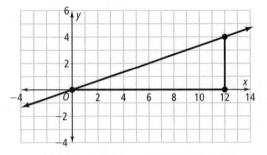

b. What is the ratio of the rise to the run of the given triangle?

c. Draw a graph which shows the triangle that is the image of the given triangle after a dilation with center (0,0) and a scale factor of $\frac{1}{4}$?

d. What do you know about the ratio of the rise to the run of the image triangle?

9. Think About the Process The slope of the given line is $\frac{1}{3}$. One slope triangle is shown. Another slope triangle with a ratio of the rise to the run of $\frac{1}{3}$ has vertices at (9,2) and (12,2).

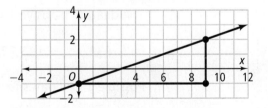

a. What do you know about the second triangle?

b. Find the coordinates of the third vertex.

CCSS: 8.G.A.3, 8.G.A.4

Part 1

Example Finding Missing Vertices After Dilations

Given $\triangle ABC \sim \triangle DEF$, use one rigid motion followed by a dilation with center (0, 0) to find possible coordinates for point D.

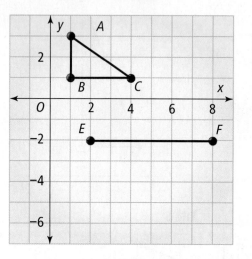

Solution

Method 1 Translate $\triangle ABC$ 2 units down.   →   Dilate its image with center (0, 0) and a scale factor of 2.

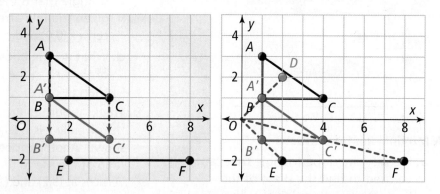

The dilation maps vertex A' to possible coordinates for point D.

$$A'(1, 1) \longrightarrow (1 \cdot 2, 1 \cdot 2) = (2, 2)$$

Possible coordinates for point D are (2, 2).

continued on next page >

Part 1

Solution continued

Method 2 Reflect $\triangle ABC$ across the *x*-axis. $\longrightarrow$ Dilate its image with center (0, 0) and a scale factor of 2.

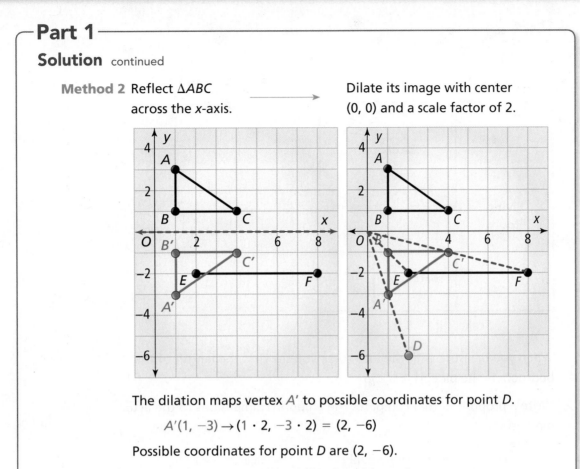

The dilation maps vertex A' to possible coordinates for point D.

$$A'(1, -3) \rightarrow (1 \cdot 2, -3 \cdot 2) = (2, -6)$$

Possible coordinates for point D are $(2, -6)$.

So, two possible coordinates for point D are $(2, 2)$ and $(2, -6)$.

Part 2

Intro

In Lesson 10-2, you learned that corresponding side lengths of similar figures are proportional. You can use this fact in applications of similarity. One application is scale drawings. A scale drawing is a dilation of the object it represents.

Example Using Scale Drawings

The blueprint shows the floor plan of an apartment.

Use an inch ruler to find measurements of rooms in the blueprint.

What are the dimensions of the actual bedroom?

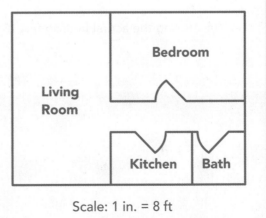

Scale: 1 in. = 8 ft

continued on next page >

Example continued

Solution

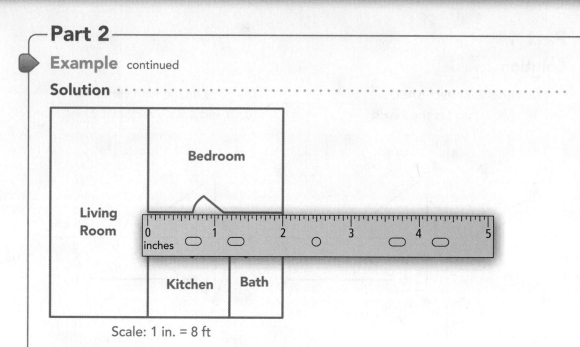

Scale: 1 in. = 8 ft

When you measure with the inch ruler, you see that the length of the bedroom in the blueprint is 2 in.

Write a proportion that compares the blueprint dimensions to the actual dimensions.

Let ℓ represents the actual length of the bedroom.

$\dfrac{1}{8} = \dfrac{2}{\ell}$ ← Blueprint (in.)
← Actual (ft)

Find a fraction equivalent to $\frac{1}{8}$ with 2 as the numerator.

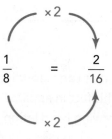

$$\frac{1}{8} = \frac{2}{16}$$

So, $\ell = 16$, and the actual bedroom is 16 ft long.

continued on next page >

Part 2

Solution continued

Next, measure the width.

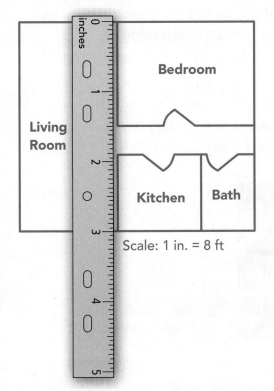

Scale: 1 in. = 8 ft

The width of the bedroom in the blueprint is 1.5 in.

Let represent the actual width of the bedroom.

$$\frac{1}{8} = \frac{1.5}{w} \quad \begin{matrix} \leftarrow \text{Blueprint (in.)} \\ \leftarrow \text{Actual (ft)} \end{matrix}$$

Find a fraction equivalent to $\frac{1}{8}$ with 1.5 as the numerator.

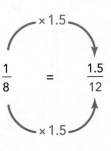

So, $w = 12$, and the actual bedroom is 12 ft wide.

The dimensions of the actual bedroom are 16 ft by 12 ft.

Part 3

Intro

Another way you can use the fact that corresponding sides of similar triangles are proportional is to help you find lengths that you cannot measure easily using a ruler or other measuring device. This is called **indirect measurement**.

Example Using Indirect Measurement

Your friend wants to find the height of a building. The building casts a shadow 15 ft long. Your friend casts a shadow 3 ft long. If your friend is 5 ft tall, what is the height of the building?

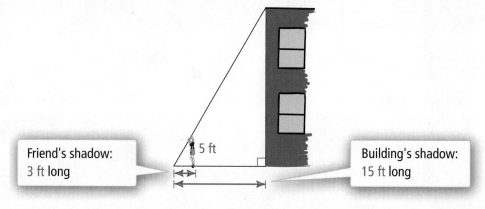

Friend's shadow: 3 ft long

5 ft

Building's shadow: 15 ft long

Solution

Know	Need	Plan
• The length of the shadow of the building • The length of the shadow of your friend • The height of your friend	The height of the building	Draw a diagram with two similar right triangles. Use what you know about corresponding side lengths and proportionality to find the height.

continued on next page >

Part 3

Solution continued

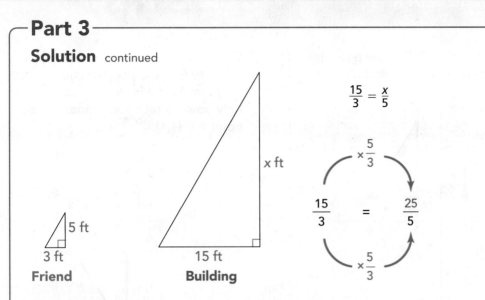

$$\frac{15}{3} = \frac{x}{5}$$

So, $x = 25$ and the height of the building is 25 ft.

1. Given △JKL ~ △XYZ, find the possible coordinates for point Y. Select all that apply.

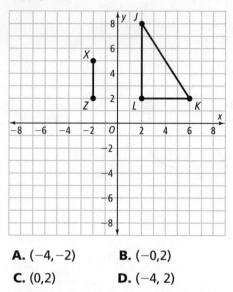

A. (−4,−2)　　**B.** (−0,2)

C. (0,2)　　**D.** (−4, 2)

2. The scale of a map is 1 cm = 80 km. What is the actual distance between two towns that are 4 cm apart on the map?

3. Find the distance d. Assume that the ratio of d to 120 ft is the same as the ratio of 50 ft to 40 ft. Simplify your answer.

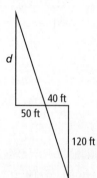

4. Barbara photographs a bird. The bird measures 8.8 cm in the photo and is actually 30.5 cm tall. Approximately how long is the bird's beak if it measures 1.1 cm in the photo? Round to two decimal places as needed.

5. Given △JKL ~ △XYZ, a student was asked to find the possible coordinates for point Y. She incorrectly said the only possible set of coordinates for point Y is (1,1).

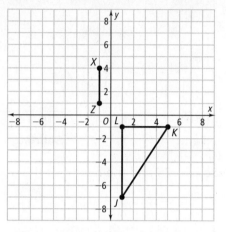

a. Find the possible coordinates for point Y. Select all that apply.

A. (−3,−1)　　**B.** (1,1)

C. (−1,1)　　**D.** (−3,1)

b. What mistake might the student have made?

6. You are building a triangular patio from a blueprint with base 5 in. and height 7 in. The base of the patio is going to be 10 ft. What will be the height of the patio, h?

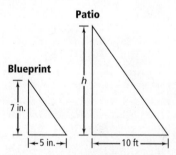

7. You are making a scale drawing of your yard. Your yard is 25 ft by 45 ft. In the drawing the 25 ft dimension is 5 in. What should the length of the 45 ft dimension be in the drawing?

8. A 6.8-ft vertical lamp post casts a 4.3-ft shadow at the same time a nearby tree house casts a 33.1-ft shadow.

   a. Round each value to the nearest whole number to estimate the height of the tree house.

   b. Find the exact height of the tree house. Round to the nearest tenth as needed.

9. a. Given $\triangle DEF \sim \triangle XYZ$, find the possible coordinates for point X. Select all that apply.

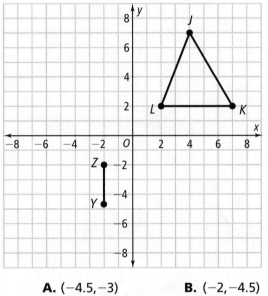

   A. $(-4.5, -3)$ **B.** $(-2, -4.5)$

   C. $(0.5, -3)$ **D.** $(4, 7)$

   b. Explain a sequence of rigid motions and dilations that could map $\triangle DEF$ to $\triangle XYZ$.

10. Think About the Process A 2-ft vertical post casts a 20-in. shadow at the same time a nearby cell phone tower casts a 125-ft shadow.

   a. What is the first step to find the height of the cell phone tower?

   b. How tall is the cell phone tower?

11. Think About the Process A model of a tractor trailer is shaped like a rectangular prism and has width 2 in., length 8 in., and height 4 in. The scale of the model is 1 in. = 48 in.

   a. What is a possible first step to compare the volume of the actual tractor trailer and the volume of the model?

   b. How many times larger is the volume of the actual tractor trailer than the volume of the model?

12. a. Given $\triangle JKL \sim \triangle XYZ$, find the possible coordinates for point X. Select all that apply.

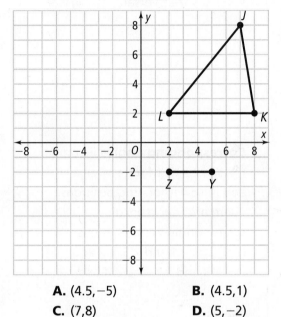

   A. $(4.5, -5)$ **B.** $(4.5, 1)$

   C. $(7, 8)$ **D.** $(5, -2)$

   b. Explain a sequence of rigid motions and dilations that could map $\triangle JKL$ to $\triangle XYZ$.

   c. Describe the result of changing the order of the rigid motions and dilations.

13. Challenge You are planning a road trip from City A to City B and then to City C. The scale of the map you are using is 1 inch = 75 miles. On the map there are 4 inches between City A and City B and 5 inches between City B and City C. If the cost of gas is $3.76 per gallon and the car you are traveling in gets 33 miles to the gallon, approximately how much will you spend on gas?

Vocabulary
alternate
interior angles,
corresponding
angles, transversal

Key Concept

A **transversal** is a line that intersects two or more lines at different points. In the diagram, line *t* is a transversal.

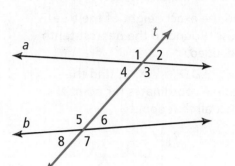

Corresponding angles lie on the same side of a transversal and in corresponding positions. There are four pairs of corresponding angles in this diagram: ∠1 and ∠5, ∠2 and ∠6, ∠3 and ∠7, and ∠4 and ∠8.

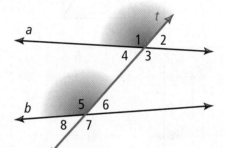

Alternate interior angles lie within a pair of lines and on opposite sides of a transversal. There are two pairs of alternate interior angles in this diagram: ∠3 and ∠5, and ∠4 and ∠6.

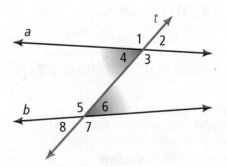

Example Identifying Corresponding Angles and Alternate Interior Angles

Name the pairs of corresponding angles and the pairs of alternate interior angles.

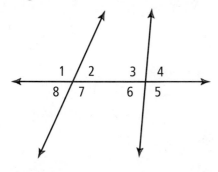

Solution

Corresponding angles lie on the same side of the transversal and in corresponding positions. The following pairs of angles are corresponding angles:

  ∠1 and ∠3
  ∠2 and ∠4
  ∠5 and ∠7
  ∠6 and ∠8

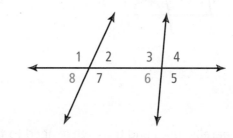

Alternate interior angles lie within a pair of lines and on opposite sides of the transversal. The following pairs of angles are alternate interior angles:

  ∠2 and ∠6
  ∠3 and ∠7

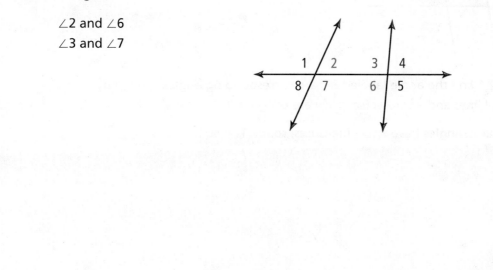

Part 2

Intro

When a transversal intersects two parallel lines, corresponding angles are congruent. Congruent angles have equal measures. You can mark angles with arcs to show that they are congruent.

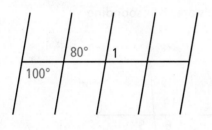

$\angle 1 \cong \angle 5$

$\angle 2 \cong \angle 6$

Example   Finding Measures of Corresponding Angles

The segments that form the parking spaces are parallel. What is $m\angle 1$?

Solution

Identify the parallel lines and transversal need to find $m\angle 1$.

Since $\angle 1$ and the angle labeled 80° are corresponding angles formed by parallel lines and a transversal, they are congruent.

Congruent angles have equal measures, so $m\angle 1 = 80°$.

Part 3

Intro

When a transversal intersects two parallel lines, alternate interior angles are congruent.

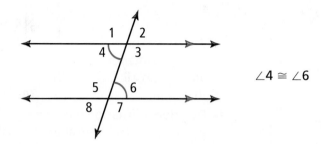

$\angle 4 \cong \angle 6$

Example Finding Measures of Alternate Interior Angles

Andie is working on a dude ranch. She is repairing fences. The rails of the fence shown are parallel. What is $m\angle 1$?

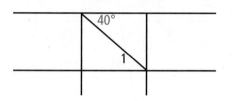

Solution ·

Since $\angle 1$ and the angle labeled 40° are alternate interior angles formed by parallel lines and a transversal, they are congruent. Congruent angles have equal measures, so $m\angle 1 = 40°$.

1. Which of the following is a pair of corresponding angles?

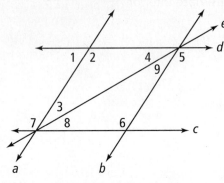

A. $\angle 5$ and $\angle 6$　　B. $\angle 6$ and $\angle 7$

C. $\angle 6$ and $\angle 8$　　D. $\angle 1$ and $\angle 4$

2. Find the measure of $\angle u$ given that $p \parallel q$.

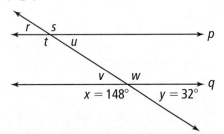

3. Streets A and B run parallel to each other. The measure of $\angle 8$ is 23°. The measure of $\angle 6$ is 157°. Find the measure of $\angle 2$.

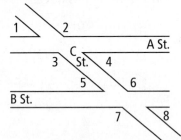

4. Find $m\angle v$ given that $p \parallel q$, $m\angle u = 75.8°$, and $m\angle w = 104.2°$.

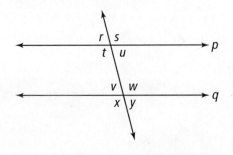

5. a. Writing Find the alternate interior angles in the figure shown, given that $m \parallel n$. Which are the alternate interior angles? List all that apply.

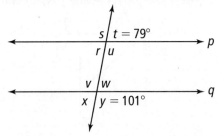

b. Describe a situation where you would use a transversal to cut a pair of parallel lines.

6. Error Analysis On a recent math test a teacher asked for the measure of $\angle w$. In the figure, $p \parallel q$. Jacob incorrectly said that the measure was 101°.

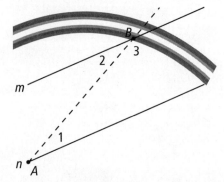

a. Find the measure of $\angle w$.

b. Which error might Jacob have made?

7. Rainbows When sunlight enters a drop of rain, different colors of light leave the drop at different angles, making a rainbow. In the figure shown, lines m and n represent the sun's rays. Assume that lines m and n are parallel and you are standing at point A.

a. For violet light at point B, $m\angle 2 = 27°$ and $m\angle 3 = 153°$. What is $m\angle 1$?

b. Justify how you can determine $m\angle 1$.

See your complete lesson at MyMathUniverse.com

8. **Open-Ended** The figure shows the design of a rectangular window pane. Note that all horizontal lines are parallel. The measure of ∠6 is 53°. The measure of ∠2 is 127°.

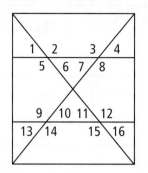

   a. Find the measure of ∠12.

   b. What other objects in your home have corresponding angles?

9. **Estimation** In the figure, $p \parallel q$. Given $m\angle x = 147.7°$ and $m\angle y = 32.3°$, round the angle measures to the nearest degree and find the estimated measure of ∠t.

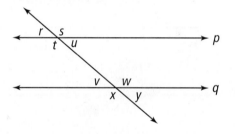

10. **Think About the Process** The figure shows a possible shot in a game of pool. The measure of ∠1 is 79°.

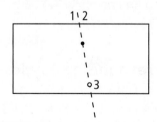

   a. How do you find the measure of ∠3?

   b. Find the measure of ∠3.

11. **Think About the Process** The figure shown represents lines being painted in a parking lot. Lines p, q, and r are parallel, $m\angle 1$ is 32° and $m\angle 2$ is 148°. Suppose you are painting the last line which is represented by the dashed line in the figure.

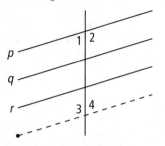

   a. To paint a parallel line, you need to angle your paint brush using $m\angle 4$. How do you find $m\angle 4$?

   b. Find the measure of ∠4.

12. **Challenge** The figure shows two possible shots in a game of pool. The easiest shots to make in pool are shots where the corresponding angles are closest to 90°. The measure of ∠1 is 86°. The measure of ∠4 is 51°.

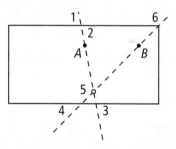

   a. Find the measures of ∠3 and ∠6.

   b. Should you aim for Ball A or Ball B?

CCSS: 8.G.A.5

Key Concept

Corresponding Angles and Parallel Lines If the corresponding angles formed by two lines and a transversal are congruent, then the lines are parallel.

Alternate Interior Angles and Parallel Lines If the alternate interior angles formed by two lines and a transversal are congruent, then the lines are parallel.

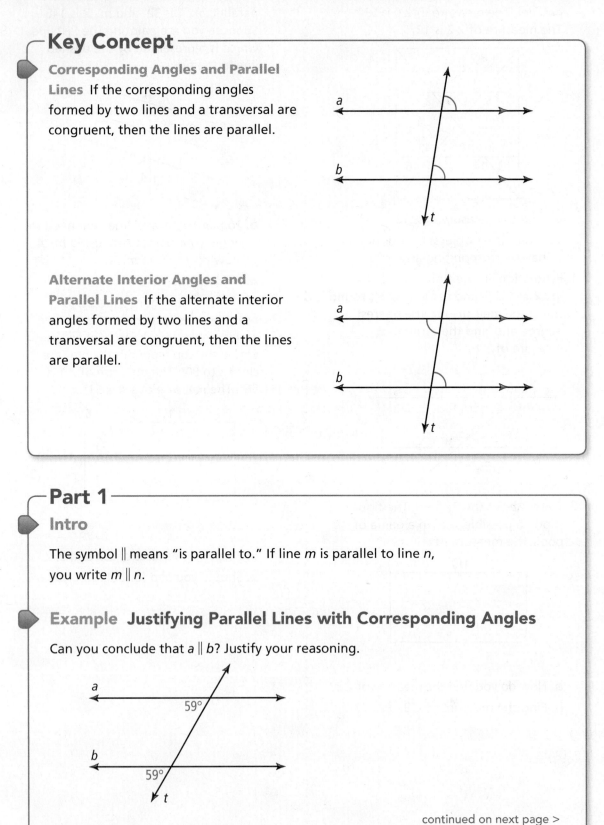

Part 1

Intro

The symbol ‖ means "is parallel to." If line m is parallel to line n, you write $m \parallel n$.

Example Justifying Parallel Lines with Corresponding Angles

Can you conclude that $a \parallel b$? Justify your reasoning.

continued on next page >

Example continued

Solution ·

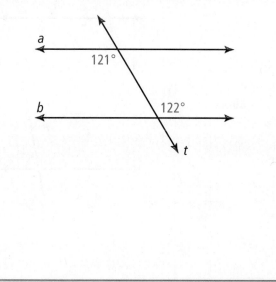

The angles labeled 59° are corresponding angles formed by two lines and a transversal. The angles have equal measures, so they are congruent. If two lines and a transversal form corresponding angles that are congruent, then the lines are parallel. So you can conclude that a ∥ b.

Part 2

Intro

The reasoning that you use to decide whether two lines are parallel based on knowing whether corresponding angles or alternate interior angles are congruent is called deductive reasoning. **Deductive reasoning** is a process of reasoning logically from given facts to a conclusion.

Example Justifying Parallel Lines with Alternate Interior Angles

Can you conclude that a ∥ b? Justify your reasoning.

continued on next page >

Example continued

Solution ·

The angles labeled 121° and 122° are alternate interior angles. If two lines
and a transversal form alternate interior angles that are congruent, then
the lines are parallel. Since the alternate interior angles do *not* have equal
measures, they are *not* congruent. So you cannot conclude that line *a* is
parallel to line *b*.

Part 3

**Example Using Angle Congruence to Justify
          Parallel Lines**

Which congruence statements justify *a* ∥ *b* or *c* ∥ *d*?

$\angle 2 \cong \angle 10$

$\angle 3 \cong \angle 6$

$\angle 4 \cong \angle 12$

$\angle 7 \cong \angle 12$

$\angle 9 \cong \angle 11$

$\angle 10 \cong \angle 15$

Solution ·

If two lines and a transversal form corresponding
angles that are congruent, then the lines are
parallel.

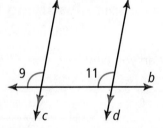

If ∠9 ≅ ∠11, then *c* ∥ *d*.

If ∠2 ≅ ∠10, then *a* ∥ *b*.

If ∠4 ≅ ∠12, then *a* ∥ *b*.

If two lines and a transversal form alternate
interior angles that are congruent, then the lines
are parallel.

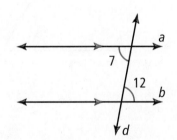

If ∠7 ≅ ∠12, then *a* ∥ *b*.

If ∠3 ≅ ∠6, then *c* ∥ *d*.

If ∠10 ≅ ∠15, then *c* ∥ *d*.

1. For the figure shown, decide if m ∥ n.

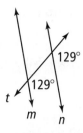

A. Yes, m ∥ n because the labeled angles are supplementary corresponding angles.

B. No, line m is not parallel to line n because the labeled angles are corresponding angles, but they are not congruent.

C. No, line m is not parallel to line n because the labeled angles are congruent, but they are not corresponding angles.

D. Yes, m ∥ n because the labeled angles are congruent corresponding angles.

2. In order for line p to be parallel to line q, what must be the value of x?

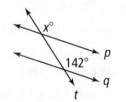

(The figure is not to scale.)

3. Use the figures to decide whether the indicated lines are parallel.

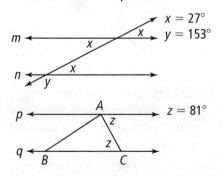

a. Are m and n parallel lines? Explain.

b. Are p and q parallel lines? Explain.

4. Find a congruence statement that justifies x ∥ y.

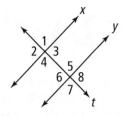

A. If ∠5 ≅ ∠6, then x ∥ y because if alternate interior angles are congruent, then the lines are parallel.

B. If ∠3 ≅ ∠6, then x ∥ y because if corresponding angles are congruent, then the lines are parallel.

C. If ∠2 ≅ ∠6, then x ∥ y because if alternate interior angles are congruent, then the lines are parallel.

D. If ∠1 ≅ ∠6, then x ∥ y because if corresponding angles are congruent, then the lines are parallel.

5. Identify each pair of parallel lines in the figure.

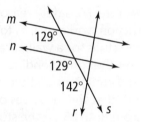

6. Error Analysis Your friend incorrectly says that line m is parallel to line n when the measure of angle X is 108°.

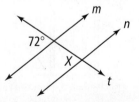

(The figure is not to scale.)

a. For which measure of angle X is line m parallel to line n?

b. What was your friend's likely mistake?

7. a. Writing If $m\angle 3 = 127°$ and $m\angle 6 = 127°$, is line m parallel to line n?

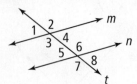

A. No, line m is not parallel to line n because $\angle 3$ and $\angle 6$ are congruent, but they are not alternate interior angles.

B. Yes, line m is parallel to line n because $\angle 3$ and $\angle 6$ are supplementary alternate interior angles.

C. Yes, line m is parallel to line n because $\angle 3$ and $\angle 6$ are congruent alternate interior angles.

D. No, line m is not parallel to line n because $\angle 3$ and $\angle 6$ are alternate interior angles, but they are not congruent.

b. If line m is parallel to line n, what must be true about the relationship between $\angle 1$ and $\angle 7$? Explain.

8. Architecture For safety reasons, a construction worker wants to make sure two studs for a wall parallel. She measures the corresponding angles formed by the floor and the two studs. She finds that the measures of the angles are both 85°. If the studs are parallel, she can leave them as they are. Otherwise, they need to be fixed. Will the worker need to fix the studs?

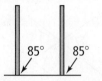

(The figure is not to scale.)

A. Yes, because the corresponding angles are not congruent.

B. Yes, because the corresponding angles do not sum to 180°.

C. No, because the corresponding angles sum to 180°.

D. No, because the corresponding angles are congruent.

9. Multiple Representations Using alternate interior angles, write an equation in terms of x that will make line m parallel to line n.

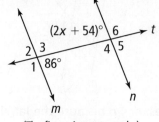

(The figure is not to scale.)

a. Write an equation which will make line m parallel to line n.

b. Find the value of x that makes line m parallel to line n.

c. Find the measures of a different pair of angles that will make line m parallel to line n. Justify your reasoning.

10. Think About the Process

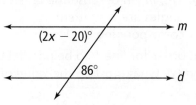

(The figure is not to scale.)

a. Write an equation in terms of x that will make $d \parallel m$.

b. Find the value of x for which $d \parallel m$.

11. Think About the Process

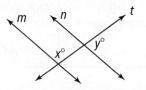

(The figure is not to scale.)

a. What must be true about the corresponding angles labeled $x°$ and $y°$ so that line m is parallel to line n?

b If the value of x is 73, for which value of y is line m parallel to line n?

See your complete lesson at MyMathUniverse.com

CCSS: 8.G.A.5

Key Concept

The sum of the measures of the interior angles of a triangle is 180°.

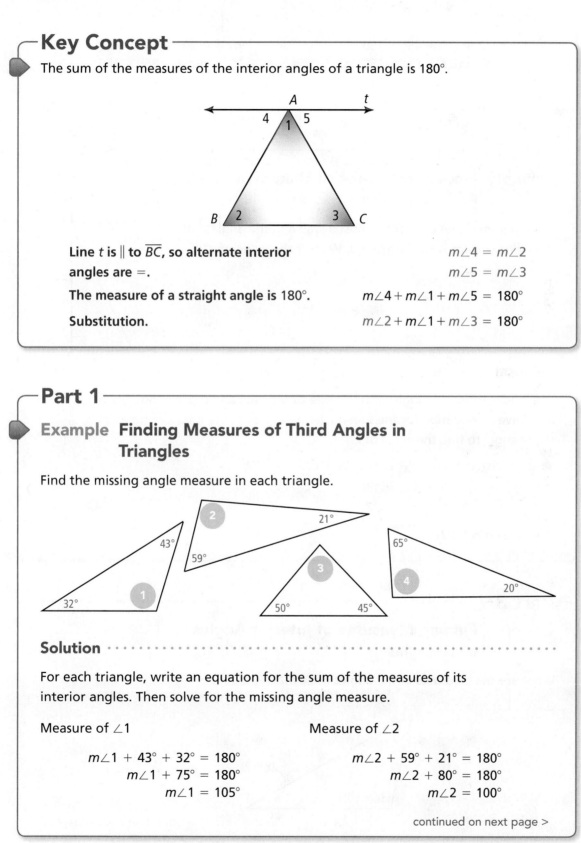

Line t is ∥ to $\overline{BC}$, so alternate interior angles are =.

$m\angle 4 = m\angle 2$
$m\angle 5 = m\angle 3$

The measure of a straight angle is 180°.

$m\angle 4 + m\angle 1 + m\angle 5 = 180°$

Substitution.

$m\angle 2 + m\angle 1 + m\angle 3 = 180°$

Part 1

Example Finding Measures of Third Angles in Triangles

Find the missing angle measure in each triangle.

Solution

For each triangle, write an equation for the sum of the measures of its interior angles. Then solve for the missing angle measure.

Measure of ∠1

$m\angle 1 + 43° + 32° = 180°$
$m\angle 1 + 75° = 180°$
$m\angle 1 = 105°$

Measure of ∠2

$m\angle 2 + 59° + 21° = 180°$
$m\angle 2 + 80° = 180°$
$m\angle 2 = 100°$

continued on next page >

Part 1

Solution continued

Measure of ∠3

$$m\angle 3 + 50° + 45° = 180°$$
$$m\angle 3 + 95° = 180°$$
$$m\angle 3 = 85°$$

Measure of ∠4

$$m\angle 4 + 20° + 65° = 180°$$
$$m\angle 4 + 85° = 180°$$
$$m\angle 4 = 95°$$

Part 2

Example Finding Measures of Unknown Angles in Right Triangles

The diagram shows a ladder against a wall and the angle that the ladder makes with the ground. What is the value of x?

Solution

The ladder forms a triangle with the side of the wall and the ground. Write and solve an equation for the sum of the measures of the interior angles of the triangle to find the value of x.

$$63° + 90° + x° = 180°$$
$$153 + x = 180$$
$$x = 27$$

The value of x is 27.

Part 3

Example Finding Measures of Interior Angles of Triangles

What are the measures of the angles of △ JKL?

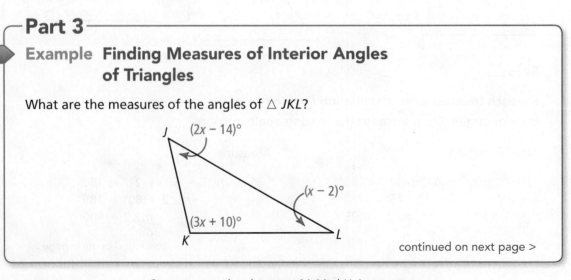

continued on next page >

Part 3

Example continued

Solution

The sum of the measures of the interior angles of a triangle is 180°.

Step 1 Write an equation to find the value of x.

$$m\angle J + m\angle K + m\angle L = 180°$$
$$(2x - 14)° + (3x + 10)° + (x - 2)° = 180°$$
$$6x - 6 = 180$$
$$6x = 186$$
$$x = 31$$

Step 2 Substitute the value of x into the expression for each angle measure.

$$
\begin{array}{lll}
m\angle J = (2x - 14)° & m\angle K = (3x + 10)° & m\angle L = (x - 2)° \\
\quad = [2(31) - 14]° & \quad = [3(31) + 10]° & \quad = (31 - 2)° \\
\quad = (62 - 14)° & \quad = (93 + 10)° & \quad = 29° \\
\quad = 48° & \quad = 103° &
\end{array}
$$

The measures of the angles of $\triangle JKL$ are 48°, 103°, and 29°.

Check

$$m\angle J + m\angle K + m\angle L = 180°$$
$$48° + 103° + 29° \stackrel{?}{=} 180°$$
$$180° = 180° \checkmark$$

1. Find the number of degrees in the third angle of the triangle.

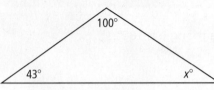

The figure is not drawn to scale.

2. An architect is designing a home. What is the measure of the missing angle of the roof?

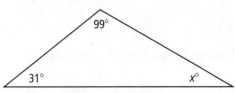

The figure is not drawn to scale.

3. There is a slide in the back of the school. The stairs for the slide go straight up. The angle made with the slide and the ground is 49°. What is the value of x?

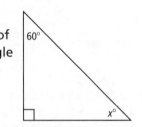

The figure is not drawn to scale.

4. Mental Math
Find the value of the missing angle of the right triangle.

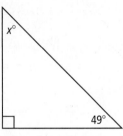

The figure is not drawn to scale.

5. In $\triangle QRS$, $m\angle R$ is 20° more than $m\angle Q$ and $m\angle S$ is 70° more than $m\angle Q$. Find $m\angle R$.

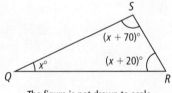

The figure is not drawn to scale.

6. For the figure, find the value of the variable x and $m\angle Q$.

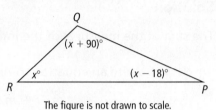

The figure is not drawn to scale.

7. a. Writing If the measures of two angles of a triangle are 100° and 19°, what is the measure of the third angle?

b. Explain how a straight angle is related to the angles of a triangle.

8. Reasoning An art class is designing a sign to put by the entrance to the school. The sign is in the shape of a triangle and has one angle that is 87° and another which is 42°.

a. What is the measure of the third angle?

b. Explain how you could determine if the triangle is acute, right, or obtuse without finding the third angle.

9. Error Analysis On a math test the students are given a right triangle. One of the acute angles has a measure of 55°. One student says that the measure of the other acute angle is 125°.

a. What is the measure of the other acute angle?

b. What error might the student have made?

A. The student only subtracted the right angle from 180°.

B. The student subtracted the sum of the two given angles from 360°.

C. The student added the right angle and the given acute angle, but did not subtract the sum from 180°.

D. The student only subtracted the acute angle from 180°.

See your complete lesson at MyMathUniverse.com

10. Statue A company is making different size statues that are in the shape of hour glasses. Use the figure to find the missing measure, $x°$.

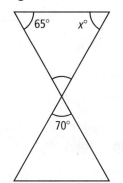

65° $x°$

70°

The figure is not drawn to scale.

11. Estimation A ramp is being built to a building to help with deliveries. The angle that the bottom of the ramp makes with the ground is 37.2°.

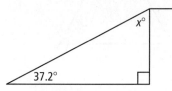

$x°$

37.2°

The figure is not drawn to scale.

a. Estimate the measure of the other acute angle.

A. 63°   **B.** 48°

C. 58°   **D.** 53°

b. Find the exact measure of the other acute angle.

12. Mental Math If $m\angle B = 130°$ and $m\angle C = 10°$ for $\triangle ABC$, what is $m\angle A$?

13. In $\triangle ABC$, angle B is 5 times $m\angle A$ and angle C is 7° less than 4 times $m\angle A$. Find $m\angle B$. Simplify your answer.

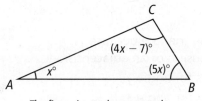

C

$(4x - 7)°$

$x°$ $(5x)°$

A   B

The figure is not drawn to scale.

14. Think About the Process Malak is building a bench. The bench comes out from the wall and there is a brace below as shown in the figure. The angle created between the wall and the brace is 53.8°.

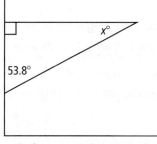

$x°$

53.8°

The figure is not drawn to scale.

a. Which of the following is the correct equation to solve for the missing angle?

A. $x° + 90° + 53.8° = 90°$

B. $x° + 100° + 53.8° = 180°$

C. $x° + 53.8° = 180°$

D. $x° + 90° + 53.8° = 180°$

b. What is the measure of the missing angle?

15. Think About the Process In $\triangle ABC$, $m\angle B$ is 4 times $m\angle A$ and $m\angle C$ is 13° less than 5 times $m\angle A$.

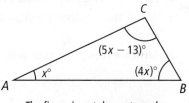

C

$(5x - 13)°$

$x°$ $(4x)°$

A   B

The figure is not drawn to scale.

a. Which of the following is the correct equation used to solve for the measure of each angle?

A $m\angle A - m\angle B - m\angle C = 180°$

B. $m\angle A + m\angle B - m\angle C = 180°$

C. $m\angle A + m\angle B + m\angle C = 180°$

D. $m\angle A - m\angle B + m\angle C = 180°$

b. Find the measure of each angle.

16. Challenge In $\triangle ABC$, $m\angle B$ is one-third the $m\angle A$ and $m\angle C$ is 37 less than the $m\angle A$. What are the measures of the angles of $\triangle ABC$?

11-4 **Exterior Angles of Triangles**

Vocabulary
exterior angle of
a triangle, remote
interior angles

CCSS: 8.G.A.5

Part 1

Intro

An **exterior angle of a triangle** is an angle formed by a side and an extension of an adjacent side. ∠1 is an exterior angle of each triangle.

For each exterior angle of a triangle, the two nonadjacent interior angles are its **remote interior angles.** ∠2 and ∠3 are remote interior angles of ∠1 in each triangle.

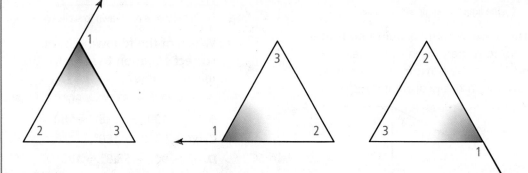

Example Identifying Interior and Exterior Angles of Triangles

a. Which of the numbered angles are exterior angles?

b. Name the remote interior angles for each exterior angle.

c. Which exterior angles are congruent? Explain.

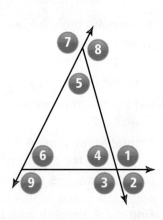

Solution

a. Angles 1, 3, 8, and 9 are exterior angles of the triangle because they are angles formed by a side and an extension of an adjacent side.

b. Angles 5 and 6 are the remote interior angles for angle 1.
Angles 5 and 6 are the remote interior angles for angle 3.
Angles 4 and 5 are the remote interior angles for angle 9.
Angles 4 and 6 are the remote interior angles for angle 8.

c. Angles 1 and 3 are vertical angles. Vertical angles have equal measures, so they are congruent.

See your complete lesson at MyMathUniverse.com

Key Concept

The measure of an exterior angle of a triangle equals the sum of the measures of its two remote interior angles.

Here is an example.

$m\angle 1 + m\angle 2 + m\angle 3 = 180°$ because the sum of the measures of the interior angles of a triangle equals 180°.

$m\angle 3 + m\angle 4 = 180°$ because $\angle 3$ and $\angle 4$ form a straight angle.

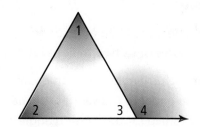

Substitute $m\angle 3 + m\angle 4$ for 180° in the first equation. Then subtract $\angle 3$ from both sides.

$$m\angle 1 + m\angle 2 + m\angle 3 = m\angle 3 + m\angle 4$$
$$m\angle 1 + m\angle 2 + m\angle 3 - m\angle 3 = m\angle 3 + m\angle 4 - m\angle 3$$
$$m\angle 1 + m\angle 2 = m\angle 4$$

So the measure of an exterior angle of a triangle equals the sum of the measures of its two remote interior angles.

Part 2

Example Finding Measures of Interior and Exterior Angles of Triangles

Find the missing angle measure in each diagram.

8°   28°   27°   17°   114°   163°   56°   124°

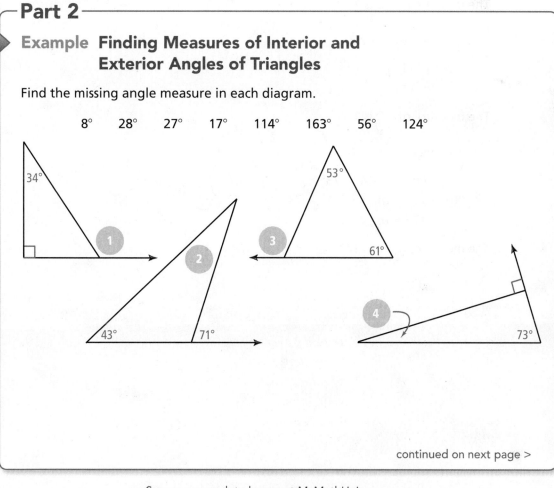

continued on next page >

Solution ·

The measure of an exterior angle of a triangle equals the sum of the measures of its two remote interior angles.

For each triangle, write an equation that sets the measure of the exterior angle equal to the sum of the measures of its two remote interior angles. Then solve for the missing angle measure.

Find the measure of $\angle 1$.

$$m\angle 1 = 34° + 90°$$
$$= 124°$$

The measure of $\angle 1$ is 124°.

Find the measure of $\angle 2$.

$$71° = m\angle 2 + 43°$$
$$71° - 43° = m\angle 2 + 43° - 43°$$
$$28° = m\angle 2$$

The measure of $\angle 2$ is 28°.

Find the measure of $\angle 3$.

$$m\angle 3 = 53° + 61°$$
$$= 114°$$

The measure of $\angle 3$ is 114°.

Find the measure of $\angle 4$.

$$90° = m\angle 4 + 73°$$
$$90° - 73° = m\angle 4 + 73° - 73°$$
$$17° = m\angle 4$$

The measure of $\angle 4$ is 17°.

Example Calculating Measures of Exterior Angles of Triangles

Given $m\angle 1 = 26°$, $m\angle 2 = (3x - 2)°$, and $m\angle 3 = (5x - 8)°$, what is $m\angle 3$?

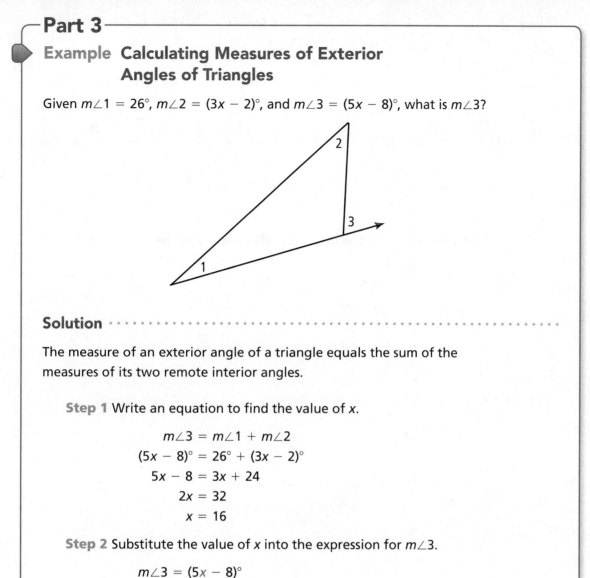

Solution ·

The measure of an exterior angle of a triangle equals the sum of the measures of its two remote interior angles.

Step 1 Write an equation to find the value of x.

$$m\angle 3 = m\angle 1 + m\angle 2$$
$$(5x - 8)° = 26° + (3x - 2)°$$
$$5x - 8 = 3x + 24$$
$$2x = 32$$
$$x = 16$$

Step 2 Substitute the value of x into the expression for $m\angle 3$.

$$m\angle 3 = (5x - 8)°$$
$$= [5(16) - 8]°$$
$$= (80 - 8)°$$
$$= 72°$$

So $m\angle 3$ is $72°$.

continued on next page >

Part 3

Solution continued

Check ·

Step 1 Find $m\angle 2$.

$$m\angle 2 = (3x - 2)°$$
$$= [3(16) - 2]°$$
$$= (48 - 2)°$$
$$= 46°$$

Step 2 Compare the sum of the measures of $\angle 1$ and $\angle 2$ to the measure of $\angle 3$.

$$m\angle 1 + m\angle 2 = 26° + 46°$$
$$= 72°$$
$$= m\angle 3 ✔$$

1. Determine which of the labeled angles are exterior angles.

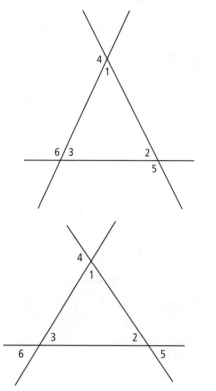

2.

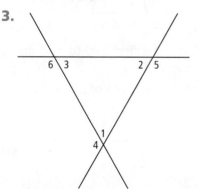

a. Which of the numbered angles in the figure are exterior angles?

b. Which of the numbered angles in the figure are congruent? List all that apply.

3.

a. What are the two remote interior angles for ∠4?

b. Which of the labeled angles are supplementary? List all that apply.

4. For the figure shown, find m∠1.

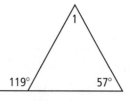

(The figure is not drawn to scale.)

5. Given that m∠4 = 68°, m∠1 = (5x − 8)°, and m∠2 = (6x − 12)°, find m∠1 and m∠2.

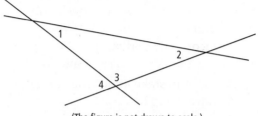

(The figure is not drawn to scale.)

6.

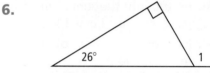

(The figure is not drawn to scale.)

a. Writing For the figure shown, find m∠1.

b. Explain two ways to find the missing angle measure of the triangle.

7.

59°

117° 1

(The figure is not drawn to scale.)

a. Reasoning For the figure shown, find m∠1.

b. Can you find the measure of ∠1 without using an exterior angle and the other remote interior angle? Explain.

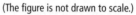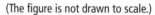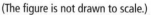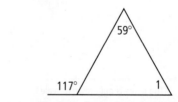

8.

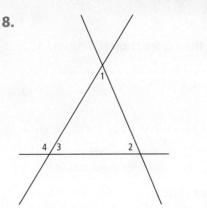

a. **Error Analysis** A student was asked to find $m\angle 1$ and $m\angle 2$ given that $m\angle 4 = 122°$, $m\angle 1 = (9x - 18)°$, and $m\angle 2 = (10x - 12)°$. He incorrectly said $m\angle 1 = 24°$ and $m\angle 2 = 34°$. Find $m\angle 1$ and $m\angle 2$.

b. What mistake might the student have made?

  A. He only solved for x.

  B. He thought the sum of $m\angle 1$, $m\angle 2$, and $m\angle 4$ was 180°.

  C. He thought the sum of $m\angle 1$ and $m\angle 2$ was 90°.

9. Airplane Spotting Two observers watch an airplane fly overhead. One observer looks up at $\angle 3$ to see the airplane, the other at $\angle 2$. If $m\angle 1 = (x + 28)°$, $m\angle 2 = (20x - 6)°$, and $m\angle 3 = 64°$, find $m\angle 1$.

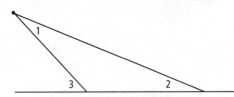

(The figure is not drawn to scale.)

10. Mental Math What is the measure of $\angle 1$?

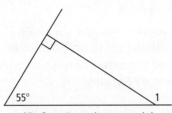

(The figure is not drawn to scale.)

11. For the figure shown, find $m\angle 1$ and $m\angle 2$.

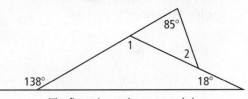

(The figure is not drawn to scale.)

12. Think About the Process

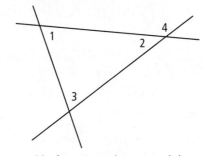

(The figure is not drawn to scale.)

a. Given that $m\angle 4 = 136°$, $m\angle 1 = (11x - 36)°$, and $m\angle 3 = (12x - 35)°$, what is the first step to find $m\angle 3$?

b. Find $m\angle 3$.

13. Think About the Process

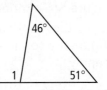

(The figure is not drawn to scale.)

a. What is the first step to find the measure of $\angle 1$?

b. Find the measure of $\angle 1$.

Angle–Angle Triangle Similarity

CCSS: 8.G.A.4, 8.G.A.5, Also 8.G.A.3

Key Concept

If two angles of one triangle are congruent to two angles of another triangle, then the triangles are similar.

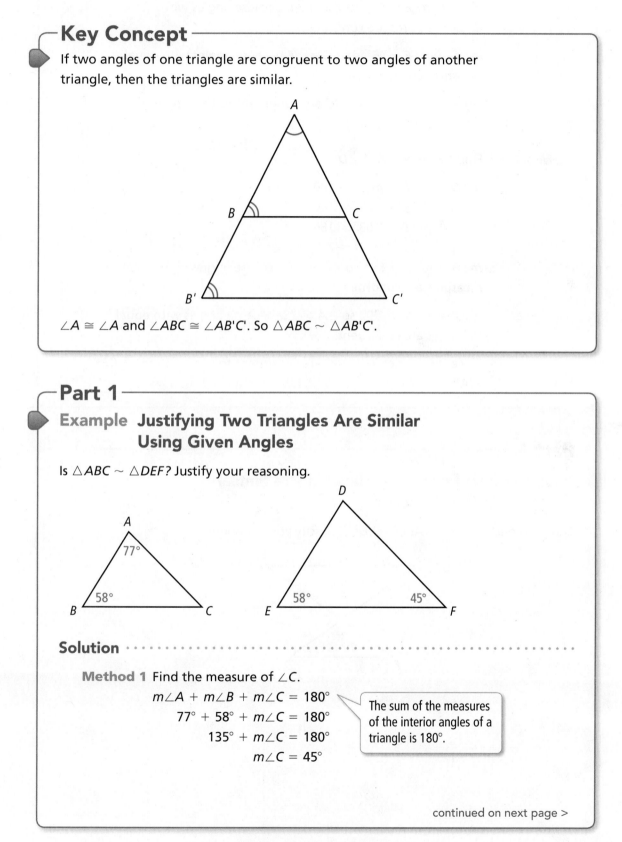

∠A ≅ ∠A and ∠ABC ≅ ∠AB'C'. So △ABC ~ △AB'C'.

Part 1

Example **Justifying Two Triangles Are Similar Using Given Angles**

Is △ABC ~ △DEF? Justify your reasoning.

Solution ·

Method 1 Find the measure of ∠C.

$$m\angle A + m\angle B + m\angle C = 180°$$
$$77° + 58° + m\angle C = 180°$$
$$135° + m\angle C = 180°$$
$$m\angle C = 45°$$

> The sum of the measures of the interior angles of a triangle is 180°.

continued on next page >

Part 1

Solution continued

$m\angle B = m\angle E = 58°$, so $\angle B \cong \angle E$ because angles with equal measures are congruent.

$m\angle C = m\angle F = 45°$, so $\angle C \cong \angle F$ because angles with equal measures are congruent.

Since two angles in $\triangle ABC$ are congruent to two angles in $\triangle DEF$, $\triangle ABC \sim \triangle DEF$.

Method 2 Find the measure of $\angle D$.

$$m\angle D + m\angle E + m\angle F = 180°$$
$$m\angle D + 58° + 45° = 180°$$
$$m\angle D + 103° = 180°$$
$$m\angle D = 77°$$

$m\angle B = m\angle E = 58°$, so $\angle B \cong \angle E$ because angles with equal measures are congruent.

$m\angle A = m\angle D = 70°$, so $\angle A \cong \angle D$ because angles with equal measures are congruent.

Since two angles in $\triangle ABC$ are congruent to two angles in $\triangle DEF$, $\triangle ABC \sim \triangle DEF$.

Part 2

Example Justifying Two Triangles Are Similar Using Vertical Angles

Can you conclude that $\triangle ABC \sim \triangle DCE$? Justify your reasoning.

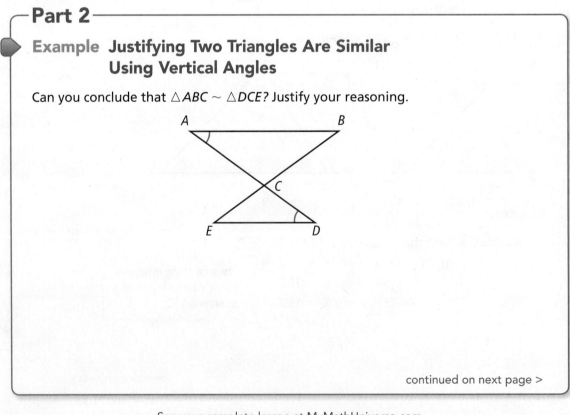

continued on next page >

Part 2

Solution ·

Know

$\angle A \cong \angle D$

↓

Need

To show that two pairs of angles are congruent.

↓

Plan

Look for another pair of congruent angles.

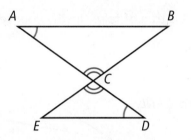

You know that $\angle A \cong \angle D$.

$\angle ACB$ and $\angle DCE$ are vertical angles. Vertical angles have equal measures, so $m\angle ACB = m\angle DCE$. Angles with equal measures are congruent, so $\angle ACB \cong \angle DCE$.

Since two angles in $\triangle ABC$ are congruent to two angles in $\triangle DEC$, you can conclude that $\triangle ABC \sim \triangle DEC$.

Part 3

Intro

Overlapping triangles may have a common side or angle.

You can simplify your work with overlapping triangles by separating and redrawing the triangles.

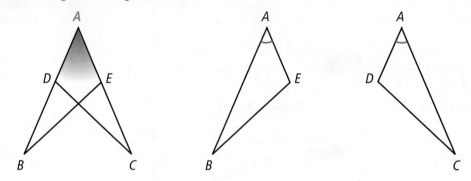

Example Finding Similar Triangles in Diagrams With Overlapping Triangles

Decide whether each statement is true of false. Justify your reasoning.

a. △LMP must be similar to △QMN.

b. △LMP must be similar to △RPQ.

c. △RPQ must be similar to △RNL.

d. △QMN must be similar to △RNL.

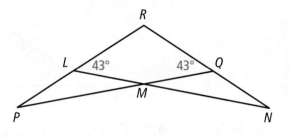

Solution

a. △LMP must be similar to △QMN.

∠MLP and ∠MQN both form a straight angle with a 43° angle, so
m∠MLP = m∠MQN = 180° − 43°, or 137°. Angles with equal
measures are congruent, so ∠MLP ≅ ∠MQN.

∠LMP and ∠QMN are vertical angles. Vertical angles have equal
measures, so m∠LMP = m∠QMN. Angles with equal measures are
congruent, so ∠LMP ≅ ∠QMN.

Since two angles of △LMP are congruent to two angles of △QMN,
△LMP must be similar to △QMN.

The statement is true.

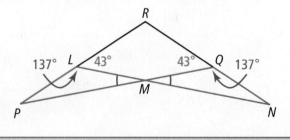

continued on next page >

Solution continued

b. △*LMP* must be similar to △*RPQ*.

There is not enough information to determine whether two angles of one triangle are congruent to two angles of the other triangle.

The statement is false.

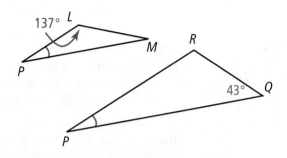

c. △*RPQ* must be similar to △*RNL*.

m∠*RQP* = *m*∠*RLN* = 43°, so ∠*RQP* ≅ ∠*RLN* because angles with equal measure are congruent.

△*RPQ* and △*RNL* share a common angle, ∠*R*. *m*∠*R* = *m*∠*R*, so ∠*R* ≅ ∠*R* because angles with equal measures are congruent.

Since two angles of △*RPQ* are congruent to two angles of △*RNL*, △*RPQ* must be similar to △*RNL*.

The statement is true.

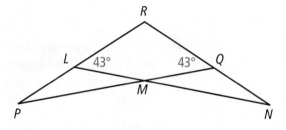

d. △*QMN* must be similar to △*RLN*.

There is not enough information to determine whether two angles of one triangle are congruent to two angles of the other triangle.

The statement is false.

1. Is △XYZ ~ △GHI? Figures are not drawn to scale.

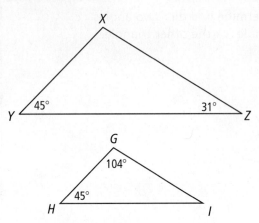

2. Is △FGH ~ △JIH? Figure is not drawn to scale.

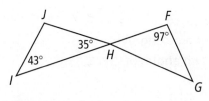

3. Which triangles are similar? Select all that apply. The figure is not drawn to scale.

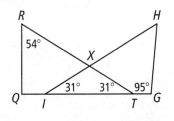

A. △TXI   **B.** △QRT

C. △GHI

4. a. Writing Is △GHI ~ △QRS? The figures are not drawn to scale.

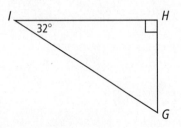

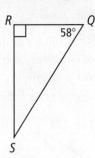

b. Describe how to use angle relationships to decide whether any two triangles are similar.

5. Error Analysis Anchil claims that the triangles △FGH and △KLJ are the only similar triangles because two angles of the triangles are congruent.

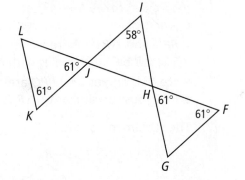

a. Which triangles are similar? Select all that apply. The figure is not drawn to scale.

A. △FGH   **B.** △KLJ

C. △JIH

b. What mistake might Anchil have made?

6. Jewelry A charm has the shape of two overlapping triangles. Is △XYZ ~ △XJK? The figure is not drawn to scale.

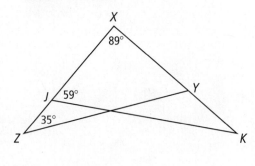

7. Is △GHI ~ △QRS? The figures are not drawn to scale.

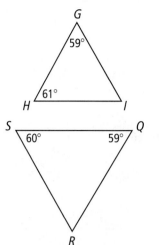

8. Find the similar triangles. Select all that apply. The figures are not drawn to scale.

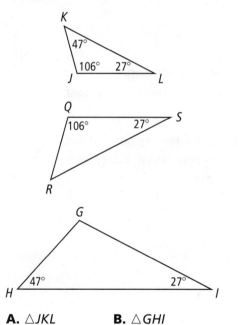

A. △JKL **B.** △GHI

C. △QRS

9. Think About the Process The figure is not drawn to scale.

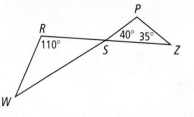

a. How can you tell if △WSR ~ △ZSP?

b. Is △WSR ~ △ZSP?

10. Think About the Process The figure is not drawn to scale.

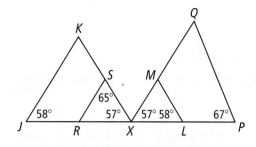

a. What facts about triangles can you use to find the similar triangles? Select all that apply.

   A. Angles with equal measures are congruent.

   B. Vertical angles have equal measures.

   C. The sum of the interior angles of any triangle is 180°.

   D. Common angles in overlapping triangles have equal measures.

b. Which triangles are similar? Select all that apply.

   A. △LMX **B.** △RSX

   C. △PQX **D.** △JKX

11. Challenge Which triangles are similar? Select all that apply. The figures are not drawn to scale.

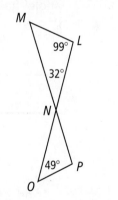

   A. △OPN **B.** △JIH

   C. △LNM **D.** △FGH

   E. △PON **F.** △LMN

CCSS: 8.G.A.5

Part 1

Example Finding Angle Measures Using Parallel Lines

In the diagram, $a \parallel b$ and $c \parallel d$. If $m\angle 1 = 60°$, what is $m\angle 6$?

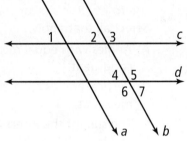

Solution

Method 1 $\angle 2$ and $\angle 1$ are corresponding angles formed by parallel lines a and b and transversal c, so they are congruent. Congruent angles have equal measures, so $m\angle 2 = 60°$.

$\angle 4$ and $\angle 2$ are corresponding angles formed by parallel lines c and d and transversal b, so they are congruent. Congruent angles have equal measures, so $m\angle 4 = 60°$.

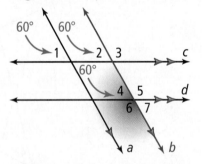

$\angle 4$ and $\angle 6$ form a straight angle, so they are supplementary angles.

$$m\angle 4 + m\angle 6 = 180°$$
$$60° + m\angle 6 = 180°$$
$$m\angle 6 = 120°$$

continued on next page >

Solution continued

Method 2 ∠2 and ∠1 are corresponding angles formed by parallel lines *a* and *b* and transversal *c*, so they are congruent. Congruent angles have equal measures, so *m*∠2 = 60°.

∠2 and ∠3 form a straight angle, so they are supplementary angles.

$$m\angle 2 + m\angle 3 = 180°$$
$$60° + m\angle 3 = 180°$$
$$m\angle 3 = 120°$$

∠3 and ∠5 are corresponding angles formed by parallel lines *c* and *d* and transversal *b*, so they are congruent. Congruent angles have the same measures, so *m*∠5 = 120°.

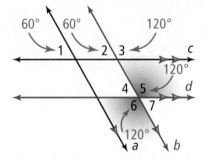

∠5 and ∠6 are vertical angles, so they have equal measures. So *m*∠6 = 120°.

Part 2

Example Finding Measures of Exterior Angles

Given $m\angle 1 = (7x - 8)°$, $m\angle 2 = (5x + 1)°$, and $m\angle 3 = (x + 11)°$, what is $m\angle 1$?

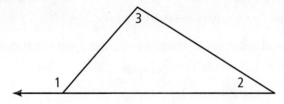

Solution

The measure of an exterior angle of a triangle equals the sum of the measures of its two remote interior angles.

Step 1 Write an equation to find the value of x.

$$m\angle 1 = m\angle 2 + m\angle 3$$

$$(7x - 8)° = (5x + 1)° + (x + 11)°$$

$$7x - 8 = 6x + 12$$

$$7x = 6x + 20$$

$$x = 20$$

Step 2 Substitute the value of x into the expression for $m\angle 1$.

$$m\angle 1 = (7x - 8)°$$

$$= [7(20) - 8]°$$

$$= (140 - 8)°$$

$$= 132°$$

So $m\angle 1$ is 132°.

Part 3

Example Justifying That Triangles are Similar

Can you conclude that the triangles are similar? Justify your reasoning.

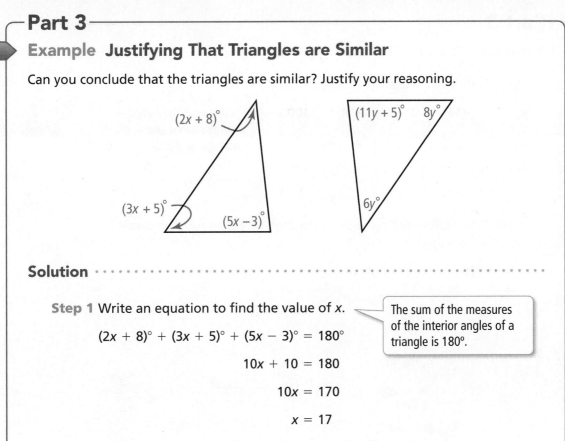

Solution

Step 1 Write an equation to find the value of *x*.

> The sum of the measures of the interior angles of a triangle is 180°.

$$(2x + 8)° + (3x + 5)° + (5x - 3)° = 180°$$

$$10x + 10 = 180$$

$$10x = 170$$

$$x = 17$$

Step 2 Substitute the value of *x* into the expression for each angle measure.

$$(2x + 8)° = [2(17) + 8]°$$

$$= (34 + 8)°$$

$$= 42°$$

$$(3x + 5)° = [3(17) + 5]°$$

$$= (51 + 5)°$$

$$= 56°$$

$$(5x + 3)° = [5(17) - 3]°$$

$$= (85 - 3)°$$

$$= 82°$$

So the measures of the angles of the first triangle are 42°, 56°, and 82°.

continued on next page >

Part 3

Solution continued

Step 3 Write an equation to find the value of y.

$$(11y + 5)° + 6y° + 8y° = 180°$$

$$25y + 5 = 180$$

$$25y = 175$$

$$y = 7$$

> The sum of the measures of the interior angles of a triangle is 180°.

Step 4 Substitute the value of y into the expression for each angle measure.

$$(11y + 5)° = [11(7) + 5]°$$

$$= (77 + 5)°$$

$$= 82°$$

$$6y° = 6(7)°$$

$$= 42°$$

$$8y° = 8(7)°$$

$$= 56°$$

So the measures of the angles of the second triangle are 82°, 42°, and 56°.

Step 5 Compare the measures of the angles of the two triangles to decide whether the triangles are similar.

The angle measures of the two triangles are equal. Angles with equal measures are congruent. Since the two angles of the first triangle are congruent to two angles of the second triangle, you can conclude that the triangles are similar.

1. In the diagram, $m \parallel n$ and $s \parallel t$. Find $m\angle 3$.

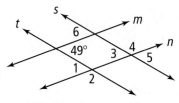

(This figure is not to scale.)

2. In the figure, $m\angle 1 = (3x + 12)°$, $m\angle 2 = (3x + 18)°$, and $m\angle 3 = (7x + 10)°$. What is $m\angle 3$?

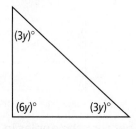

(This figure is not to scale.)

3. Are the two triangles similar?

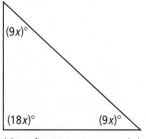

(These figures are not to scale.)

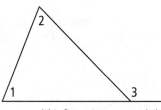

A. Yes, because the triangles looks the same.

B. Yes, because the angles in one triangle are congruent to the angles in the other triangle.

C. No, because the angles in one triangle are not congruent to the angles in the other triangle.

D. You cannot determine if two triangles are similar without knowing their side lengths.

4. In the figure, $m \parallel n$ and $p \parallel q$.

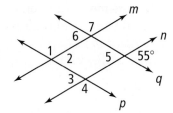

(This figure is not to scale.)

a. Describe a method you can use to find $m\angle 2$.

b. Find $m\angle 2$.

c. Is there another method you can use to find $m\angle 2$? Explain.

5. In the figure, $m\angle 1 = (8x + 7)°$, $m\angle 2 = (4x + 14)°$, and $m\angle 4 = (13x + 12)°$. Your friend incorrectly says that $m\angle 4 = 51°$.

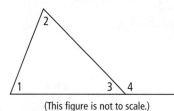

(This figure is not to scale.)

a. What is $m\angle 4$?

b. What mistake might your friend have made?

   A. Your friend found $m\angle 3$, not $m\angle 4$.

   B. Your friend found $m\angle 2$, not $m\angle 4$.

   C. Your friend found $m\angle 1$, not $m\angle 4$.

6. In the figure, $m\angle 1 = (4x + 7)°$, $m\angle 2 = (2x + 9)°$, and $m\angle 4 = (7x - 4)°$. What is $m\angle 2$? $m\angle 3$?

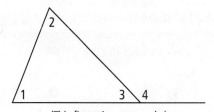

(This figure is not to scale.)

See your complete lesson at MyMathUniverse.com

7. In a certain city, four streets intersect as shown. A Street and B Street are parallel, and C Street and D Street are parallel. If the measure of an angle formed by B Street and D Street is as shown, what is $m\angle 2$?

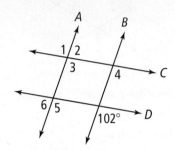

(This figure is not to scale.)

8.

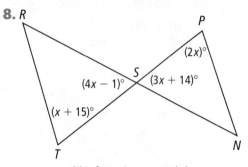

(This figure is not to scale.)

a. Are $\triangle RST$ and $\triangle NSP$ similar?

b. Find the measure of the angles in each triangle.

9. Think About the Process

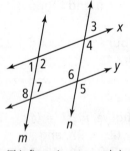

(This figure is not to scale.)

a. If you are given $m\angle 1$, what is the minimum number of steps you need to find $m\angle 5$?

A. 4   **B.** 5

C. 3   **D.** 2

b. If $m\angle 1 = 63°$, what is $m\angle 5$?

10. Think About the Process In the figure,
$m\angle 1 = (5x + 11)°$,
$m\angle 2 = (3x + 22)°$, and
$m\angle 3 = (9x + 28)°$.

(This figure is not to scale.)

a. Write an equation you could use to find $m\angle 1$.

b. What is $m\angle 1$?

11. Challenge In the figure,
$m\angle 1 = (x + 4)°$, $m\angle 2 = (2x + 11)°$, and $m\angle 4 = (4x - 4)°$.

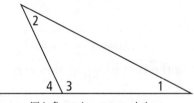

(This figure is not to scale.)

a. Find $m\angle 1$, $m\angle 2$, $m\angle 3$, and $m\angle 4$.

b. Write four other algebraic expressions for the diagram that you can use to get the same angle measures.

12. Challenge Are the triangles similar?

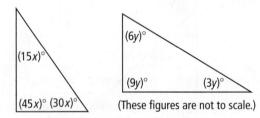

(These figures are not to scale.)

A. Yes, because the angles in one triangle are congruent to the angles in the other triangle.

B. Yes, because they both have three sides.

C. No, because the angles in one triangle are not congruent to the angles in the other triangle.

D. Yes, because all six angles are congruent to each other.

CCSS: 8.G.B.6

Key Concept

A **proof** is a logical, deductive argument in which every statement of fact is supported by a reason. Reasons can be properties, definitions, assumptions, or given facts. A **theorem** is a conjecture that is proven.

Part 1

Example Justifying Steps of Proofs

Given $3(x + 5) = 45$, prove $x = 10$. Complete the proof by writing the reason that justifies each statement.

- Division Property of Equality
- Subtraction Property of Equality
- Distributive Property
- Given

Statements	Reasons
1. $3(x + 5) = 45$	**1.** ■
2. $3x + 15 = 45$	**2.** ■
3. $3x = 30$	**3.** ■
4. $x = 10$	**4.** ■

Solution

Statements	Reasons
1. $3(x + 5) = 45$	**1.** Given
2. $3x + 15 = 45$	**2.** Distributive Property
3. $3x = 30$	**3.** Subtraction Property of Equality
4. $x = 10$	**4.** Division Property of Equality

Part 2

Example Writing Proofs

It is given that *a* intersects *b*. Write the missing statements and reasons in this proof that $m\angle 2 = m\angle 3$.

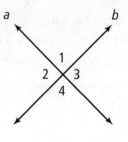

- It is given that ■.
- $m\angle 1 + m\angle 2 = 180°$ because ■ are adjacent angles that form a straight angle.
- $m\angle 1 + m\angle 3 = 180°$ because ■ are adjacent angles that form a straight angle.
- By ■, $m\angle 1 + m\angle 2 = m\angle 1 + m\angle 3$.
- By the Subtraction Property of Equality, ■.

Solution ·

It is given that *a* intersects *b*.

$m\angle 1 + m\angle 2 = 180°$ because $\angle 1$ and $\angle 2$ are adjacent angles that form a straight angle.

$m\angle 1 + m\angle 3 = 180°$ because $\angle 1$ and $\angle 3$ are adjacent angles that form a straight angle.

By substitution, $m\angle 1 + m\angle 2 = m\angle 1 + m\angle 3$.

By the Subtraction Property of Equality, $m\angle 2 = m\angle 3$.

1. Given $4x + 5 = 25$, prove $x = 5$.

Statements	Reasons
1. $4x + 5 = 25$	1. Given
2. $4x = 20$	2. ■
3. $x = 5$	3. ■

2. If $\frac{x}{3} - 2 = 13$, prove that $x = 45$.

Statements	Reasons
1. $\frac{x}{3} - 2 = 13$	1. ■
2. $\frac{x}{3} = ■$	2. Addition Property of Equality
3. $x = 45$	3. ■

3. If $0.50(x - 2) = 8$, prove $x = 20$.

Statements	Reasons
1. $0.50(x - 4) = 8$	1. Given
2. $0.50x - 2 = 8$	2. ■
3. $0.50x = 10$	3. ■
4. $x = 20$	4. ■

4. a. Writing Given $\frac{x + 1}{4} = 9$, prove $x = 35$.

Statements	Reasons
1. $\frac{x + 1}{4} = 9$	1. Given
2. $x + 1 = 36$	2. ■
3. $x = 35$	3. ■

b. Explain why it is important to justify each step in a proof.

5. a. Reasoning Complete the following proof.

Given: C is the midpoint of $\overline{AD}$.

Prove: $x = 4$

$$\overset{7x}{\underset{A}{\rule{0pt}{0pt}}} \qquad \overset{4x + 12}{\underset{C \qquad\qquad D}{\rule{0pt}{0pt}}}$$

Statements	Reasons
1. C is the midpoint of $\overline{AD}$	1. Given
2. $\overline{AC} \cong \overline{CD}$	2. ■
3. $AC = CD$	3. Congruent segments have equal length.
4. $7x = 4x + 12$	4. ■
5. $3x = 12$	5. ■
6. $x = 4$	6. ■

b. Explain if there is another way to prove $x = 4$.

6. Streets The following is a diagram of streets in a city. Street A intersects Streets B, and C and B is parallel to C. If $m\angle 2 = 116°$, prove that the $m\angle 2 = m\angle 8$.

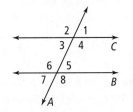

It is given that Street A intersects Street B and C, B is parallel to C, and $m\angle 2 = ■°$. By vertical angles, $m\angle 2 = m\angle ■$. Then $m\angle 4 = m\angle 6$ because of ■. Again by vertical angles, $m\angle 6 = m\angle ■$. By the ■, $m\angle 2 = m\angle 8$.

7. Open-Ended

a. Prove $x = 8$ if $2x - 7 + 7x = 65$.

Statements
1. $2x - 7 + 7x = 65$
2. $2x + 7x - 7 = 65$
3. $■ = 65$
4. $9x = 72$
5. $x = 8$

Reasons
1. Given
2. ■
3. Combine like terms
4. ■
5. ■

b. Write a similar proof and have a friend complete the missing statements and reasons.

8. *E* intersects line *F* and *G*. Line *F* is parallel to *G*. The $m\angle 2 = 126°$. Prove that $m\angle 2 + m\angle 7 = 180°$.

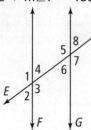

It is given that *E* intersects lines *F* and *G*, line *F* is parallel to *G*, and $m\angle 2 = $ ■°. Then $m\angle 2 + m\angle 3 = 180°$ because $\angle$■ and $\angle 3$ are adjacent angles that form a straight line. $m\angle 3 = m\angle 5$ by ■. By ■, $m\angle 5 = m\angle 7$. By the Transitive Property, $m\angle 3 = m\angle$■. By ■, $m\angle 2 + m\angle 7 = 180°$.

9. Think About the Process

a. Which statements should be compared to come up with each reason?

A. The current statement and the previous statement

B. The first statement and the last statement

C. The current statement and the next statement

b. Prove that $m\angle C = 43°$ for $\triangle ABC$, if $m\angle A = 62°$ and $m\angle B = 75°$.

Statements
1. $m\angle A = 62°$ and $m\angle B = 75°$
2. $m\angle A + m\angle B + m\angle C = 180$
3. $\qquad 62 + 75 + x = 180$
4. $\qquad\qquad 137 + x = 180$
5. $\qquad\qquad\qquad x = 43$

Reasons
1. Given
2. ■
3. ■
4. ■
5. ■

10. Think About the Process

a. What should be the first step to starting a proof?

A. Find the given information.

B. See what the second statement should be.

C. See what the last statement should be.

D. See what the second reason should be.

b. Prove that $x = 8$ for the equation $3(x + 5) + 9 = 56 - x$.

Statements
1. $\qquad 3(x + 5) + 9 = 56 - x$
2. $\qquad\qquad\quad ■ = 56 - x$
3. $\quad 3x + 15 + 9 + x = 56$
4. $\qquad\qquad 4x + 24 = 56$
5. $\qquad\qquad\qquad 4x = ■$
6. $\qquad\qquad\qquad x = 8$

Reasons
1. ■
2. Distributive Property
3. ■
4. ■
5. Subtraction Property of Equality
6. ■

The Pythagorean Theorem

Vocabulary
hypotenuse, leg
of a right triangle,
Pythagorean
Theorem

CCSS: 8.G.B.6, 8.G.B.7

Key Concept

In a right triangle, the two shortest sides are **legs**.

The longest side, which is opposite the right angle, is the **hypotenuse**.

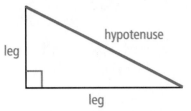

You can represent the lengths of the legs of the triangle with *a* and *b*, and the length of the hypotenuse with *c*.

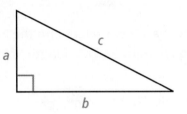

In any right triangle, the sum of the squares of the lengths of the legs is equal to the square of the length of the hypotenuse. This equation is known as the Pythagorean Theorem.

$$(\text{leg})^2 + (\text{leg})^2 = (\text{hypotenuse})^2$$
$$a^2 + b^2 = c^2$$

Part 1

Intro

You can use the Pythagorean Theorem to find the length of the hypotenuse of a right triangle when you know the lengths of the legs.

Example Finding Lengths of Hypotenuses Using the Pythagorean Theorem

What is the length of the hypotenuse of each triangle?

a. 3 cm
4 cm

continued on next page >

Example continued

b.

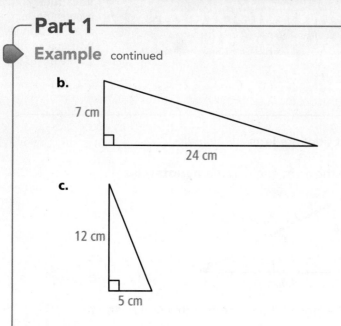

c.

Solution

For each triangle, substitute the known values into the Pythagorean theorem. Then solve the equation to find the length of the hypotenuse.

a.

Let c represent the length of the hypotenuse.

Use the Pythagorean Theorem.	$a^2 + b^2 = c^2$
Substitute 3 for *a* and 4 for *b*.	$3^2 + 4^2 = c^2$
Simplify.	$9 + 16 = c^2$
Add.	$25 = c^2$
Find the positive square root of each side.	$\sqrt{25} = \sqrt{c^2}$
Simplify.	$5 = c$

The length of the hypotenuse of the triangle is 5 cm.

continued on next page >

Solution continued

b.

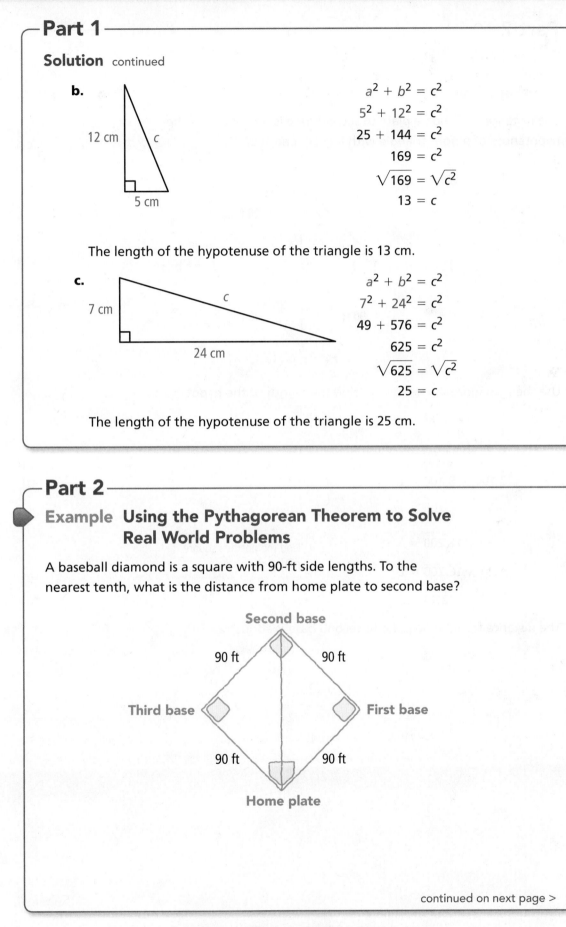

12 cm c

5 cm

$$a^2 + b^2 = c^2$$
$$5^2 + 12^2 = c^2$$
$$25 + 144 = c^2$$
$$169 = c^2$$
$$\sqrt{169} = \sqrt{c^2}$$
$$13 = c$$

The length of the hypotenuse of the triangle is 13 cm.

c.

7 cm c

24 cm

$$a^2 + b^2 = c^2$$
$$7^2 + 24^2 = c^2$$
$$49 + 576 = c^2$$
$$625 = c^2$$
$$\sqrt{625} = \sqrt{c^2}$$
$$25 = c$$

The length of the hypotenuse of the triangle is 25 cm.

Part 2

Example Using the Pythagorean Theorem to Solve Real World Problems

A baseball diamond is a square with 90-ft side lengths. To the nearest tenth, what is the distance from home plate to second base?

Second base

90 ft   90 ft

Third base   First base

90 ft   90 ft

Home plate

continued on next page >

Example continued

Solution

The distance from home plate to second base is the length of the hypotenuse of a right triangle with legs of length 90 ft.

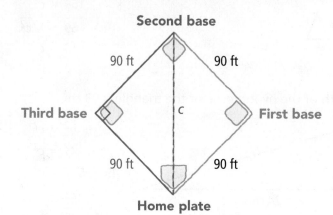

Use the Pythagorean Theorem to find the length of the hypotenuse.

$$a^2 + b^2 = c^2$$

$$90^2 + 90 = c^2$$

$$8{,}100 + 8{,}100 = c^2$$

$$16{,}200 = c^2$$

$$\sqrt{16{,}200} = \sqrt{c^2}$$

Find the positive square root of each side.

$$\sqrt{16{,}200} = c$$

$$127.3 \approx c$$

The distance from home plate to second base is about 127.3 ft.

Part 3

Example Finding Slant Heights of Pyramids

The Great Pyramid is a square pyramid. To the nearest hundredth, what is the slant height of the Great Pyramid?

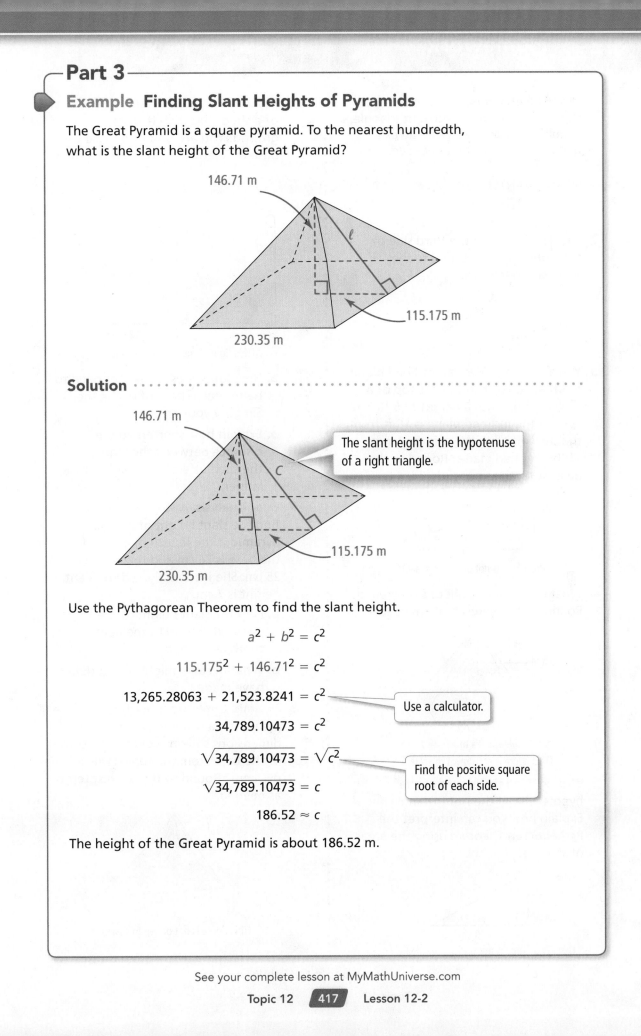

146.71 m

ℓ

115.175 m

230.35 m

Solution

146.71 m

The slant height is the hypotenuse of a right triangle.

c

115.175 m

230.35 m

Use the Pythagorean Theorem to find the slant height.

$$a^2 + b^2 = c^2$$

$$115.175^2 + 146.71^2 = c^2$$

$$13{,}265.28063 + 21{,}523.8241 = c^2$$

Use a calculator.

$$34{,}789.10473 = c^2$$

$$\sqrt{34{,}789.10473} = \sqrt{c^2}$$

Find the positive square root of each side.

$$\sqrt{34{,}789.10473} = c$$

$$186.52 \approx c$$

The height of the Great Pyramid is about 186.52 m.

1. Use the Pythagorean Theorem to find the unknown side of the right triangle. Simplify your answer. Write an exact answer, using radicals as needed.

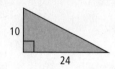

10

24

2. Find the length of the third side of the right triangle. Round to the nearest thousandth.

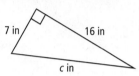

7 in   16 in

c in

3. You are going to use an inclined plane to lift a heavy object to the top of a shelving unit with a height of 6 ft. The base of the inclined plane is 16 ft from the shelving unit. What is the length of the inclined plane? Round to the nearest tenth as needed.

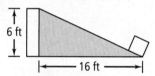

6 ft

|← 16 ft →|

(This figure is not drawn to scale.)

4. What is the slant height of the pyramid? Round to the nearest tenth as needed.

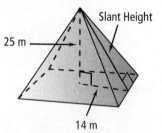

Slant Height

25 m

14 m

(This figure is not drawn to scale.)

5. **Writing** Find the length of the hypotenuse of the right triangle. Explain how you can interpret the Pythagorean Theorem using the areas of squares.

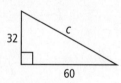

c

32

60

(This figure is not drawn to scale.)

6. **Reasoning** You are painting the roof of a shed that is 35 ft from the ground. You are going to place the base of a ladder 12 ft from the shed.

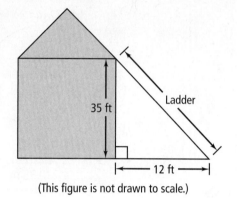

Ladder

35 ft

|← 12 ft →|

(This figure is not drawn to scale.)

a. How long does the ladder need to be to reach the roof of the shed? Simplify your answer.

b. Explain how shortening the distance between the ladder and the shed affects the height of the ladder.

7. **Error Analysis** A student was asked to find the slant height of a square pyramid if the length of each side of the base is 24 cm and the height is 25 cm. She incorrectly said the slant height is 7 cm.

a. Find the slant height of the pyramid. Round to the nearest tenth as needed.

b. What mistake might the student have made?

8. **Pyramid Dimensions** Each face of the pyramid is a triangle with the dimensions shown. How far is a corner of the base from the top of the pyramid? Round to the nearest tenth as needed.

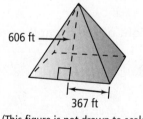

606 ft

367 ft

(This figure is not drawn to scale.)

See your complete lesson at MyMathUniverse.com

9. **Mental Math** What is the length of the hypotenuse of the triangle? Simplify your answer.

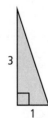

3

1

(This figure is not drawn to scale.)

10. **Open-Ended** A builder constructs a roof using wooden beams. The longest vertical beam divides the horizontal beam in half.

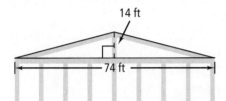

14 ft

74 ft

(This figure is not drawn to scale.)

a. What is the length of a sloping beam?

b. Find an object with a right angle. Measure the leg lengths and find the hypotenuse.

11. In a square pyramid, the length of each side of the base is $(28x - 18)$ ft. The height is $(24x + 6)$ ft. Find the slant height of the pyramid when $x = 11$. Round to the nearest tenth as needed.

12. **Think About the Process**

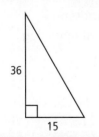

36

15

(This figure is not drawn to scale.)

a. What is the first step to find the length of the hypotenuse of the right triangle?

   A. Substitute the side lengths for a and b in the equation $a^2 + b^2 = c^2$.

B. Substitute the side lengths for b and c in the equation $a^2 + b^2 = c^2$.

C. Find the sum of the side lengths.

D. Substitute the side lengths for a and c in the equation $a^2 + b^2 = c^2$.

b. Find the length of the hypotenuse of the right triangle in the figure.

13. **Think About the Process** You roll a ball down the ramp shown.

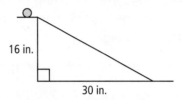

16 in.

30 in.

(This figure is not drawn to scale.)

a. How can you find the distance the ball travels down the ramp?

b. Find the distance.

14. **Challenge** You are going to the library from school. You can either walk on the sidewalk or go through the park. These paths are shown as dashed lines in the figure. The path through the park forms two congruent triangles.

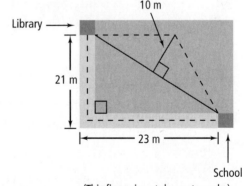

Library

10 m

21 m

23 m

School

(This figure is not drawn to scale.)

a. Find the distance you have to walk if you go through the park. Round to the nearest tenth as needed.

b. Is it shorter to go through the park or walk on the sidewalk?

CCSS: 8.G.B.7

Key Concept

You used the Pythagorean Theorem to find the hypotenuse of a right triangle when you knew the lengths of the legs. You can also use the Pythagorean Theorem to find the length of a leg when you know the hypotenuse and the length of the other leg.

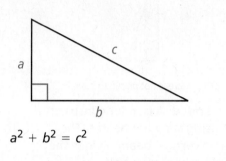

$$a^2 + b^2 = c^2$$

Part 1

Example Calculating Unknown Leg Lengths Using the Pythagorean Theorem

What is the length of the unknown leg in each triangle?

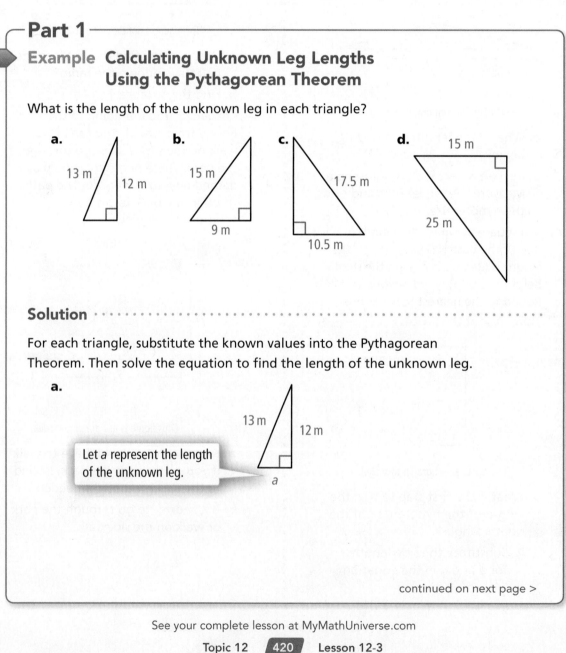

Solution

For each triangle, substitute the known values into the Pythagorean Theorem. Then solve the equation to find the length of the unknown leg.

a.

Let a represent the length of the unknown leg.

continued on next page >

Solution continued

Use the Pythagorean Theorem.	$a^2 + b^2 = c^2$
Substitute 12 for *b* and 13 for *c*.	$a^2 + 12^2 = 13^2$
Simplify.	$a^2 + 144 = 169$
Subtract 144 from each side.	$a^2 = 25$
Find the positive square root of each side.	$\sqrt{a^2} = \sqrt{25}$
Simplify.	$a = 5$

The length of the unknown leg of the triangle is 5 m.

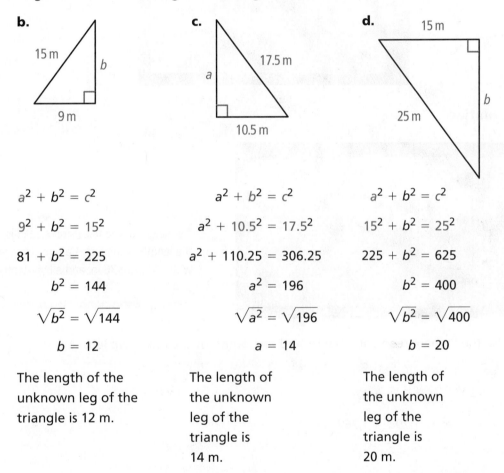

b.

$a^2 + b^2 = c^2$

$9^2 + b^2 = 15^2$

$81 + b^2 = 225$

$b^2 = 144$

$\sqrt{b^2} = \sqrt{144}$

$b = 12$

The length of the unknown leg of the triangle is 12 m.

c.

$a^2 + b^2 = c^2$

$a^2 + 10.5^2 = 17.5^2$

$a^2 + 110.25 = 306.25$

$a^2 = 196$

$\sqrt{a^2} = \sqrt{196}$

$a = 14$

The length of the unknown leg of the triangle is 14 m.

d.

$a^2 + b^2 = c^2$

$15^2 + b^2 = 25^2$

$225 + b^2 = 625$

$b^2 = 400$

$\sqrt{b^2} = \sqrt{400}$

$b = 20$

The length of the unknown leg of the triangle is 20 m.

Part 2

Example Calculating the Diagonal of a Rectangle Using the Pythagorean Theorem

The length of the diagonal of a television screen is 42 in. The length of the bottom of the screen is 36 in. To the nearest tenth, what is the height of the television screen?

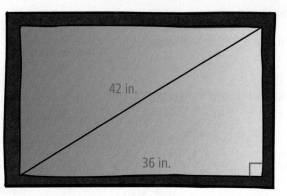

Solution

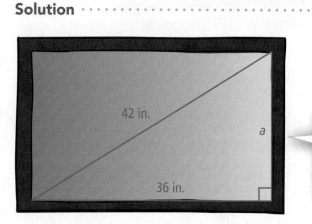

The height of the television screen is the length of the leg of a right triangle with a base of 36 in. and a hypotenuse of 42 in.

Use the Pythagorean Theorem to find the length of the unknown leg.

$$a^2 + b^2 = c^2$$

$$a^2 + 36^2 = 42^2$$

$$a^2 + 1{,}296 = 1{,}764$$

$$a^2 = 468$$

$$\sqrt{a^2} = \sqrt{468}$$

Find the positive square root of each side.

$$a \approx 21.6$$

The height of the television screen is about 21.6 in.

Example Calculating the Height of a Pyramid Using the Pythagorean Theorem

The entrance to the Louvre Museum in Paris, France is a square pyramid. To the nearest tenth, what is the height of the pyramid?

Solution

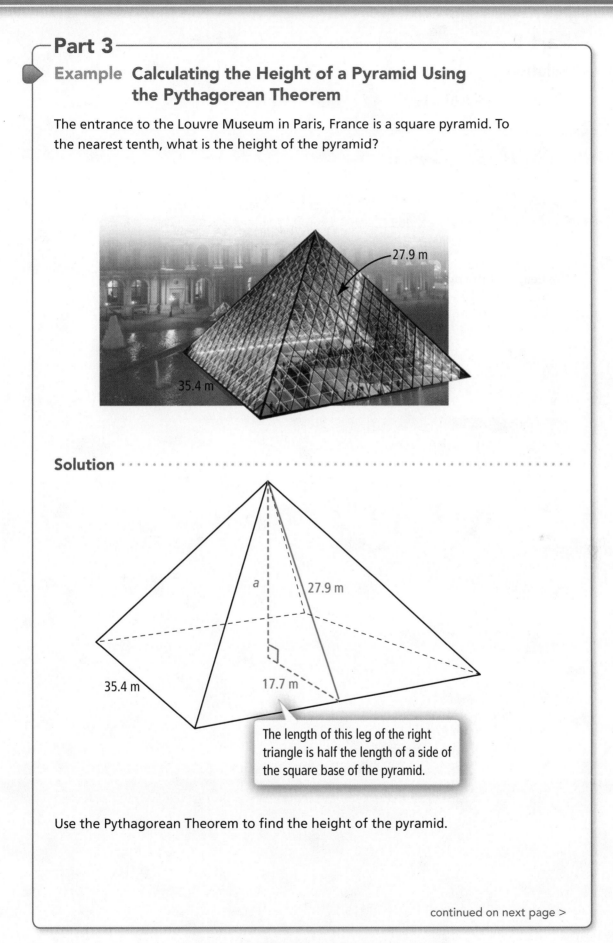

The length of this leg of the right triangle is half the length of a side of the square base of the pyramid.

Use the Pythagorean Theorem to find the height of the pyramid.

continued on next page >

Part 3

Solution continued

$$a^2 + b^2 = c^2$$

$$a^2 + 17.7^2 = 27.9^2$$

$$a^2 + 313.29 = 778.41$$

$$a^2 = 465.12$$

$$\sqrt{a^2} = \sqrt{465.12}$$

Find the positive square root of each side.

$$a \approx 21.6$$

The height of the pyramid is about 21.6 m.

1. Find the length of the third side of the right triangle. Simplify your answer.

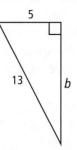

5

13   b

2. Tyler is flying a kite on 500 feet of string. How high is it above the ground if the horizontal distance between Tyler and the kite is 300 feet? Simplify your answer.

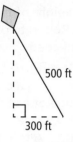

500 ft

300 ft

3. You are flying your dragon kite. It's connected to 34 yd of string. The kite is directly above the edge of a pond. The edge of the pond is 29 yd from where the kite is tied to the ground. How high is the kite above the edge of the pond? Round to one decimal place as needed.

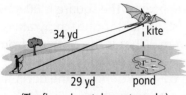

34 yd   kite

29 yd   pond

(The figure is not drawn to scale.)

4. Think About the Process A 10-foot ladder is leaning against a building with the base of the ladder 2 feet from the building.

a. How can you find how high on the building the top of the ladder will reach?

A. Subtract the two given values.

B. Add the two given values.

C. Substitute the values for *a* and *b* in the equation $a^2 + b^2 = c^2$ and solve for *c*.

D. Substitute the values for *a* and *c* in the equation $a^2 + b^2 = c^2$ and solve for *b*.

b. How far up the building will the top of the ladder reach?

5. Find the height of the square pyramid.

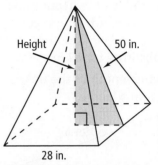
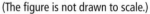

Height   50 in.

28 in.
(The figure is not drawn to scale.)

6. A stainless steel patio heater is a square pyramid. The length of one side of the base is 19.8 in. The slant height of the pyramid is 92.8 in. What is the height of the pyramid? Round to one decimal place as needed.

7. The base of a square pyramid is 13 ft long. Its slant height is 34.2 ft. Find the height of the square pyramid. Round to one decimal place as needed.

8.

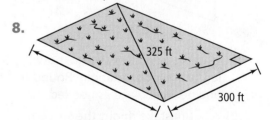

325 ft

300 ft

(The figure is not drawn to scale.)

a. Writing What is the length of the rectangular plot of land shown?

b. How are the lengths of the legs of a right triangle related to the lengths of the sides of a rectangle?

9.

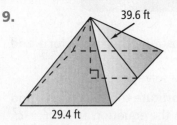

39.6 ft

29.4 ft

(The figure is not drawn to scale.)

a. Reasoning What is the height of the square pyramid? Round to one decimal place as needed.

b. Once you know which length represents the hypotenuse, does it matter which length you substitute for *a* and which length you substitute for *b*? Explain.

10. Find the length of the unknown leg of the right triangle.

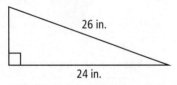

26 in.

24 in.

(The figure is not drawn to scale.)

11. Error Analysis A student was asked to find the length of the unknown leg of the right triangle. She incorrectly said that the length of the unknown leg of the right triangle is about 6.2 cm.

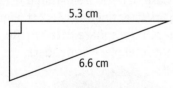

5.3 cm

6.6 cm

(The figure is not drawn to scale.)

a. Find the length of the unknown leg of the right triangle. Round to one decimal place as needed.

b. What mistake might the student have made?

12. Camping A guy rope is attached to the top of a tent pole. The guy rope is pegged into the ground 6 feet from the tent. If the guy rope is 11 feet long, how long is the tent pole? Round to one decimal place as needed.

13. The area of the base of a square pyramid is 100 cm². Its slant height is 36.8 cm. Find the height of the square pyramid. Round to one decimal place as needed.

14. Think About the Process A lamp base is a square pyramid. One side of the base is 13 cm long. The slant height is 35.6 cm.

a. What is the first step in finding the height of the square pyramid?

A. Substitute the given values into $a^2 + b^2 = c^2$.

B. Divide the length of one side of the base by 2.

C. Add the two given values.

D. Subtract the two given values.

b. Find the height of the square pyramid. Round to one decimal place as needed.

15. Challenge To get to a cabin, Diana can bike west from a parking lot along the edge of a rectangular reservoir for 0.5 miles and then south along the edge. Alternatively, she can row a boat directly from the parking lot for 1.3 miles. If Diana can ride 1.4 times as fast as she can row, which method of travel will get Diana to the cabin faster?

16. Challenge An 8-sided game piece has the shape of two identical square pyramids attached at their bases. The perimeter of the square is 80 mm and the slant height of each pyramid is 17 mm. What is the distance from the apex of one pyramid to the apex of the other? Round to one decimal place as needed.

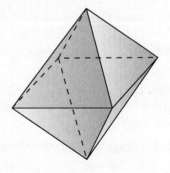

The Converse of the Pythagorean Theorem

Vocabulary
Converse of the
Pythagorean Theorem

CCSS: 8.G.B.6

Key Concept

The Pythagorean Theorem states that in any right triangle, the sum of the squares of the lengths of the legs is equal to the square of the length of the hypotenuse.

If $\triangle ABC$ is a right triangle, then $a^2 + b^2 = c^2$.

The converse is also true.

The sum of the squares of the lengths of two sides of a triangle is equal to the square of the length of the third side, then the triangle is a right triangle.

If then $a^2 + b^2 = c^2$, then $\triangle ABC$ is a right triangle.

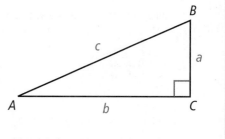

Part 1

Example Identifying Right Triangles

Decide if each of the following is a right triangle. Justify your reasoning.

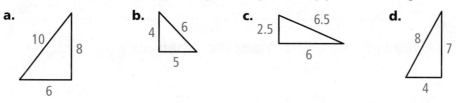

a.

b.

c.

d.

Solution ·

Use the converse of the Pythagorean Theorem to determine whether each triangle is a right triangle.

a.

$$a^2 + b^2 \overset{?}{=} c^2$$
$$6^2 + 8^2 \overset{?}{=} 10^2$$
$$36 + 64 \overset{?}{=} 100$$
$$100 = 100 \checkmark$$

Yes, the triangle is a right triangle because $6^2 + 8^2 = 10^2$.

continued on next page >

See your complete lesson at MyMathUniverse.com

Part 1

Solution continued

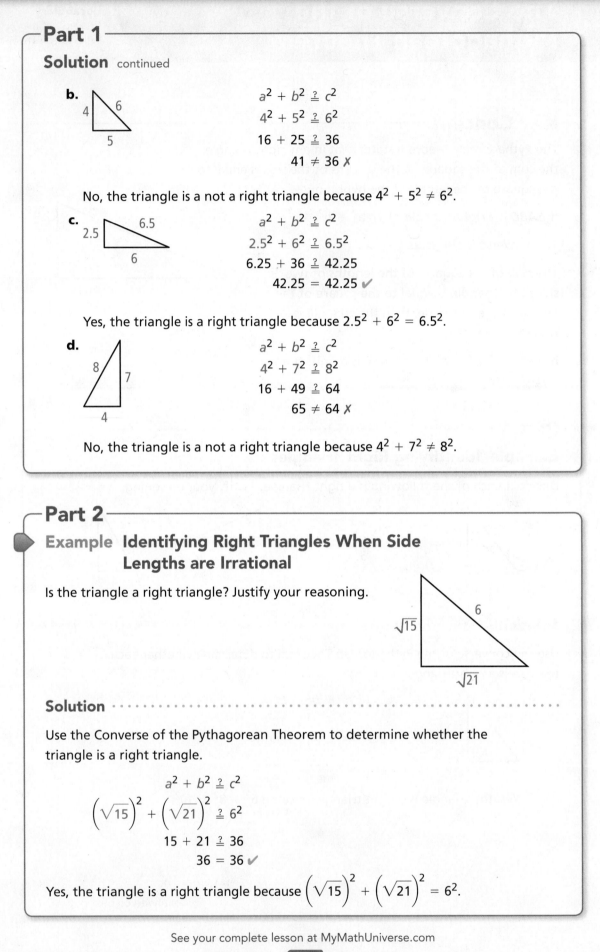

b.

4, 6, 5 (triangle)

$a^2 + b^2 \stackrel{?}{=} c^2$

$4^2 + 5^2 \stackrel{?}{=} 6^2$

$16 + 25 \stackrel{?}{=} 36$

$41 \neq 36$ ✗

No, the triangle is a not a right triangle because $4^2 + 5^2 \neq 6^2$.

c.

2.5, 6.5, 6 (triangle)

$a^2 + b^2 \stackrel{?}{=} c^2$

$2.5^2 + 6^2 \stackrel{?}{=} 6.5^2$

$6.25 + 36 \stackrel{?}{=} 42.25$

$42.25 = 42.25$ ✔

Yes, the triangle is a right triangle because $2.5^2 + 6^2 = 6.5^2$.

d.

8, 7, 4 (triangle)

$a^2 + b^2 \stackrel{?}{=} c^2$

$4^2 + 7^2 \stackrel{?}{=} 8^2$

$16 + 49 \stackrel{?}{=} 64$

$65 \neq 64$ ✗

No, the triangle is a not a right triangle because $4^2 + 7^2 \neq 8^2$.

Part 2

Example Identifying Right Triangles When Side Lengths are Irrational

Is the triangle a right triangle? Justify your reasoning.

Solution

Use the Converse of the Pythagorean Theorem to determine whether the triangle is a right triangle.

$$a^2 + b^2 \stackrel{?}{=} c^2$$

$$\left(\sqrt{15}\right)^2 + \left(\sqrt{21}\right)^2 \stackrel{?}{=} 6^2$$

$$15 + 21 \stackrel{?}{=} 36$$

$$36 = 36 ✔$$

Yes, the triangle is a right triangle because $\left(\sqrt{15}\right)^2 + \left(\sqrt{21}\right)^2 = 6^2$.

1. Is the triangle a right triangle?

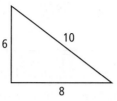

2. Is the triangle a right triangle? The figure is not drawn to scale.

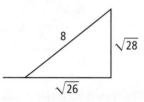

3. Which lengths could represent the side lengths of a right triangle?

   I. $7, 10, \sqrt{132}$

   II. $5, 11, \sqrt{146}$

   III. $6, 7, \sqrt{87}$

4.

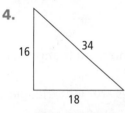

   a. Writing Decide if the triangle is a right triangle. The figure is not drawn to scale.

   A. No, because $16^2 + 18^2 \neq 34^2$.

   B. Yes, because $16^2 + 18^2 = 34^2$.

   C. No, because $16 + 18 \neq 34$.

   D. Yes, because $16 + 18 = 34$.

   b. How can you use your results to decide if a triangle with side lengths 8, 9, and 17 is a right triangle?

5. Reasoning Is the triangle a right triangle? The figure is not drawn to scale.

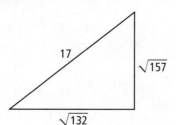

A. No, because $a + b \neq c$.

B. Yes, because $a^2 + b^2 = c^2$.

C. No, because $a^2 + b^2 \neq c^2$.

D. Yes, because $a + b = c$.

6. Error Analysis Three students draw triangles with the side lengths listed below. Each student says his triangle is a right triangle.

   Student 1: 24, 18, 42

   Student 2: 30, 72, 78

   Student 3: 12, 18, 30

   a. Which students are incorrect?

   b. What mistake might they have made?

7. Multiple Representations Which lengths represent the side lengths of a right triangle? Draw each triangle to verify your answer.

   Triangle 1: 12, 9, 21

   Triangle 2: 15, 36, 39

   Triangle 3: 9, 12, 15

8. Metalworking A machine in a factory cuts out triangular sheets of metal. Which of the triangles are right triangles? Select all that apply.

Triangle Side Lengths

Triangle	Side Lengths (in.)		
1	12	19	$\sqrt{505}$
2	16	19	$\sqrt{467}$
3	14	20	$\sqrt{596}$
4	11	23	$\sqrt{421}$

9. The lengths of the sides of a triangle are 4.5, 6, and 7. Is the triangle a right triangle?

See your complete lesson at MyMathUniverse.com

10.

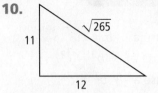

a. Open-Ended Use the Converse of the Pythagorean Theorem to decide if this triangle is a right triangle. The figure is not drawn to scale.

  A. Yes, because
  $11^2 + 12^2 = (\sqrt{265})^2$.

  B. No, because
  $11^2 + 12^2 \neq (\sqrt{265})^2$.

  C. No, because
  $11^2 + 12^2 = (\sqrt{265})^2$.

  D. Yes, because
  $11^2 + 12^2 \neq (\sqrt{265})^2$.

b. Write a situation you could model with this triangle.

11. Decide if this triangle is a right triangle. The figure is not drawn to scale.

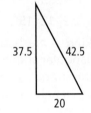

  A. No, because $37.5^2 + 20^2 \neq 42.5^2$.

  B. No, because $37.5 + 20 \neq 42.5$.

  C. Yes, because $37.5 + 20 = 42.5$.

  D. Yes, because $37.5^2 + 20^2 = 42.5^2$.

12. Think About the Process

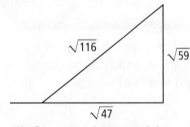

(The figure is not drawn to scale.)

a. What is a good first step when deciding if a triangle is a right triangle?

b. Is the triangle a right triangle?

13. Think About the Process

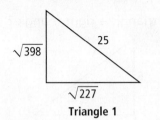

Triangle 1
(The figure is not drawn to scale.)

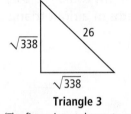

Triangle 2
(The figure is not drawn to scale.)

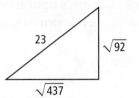

Triangle 3
(The figure is not drawn to scale.)

a. How do you know if a triangle is a right triangle?

b. Which triangles are right triangles?

14. a. Challenge Which of the triangles described are right triangles?

Triangle Side Lengths

Triangle	Side Lengths		
1	$\sqrt{229}$	$\sqrt{225}$	22
2	$\sqrt{11\frac{1}{3}}$	$\sqrt{13\frac{2}{3}}$	5
3	16	17	$\sqrt{555}$

b. For any triangles that are not right triangles, use two of the sides to create a right triangle.

Distance in the Coordinate Plane

CCSS: 8.G.B.8

Key Concept

You can use the Pythagorean Theorem to find distances in the coordinate plane.

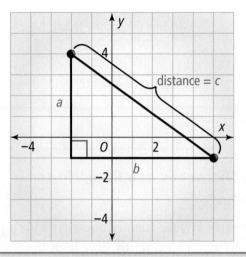

Part 1

Example **Finding Distances Between Two Points on the Coordinate Plane**

What is the distance between $A(-2,-3)$ and $B(4, 5)$?

Solution ·

Graph a right triangle with $\overline{AB}$ as the hypotenuse. Then use the Pythagorean Theorem to find the distance between points A and B.

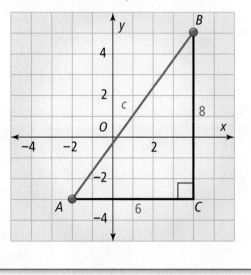

continued on next page >

Part 1

Solution continued

$$a^2 + b^2 = c^2$$
$$6^2 + 8^2 = c^2$$
$$36 + 64 = c^2$$
$$100 = c^2$$
$$\sqrt{100} = \sqrt{c^2}$$
$$10 = c$$

Find the positive square root of each side.

The distance between $A\,(-2, -3)$ and $B\,(4, 5)$ is 10 units.

Part 2

Example Finding Distances in a Real-World Situation

The post office is 4 km north of your friend's house. The library is 7 km east of your friend's house. To the nearest tenth, how far is the post office from the library?

continued on next page >

Part 2

Example continued

Solution ·

Your friend's house, the post office, and the library form a right triangle.

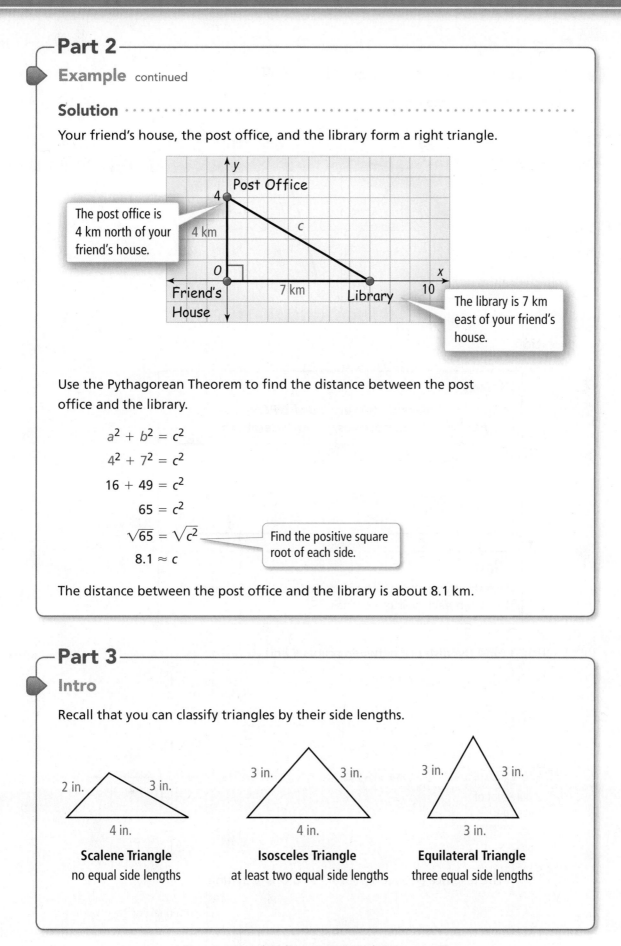

Use the Pythagorean Theorem to find the distance between the post office and the library.

$$a^2 + b^2 = c^2$$
$$4^2 + 7^2 = c^2$$
$$16 + 49 = c^2$$
$$65 = c^2$$
$$\sqrt{65} = \sqrt{c^2}$$
$$8.1 \approx c$$

Find the positive square root of each side.

The distance between the post office and the library is about 8.1 km.

Part 3

Intro

Recall that you can classify triangles by their side lengths.

2 in. 3 in. 4 in.	3 in. 3 in. 4 in.	3 in. 3 in. 3 in.
Scalene Triangle no equal side lengths	**Isosceles Triangle** at least two equal side lengths	**Equilateral Triangle** three equal side lengths

Example Classifying Triangles by Side Lengths

Classify △PQR by its side lengths.

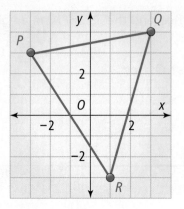

Solution · >

> **Know**
> • The coordinates of the vertices of △PQR
> • △PQR is scalene, isosceles, or equilateral

⬇

> **Need**
> The side lengths of △PQR

⬇

> **Plan**
> Use the Pythagorean Theorem to find the distance between each pair of vertices.

Step 1 Find the distance between points P and Q.

$$a^2 + b^2 = c^2$$
$$6^2 + 1^2 = c^2$$
$$36 + 1 = c^2$$
$$37 = c^2$$
$$\sqrt{37} = \sqrt{c^2}$$
$$\sqrt{37} = c$$

> Find the positive square root of each side.

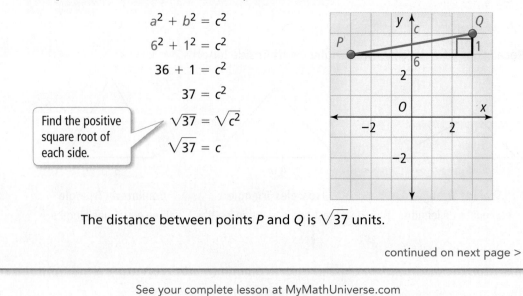

The distance between points P and Q is $\sqrt{37}$ units.

continued on next page >

Part 3

Solution continued

Step 2 Find the distance between points Q and R.

$$a^2 + b^2 = c^2$$
$$2^2 + 7^2 = c^2$$
$$4 + 49 = c^2$$
$$53 = c^2$$

> Find the positive square root of each side.

$$\sqrt{53} = \sqrt{c^2}$$
$$\sqrt{53} = c$$

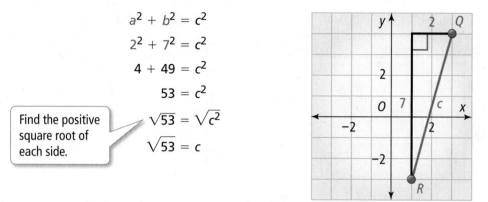

The distance between points Q and R is $\sqrt{53}$ units.

Step 3 Find the distance between points P and R.

$$a^2 + b^2 = c^2$$
$$6^2 + 4^2 = c^2$$
$$36 + 16 = c^2$$
$$52 = c^2$$

> Find the positive square root of each side.

$$\sqrt{52} = \sqrt{c^2}$$
$$\sqrt{52} = c$$

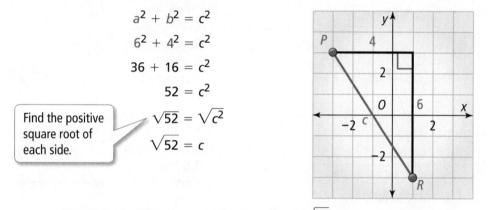

The distance between points P and R is $\sqrt{52}$ units.

Step 4 Classify $\triangle PQR$.

Since $\triangle PQR$ has three different side lengths, it is a scalene triangle.

1. In the graph shown, the post office is located at P and the market is located at Q. The axes show distances in miles. Find the distance in miles from the post office to the market.

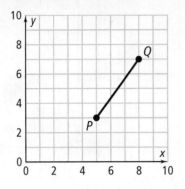

2. Find the distance between P and Q.

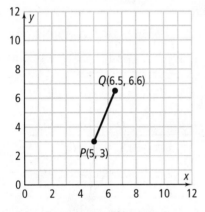

3. Is this triangle isosceles, scalene, or equilateral? **(Figure 1)**

4. Reasoning You are on your way back to school from a field trip to the zoo. The point P on the graph represents the location of your school. You are on the bus located at point Q. Your friend is on the bus located at point R.

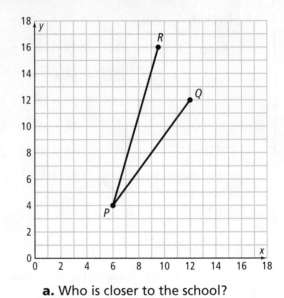

a. Who is closer to the school?

b. Explain your reasoning.

5. Think About the Process Suppose your home is located at H. The park is 3.6 miles east of your home. The library is 4.8 miles north of the park.

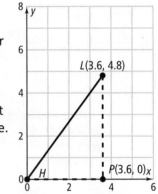

a. How can you use a coordinate plane to map the distance from the library to your home?

b. What is the distance from the library to your home?

(Figure 1)

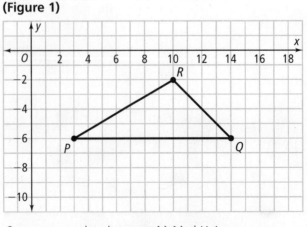

See your complete lesson at MyMathUniverse.com

6. Estimation You are at a concert with friends and decide to go to the concession stand to get snacks. The end of the line is located at point, *P*. The concession stand is located at point *Q*. Round the coordinates of each point to the nearest whole number to estimate the distance between your position and the front of the line in yards.

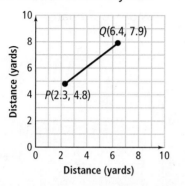

7. At Parlee Farms, the individual fields are laid out in rectangles like the one shown in the graph. What is the shortest distance from the shed, *A*, to the well, *B*? Round to the nearest tenth as needed.

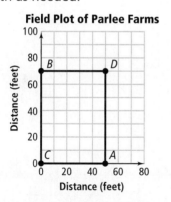

8. Find the distance between *P*(1,5) and *Q*(5.5,9.25). Round to the nearest tenth as needed.

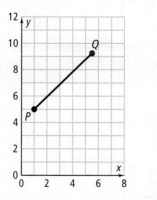

9. Think About the Process

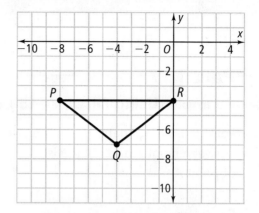

a. What must you do first to classify the triangle shown?

b. Determine whether the triangle, defined by the points *P*(−8,−4), *Q*(−4,−7), and *R*(0,−4), is isosceles, scalene, or equilateral.

10. Challenge You are given the points $Q\left(-\frac{5}{2}, \frac{5\sqrt{3}}{2}\right)$ and $R\left(-\frac{5}{2}, -\frac{5\sqrt{3}}{2}\right)$. Which of the following points will make an equilateral triangle?

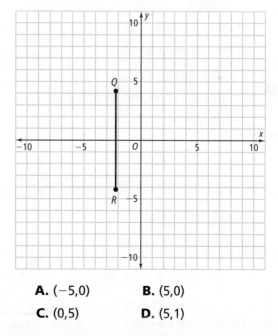

A. (−5,0)   **B.** (5,0)

C. (0,5)   **D.** (5,1)

See your complete lesson at MyMathUniverse.com

CCSS: 8.G.B.7, 8.G.B.8

Part 1

Example Using Distance to Locate Points

Point B has coordinates (1, 5). The y-coordinate of point A is -3. The distance between point A and point B is 10 units. What are the possible coordinates of point A?

Solution

Point B has coordinates (1, 5).

Point A has y-coordinate of -3, so it is somewhere along the line $y = -3$.

Points A, B, and C form a right triangle with $\overline{AB}$ as the hypotenuse.

The distance between points A and B is 10 units. The length of $\overline{BC}$ is 8 units.

Use the Pythagorean Theorem to find the length of the unknown leg.

$$a^2 + b^2 = c^2$$

$$8^2 + b^2 = 10^2$$

$$64 + b^2 = 100$$

$$b^2 = 36$$

$$\sqrt{b^2} = \sqrt{36}$$

$$b = 6$$

Point A can be 6 units to the left of point C, or 6 units to the right of point C. So the possible coordinates of point A are $(-5, -3)$ and $(7, -3)$.

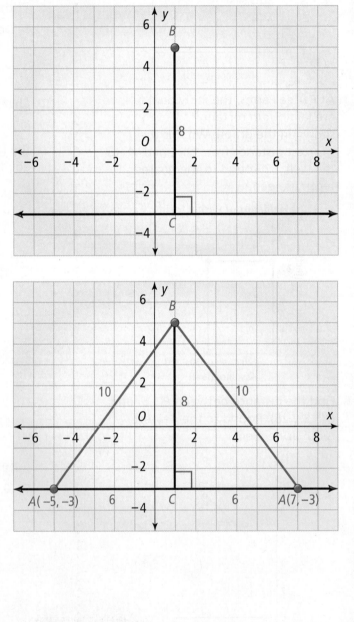

See your complete lesson at MyMathUniverse.com

Example Finding Surface Areas of Pyramids

The base of a square pyramid has a side length of 10 in. The height of the pyramid is 12 in. What is the surface area of the pyramid?

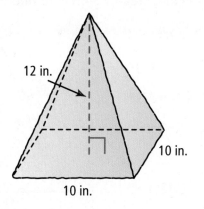

12 in.

10 in.

10 in.

Solution

Method 1 Use a net.

Step 1 Draw and label a net of the square pyramid.

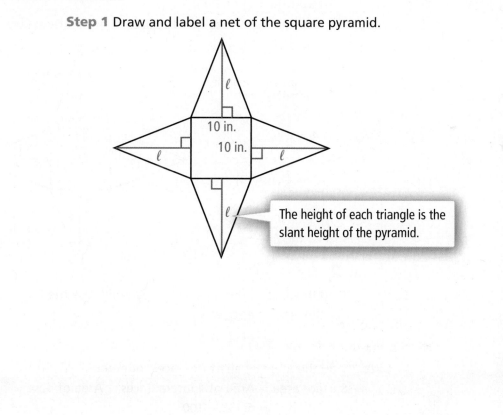

ℓ

10 in.
10 in.

ℓ   ℓ

ℓ

The height of each triangle is the slant height of the pyramid.

continued on next page >

Step 2 Find the area of each face of the square pyramid.
Use the Pythagorean Theorem to find the slant height.

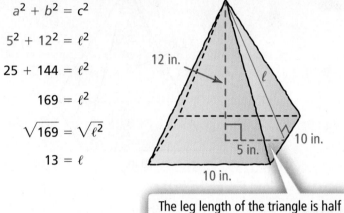

$$a^2 + b^2 = c^2$$
$$5^2 + 12^2 = \ell^2$$
$$25 + 144 = \ell^2$$
$$169 = \ell^2$$
$$\sqrt{169} = \sqrt{\ell^2}$$
$$13 = \ell$$

The leg length of the triangle is half the side length of the square base.

Use the slant height to find the area of each lateral face.

Use the formula for the area of a triangle.

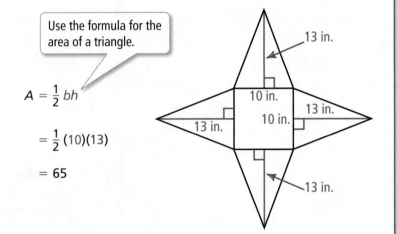

$$A = \frac{1}{2}bh$$
$$= \frac{1}{2}(10)(13)$$
$$= 65$$

Find the area of the base of the pyramid. Use the formula for the area of a square.

$$A = s^2 = 10^2 = 100$$

Step 3 Add the areas of all of the faces together.

Surface area = Area of 4 lateral faces + Area of base
$$= 4(65) + 100$$
$$= 260 + 100$$
$$= 360$$

The surface area of the square pyramid is 360 in.².

continued on next page >

Part 2

Solution continued

> **Method 2** Use the formula S.A. = L.A. + B.
>
> **Step 1** Find the lateral area.
>
> L.A. = Lateral Area
>
> $= \frac{1}{2} p\ell$
>
> > *p* represents the perimeter of the base
> > *ℓ* represents the slant height of the pyramid.
>
> The perimeter of the base is 4 · 10, or 40 in.
>
> Use the Pythagorean Theorem to find the slant height.
>
> $a^2 + b^2 = c^2$
>
> $5^2 + 12^2 = \ell^2$
>
> $25 + 144 = \ell^2$
>
> $169 = \ell^2$
>
> $\sqrt{169} = \sqrt{\ell^2}$
>
> $13 = \ell$

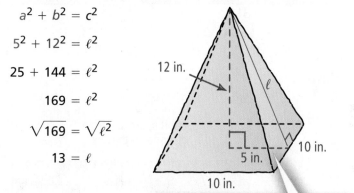

> The leg length of the triangle is half the side length of the square base.

> Substitute 13 for *ℓ* in the formula for lateral area.
>
> L.A. $= \frac{1}{2} p\ell$
>
> $= \frac{1}{2}(40)(30)$
>
> $= 260$
>
> **Step 2** Find the area of the base.
>
> B = Lateral Area
>
> $= s^2$
>
> > Use the formula for the area of a square.
>
> $= 10^2$
>
> $= 100$
>
> **Step 3** Find the surface area.
>
> S.A. = L.A. + B
>
> $= 260 + 100$
>
> $= 360$
>
> The surface area of the square pyramid is 360 in.².

Example Calculating Diagonals in Real-World Problems

Bat A and Bat B are packed into two identical boxes as shown. Each box is a right rectangular prism. Which baseball bat is longer? If the length of a baseball bat is in whole inches, how much longer is the longer bat?

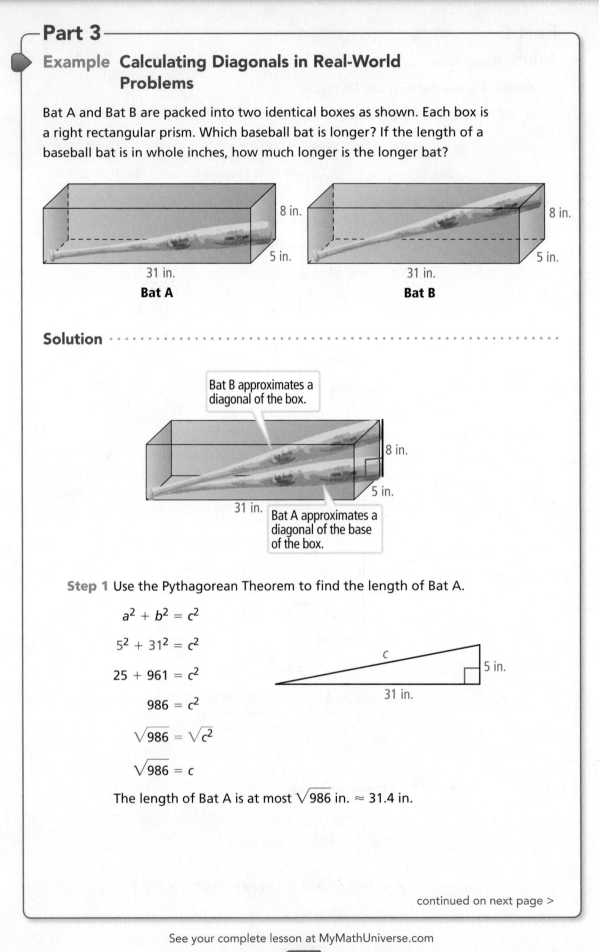

8 in.

5 in.

31 in.

Bat A

8 in.

5 in.

31 in.

Bat B

Solution ·

Bat B approximates a diagonal of the box.

8 in.

5 in.

31 in.

Bat A approximates a diagonal of the base of the box.

Step 1 Use the Pythagorean Theorem to find the length of Bat A.

$$a^2 + b^2 = c^2$$

$$5^2 + 31^2 = c^2$$

$$25 + 961 = c^2$$

$$986 = c^2$$

$$\sqrt{986} = \sqrt{c^2}$$

$$\sqrt{986} = c$$

c

5 in.

31 in.

The length of Bat A is at most $\sqrt{986}$ in. $\approx$ 31.4 in.

continued on next page >

Part 3

Solution continued

Step 2 Use the Pythagorean Theorem to find the length of Bat B.

$$a^2 + b^2 = c^2$$

$$(\sqrt{986})^2 + 8^2 = c^2$$

$$986 + 64 = c^2$$

$$1{,}050 = c^2$$

$$\sqrt{1{,}050} = \sqrt{c^2}$$

$$\sqrt{1{,}050} = c$$

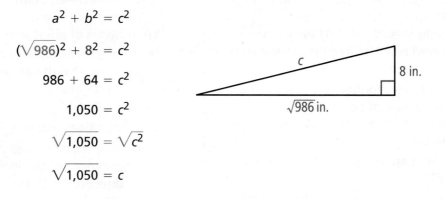

The length of Bat A is at most $\sqrt{1{,}050}$ in. $\approx$ 32.4 in.

The length of each bat is in whole inches.

Length of Bat A = 31 in.

Length of Bat B = 32 in.

32 − 31 = 1

Bat B is longer by 1 in.

1. Point B has coordinates (2,1). The x-coordinate of point A is −10. The distance between point A and point B is 15 units. What are the possible coordinates of point A? Write an ordered pair. Use a comma to separate answers as needed.

2. Point B has coordinates (−4,−2). The x-coordinate of point A is 5. The distance between point A and point B is 12 units.

a. What are the possible coordinates of point A?

b. Find the possible coordinates of point A if point B were moved to (−2,−4).

3. A square pyramid has base edge length 22 ft. The slant height of the pyramid is 61 ft. What is the volume of the pyramid?

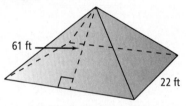

61 ft

22 ft

(The figure is not to scale.)

4. What is the longest line segment that can be drawn in a right rectangular prism that is 16 cm long, 9 cm wide, and 7 cm tall? Round to one decimal place as needed.

5. a. What is true about the longest distance between any two vertices in a right rectangular prism that is 14 cm long, 13 cm wide, and 8 cm high? Select all that apply.

   A. The distance is the square root of the sum of the two longest lengths squared.

   B. The distance is greater than 14 cm.

   C. The distance can be found using the Pythagorean Theorem.

   D. The distance is at most 14 cm.

b. Find the longest distance between any two vertices in this right rectangular prism. Round to one decimal place as needed.

6. Point A has coordinates (4,1). The x-coordinate of point B is 7. The distance between point A and point B is 5 units. Your friend says the coordinates of point B could be (8,4).

a. What are the possible coordinates of point B? Write an ordered pair. Use a comma to separate answers as needed.

b. What mistake did your friend make?

   A. Your friend moved the correct distance but the incorrect direction on the coordinate plane.

   B. Your friend used the given distance as one of the leg lengths instead of the hypotenuse length.

   C. Your friend switched the hypotenuse length for one of the leg lengths.

   D. Your friend's point does not have the same x-coordinate as point A. Your friend switched the leg lengths of the right triangle.

7. You are painting a square pyramid for a diorama. The square pyramid has base edge length 10 in. The height of the pyramid is 12 in.

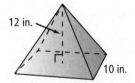

12 in.

10 in.

(The figure is not to scale.)

a. Find the surface area of the square pyramid.

b. You have enough paint to cover 400 in.². Do you have enough paint for the pyramid?

8. Point A has coordinates (1,0). The x-coordinate of point B is 4. The distance between point A and point B is 5 units. What are the possible coordinates of point B? Write an ordered pair. Use a comma to separate answers as needed.

See your complete lesson at MyMathUniverse.com

9. Think About the Process A square pyramid has a base edge length of 30 mm. The slant height of the pyramid is 17 mm.

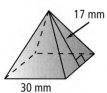

17 mm

30 mm

(The figure is not to scale.)

a. How can you find the height of the pyramid?

  A. Use the Pythagorean Theorem to find the height of the pyramid using the slant height as the hypotenuse and half the length of the base edge as one of the legs.

  B. Use the Pythagorean Theorem to find the height of the pyramid using half the length of the base edge as the hypotenuse and the slant height as one of the legs.

  C. Use the Pythagorean Theorem to find the height of the pyramid using the slant height as the hypotenuse and length of the base edge as one of the legs.

b. What is the height of the square pyramid?

c. Find the volume of the square pyramid.

10. A square pyramid has base edge length 26 in. The height of the pyramid is 84 in.

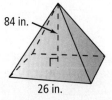

84 in.

26 in.

(The figure is not to scale.)

a. Find the surface area of the pyramid.

b. Draw a net for the figure and find the surface area.

11. Point *B* has coordinates (−1,2). The *y*-coordinate of point *A* is 5. The distance between point *A* and point *B* is 5 units. What are the possible coordinates of point *A*? Write an ordered pair. Use a comma to separate answers as needed.

12. Think About the Process A box is 18 in. high, 18 in. long, and 8 in. wide.

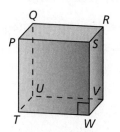

Q   *R*

P   *S*

U *V*

T *W*

(The figure is not to scale.)

a. What is the first step in finding the distance between vertex *P* and vertex *V*?

  A. Find the length of the diagonal between vertex *P* and *R*.

  B. Find the length of the diagonal between vertex *P* and *U*.

  C. Find the length of the diagonal between vertex *P* and *W*.

b. Find the distance between vertex *P* and vertex *V*.

13. Challenge Find the surface area of a square pyramid if the area of the base is 324 cm² and the height is 40 cm.

40 cm

(The figure is not to scale.)

14. Challenge A box is 12 in. high, 20 in. long, and 8 in. wide.

a. What is the longest poster you could fit in the box? Round to one decimal place as needed.

b. Explain why you can only fit one maximum-length poster in the box but you can fit multiple 23-in. posters in the same box.

See your complete lesson at MyMathUniverse.com

Surface Areas of Cylinders

Vocabulary
base of a cylinder, cylinder, height of a cylinder, lateral area of a cylinder, lateral surface of a cylinder, right cylinder, surface area of a cylinder

CCSS: 8.G.C.9

Part 1

Intro

Parts of a Cylinder

A **cylinder** is a three-dimensional figure with two parallel circular bases that are the same size.

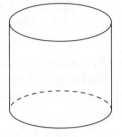

A **base of a cylinder** is one of a pair of parallel circular faces that are the same size.

The **height of a cylinder** is the length of a perpendicular segment that joins the planes of the bases. In a **right cylinder**, a segment representing the height joins the centers of the bases. In this Topic, you may assume that all cylinders are right cylinders unless otherwise noted.

Right Cylinder

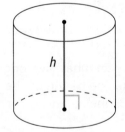

The **lateral surface of a cylinder** is the curved surface not included in the bases.

Part 1

Example Finding Surface Areas of Cylinders Using Nets

A set of candles comes in a cylindrical package. Use the net to find the surface area of the cylindrical package. Use 3.14 for π.

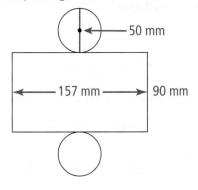

Solution

To find the surface area of the cylindrical package, find the sum of the areas of the two circles and the rectangle.

Step 1 Find the area of each circle. First find the radius.

Use the formula for radius.	radius $= \dfrac{\text{diameter}}{2}$
Substitute 50 for diameter.	$= \dfrac{50}{2}$
Divide.	$= 25$

Then find the area of the circle.

Use the area formula for a circle.	$A = \pi r^2$
Substitute 25 for r and 3.14 for π.	$\approx 3.14(25)^2$
Simplify.	$= 1{,}962.5$

Since the bases of the cylinder are congruent, the areas of circles in the net are equal.

Step 2 Find the area of the rectangle.

Use the area formula for a rectangle.	Area of rectangle $= bh$
Substitute 157 for b and 90 for h.	$= 157 \cdot 90$
Multiply.	$= 14{,}130$

continued on next page >

Solution continued

Step 3 Add the areas to find the surface area of the cylinder.

Surface Area of cylinder	$=$ area of circle $+$ area of circle $+$ area of rectangle
	$\approx 1{,}962.5 + 1{,}962.5 + \quad 14{,}130$
	$= 18{,}055$

The surface area of the cylinder is about 18,055 mm².

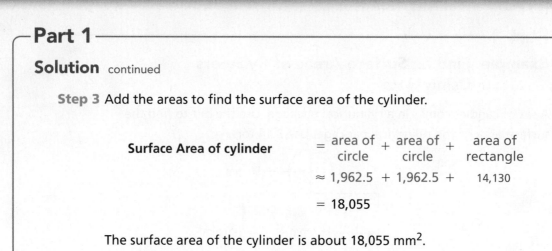

Key Concept

▶ **Finding S.A. of Cylinders**

The **lateral area of a cylinder** is the area of its lateral surface. To find the area of the lateral surface, visualize "unrolling" it. The area of the resulting rectangle is $2\pi rh$.

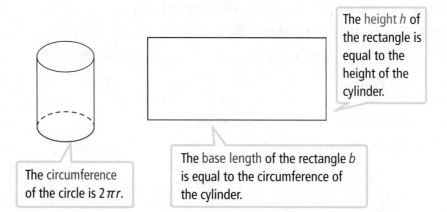

The height *h* of the rectangle is equal to the height of the cylinder.

The circumference of the circle is $2\pi r$.

The base length of the rectangle *b* is equal to the circumference of the cylinder.

The **base area of a cylinder** is the area of the circular bases. When a cylinder is "unrolled" the resulting net shows 2 circles. The area of a circle is πr^2.

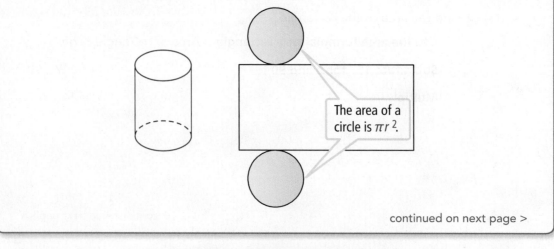

The area of a circle is πr^2.

continued on next page >

Key Concept

continued

The **surface area of a cylinder** is the sum of the lateral area and the areas of the two circular bases.

$$\text{Surface Area} = \text{Lateral Area} + \text{Area of 2 Bases}$$

$$\text{S.A.} = \text{L.A.} + 2B$$
$$= 2\pi rh + 2(\pi r^2)$$
$$= 2\pi rh + 2\pi r^2$$

> The base of a cylinder is always a circle.

Part 2

Example Finding Surface Areas of Cylinders Using Formulas

What is the surface area of the cylinder? Use 3.14 for π. Round your answer to the nearest tenth of a square foot.

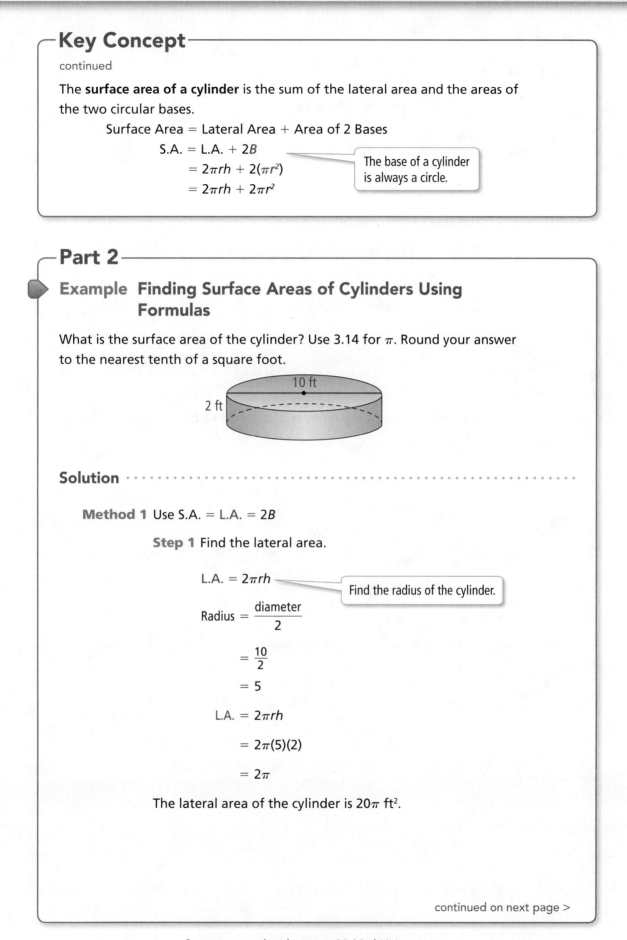

Solution ·

Method 1 Use S.A. = L.A. = $2B$

Step 1 Find the lateral area.

$$\text{L.A.} = 2\pi rh$$

> Find the radius of the cylinder.

$$\text{Radius} = \frac{\text{diameter}}{2}$$
$$= \frac{10}{2}$$
$$= 5$$

$$\text{L.A.} = 2\pi rh$$
$$= 2\pi(5)(2)$$
$$= 2\pi$$

The lateral area of the cylinder is 20π ft².

continued on next page >

Solution continued

Step 2 Find the area of the base.

$$B = \pi r^2$$

$$= \pi(5)^2$$

$$= 25\pi$$

The area of one base of the cylinder is 25π ft².

Step 3 Find the surface area of the cylinder.

$$S.A. = L.A. = 2B$$

$$= 20\pi + 2(25\pi)$$

$$= 70\pi$$

$$\approx 70(3.14)$$

$$\approx 219.8$$

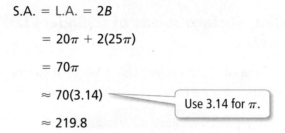

Use 3.14 for π.

The surface area of the cylinder is about 219.8 ft².

Method 2 Use S.A. $\approx 2\pi rh + 2\pi r^2$

$$S.A. = 2\pi rh + 2\pi r^2$$

$$= 2\pi(5)(2) + 2\pi(5)^2$$

$$= 20\pi + 50\pi$$

$$= 70\pi$$

$$\approx 70(3.14)$$

$$= 219.8$$

Use 3.14 for π.

The surface area of the cylinder is about 219.8 ft².

Part 3

Example Finding Surface Area of Cylinders

A manufacturer is making a prototype of a collapsible laundry hamper. The hamper does not have a top. Approximately how much polyester does the manufacturer need for the hamper?

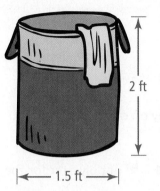

2 ft

← 1.5 ft →

Solution

Method 1 Use 3.14 to approximate π.

Since there is only one base, surface area will be the sum of the lateral area and the base, or S.A. = L.A. + B.

First find the radius.

Use the formula for radius.	Radius $= \dfrac{\text{diameter}}{2}$
Substitute.	$= \dfrac{1.5}{2}$
Divide.	$= 0.75$

Next find the surface area.

Write the formula.	**S.A. = L.A. + B.**
	$= 2\pi rh + \pi r^2$
Substitute 0.75 for r and 2 for h.	$= 2\pi(0.75)(2) + \pi(0.75)^2$
Simplify.	$= 3\pi + 0.5625\pi$
Add.	$= 3.5625\pi$
Substitute 3.14 for π.	$\approx 3.5625(3.14)$
Multiply.	≈ 11.19

The manufacturer needs about 11.2 ft² of polyester for the hamper.

continued on next page >

Part 3

Solution continued

Method 2 Use the π key on your calculator.

Use S.A. = L.A. + B since there is only one base.

$$S.A. = L.A. + B$$
$$= 2\pi rh + \pi r^2$$
$$= 2\pi(0.75)(2) + \pi(0.75)^2$$

> Substitute the values 0.75 for r and 2 for h.

> Use the π key on calculator.

$$\approx 11.19$$

The manufacturer needs about 11.2 ft² of polyester for the hamper.

1. Use a net to find the surface area of the cylinder. Use 3.14 for π. Round to the nearest tenth as needed.

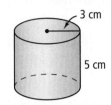

3 cm

5 cm

(The figure is not to scale.)

2. Use a formula to find the surface area of the open cylinder with only one base. Use 3.14 for π.

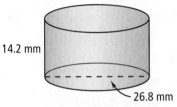

14.2 mm

26.8 mm

(The figure is not to scale.)

3. Use a net to find the surface area of the cylinder. Use 3.14 for π.

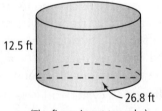

12.5 ft

26.8 ft

(The figure is not to scale.)

4. Use a formula to find the amount of wrapping paper you need to wrap a gift in the cylindrical box shown. You need to cover the top, bottom, and all the way around the box. Use 3.14 for π. Round to the nearest tenth as needed.

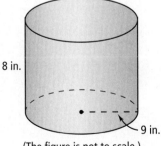

8 in.

9 in.

(The figure is not to scale.)

5. A company has designed cylindrical plastic drinking cups with the dimensions shown. Approximately how much plastic does the company need to make each cup? Use 3.14 for π. Round to the nearest tenth as needed.

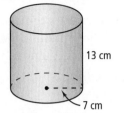

13 cm

7 cm

(The figure is not to scale.)

6.

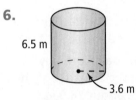

6.5 m

3.6 m

(The figure is not to scale.)

a. **Writing** Use a net to find the surface area of the cylinder. Use 3.14 for π. Round to the nearest tenth as needed.

b. What types of things can you model with a cylinder? Why might you want to find the surface area of a cylinder?

7.

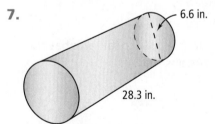

6.6 in.

28.3 in.

(The figure is not to scale.)

a. **Reasoning** Use a net to find the surface area of the open cylinder with only one base. Use 3.14 for π. Round to the nearest tenth as needed.

b. Without doing any calculations, would you expect the lateral area or the area of a base of the cylinder to increase by a greater amount if the diameter were doubled? Explain your reasoning.

8. Think About the Process

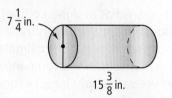

$7\frac{1}{4}$ in.

$15\frac{3}{8}$ in.

(The figure is not to scale.)

a. To use a formula to find the surface area of the cylinder, what other dimension do you need to find?

A. The radius

B. The height

C. The diameter

D. The width

b. Use a formula to find the surface area of the cylinder. Use 3.14 for π.

9. Error Analysis Sacha incorrectly claimed that the surface area of the cylinder shown is about 76.9 in.².

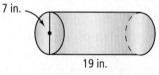

7 in.

19 in.

(The figure is not to scale.)

a. Use a formula to find the surface area of the cylinder. Use 3.14 for π. Round to the nearest tenth as needed.

b. What was her likely error?

10. Painting A cylindrical tank has the dimensions shown.

5.5 ft

16 ft

(The figure is not to scale.)

a. Use a formula to find the surface area of the tank. Round to the nearest tenth as needed.

b. If one gallon of paint covers 140 ft², how many full gallons would you need to put two coats of paint on the entire surface of the tank? Use 3.14 for π. Round up to the nearest whole number as needed.

11. Think About the Process A manufacturer produces cylindrical cans of fruit as shown. To use a formula to find the surface area of each can, you need to find the radius of each can.

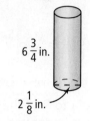

$6\frac{3}{4}$ in.

$2\frac{1}{8}$ in.

(The figure is not to scale.)

a. What step should you perform to find the radius of each can?

A. Multiply $6\frac{3}{4}$ by 2.

B. Divide $6\frac{3}{4}$ by 2.

C. Multiply $2\frac{1}{8}$ by 2.

D. Divide $2\frac{1}{8}$ by 2.

b. Use a formula to find the surface area of each can. Use 3.14 for π.

12. An open cylinder has only one base. Its diameter is 18 cm and its height is three less than five times its radius. Use a formula to find the surface area of the cylinder. Use 3.14 for π. Round to the nearest tenth as needed.

13. Challenge A cylindrical vase has height 17 in. and radius 3 in.

a. Find the exact surface area of the vase in terms of π.

b. Suppose a second vase has double the radius, but the same surface area. What is the height of this vase? Write an integer or a decimal.

CCSS: 8.G.C.9

Key Concept

Volume of a Cylinder

The **volume of a cylinder** is the
number of unit cubes, or cubic units,
needed to fill the cylinder.

If each layer is one unit high, then the
height h represents the number of
layers.

The formula for the volume of a cylinder
is the area of the base times the height.

$v = Bh$ ── The area of the circular base
$\quad = (\pi r^2)h$ — is represented by $\pi r^2 h$
$\quad = \pi r^2 h$

The volume of a cylinder is represented by $\pi r^2 h$.

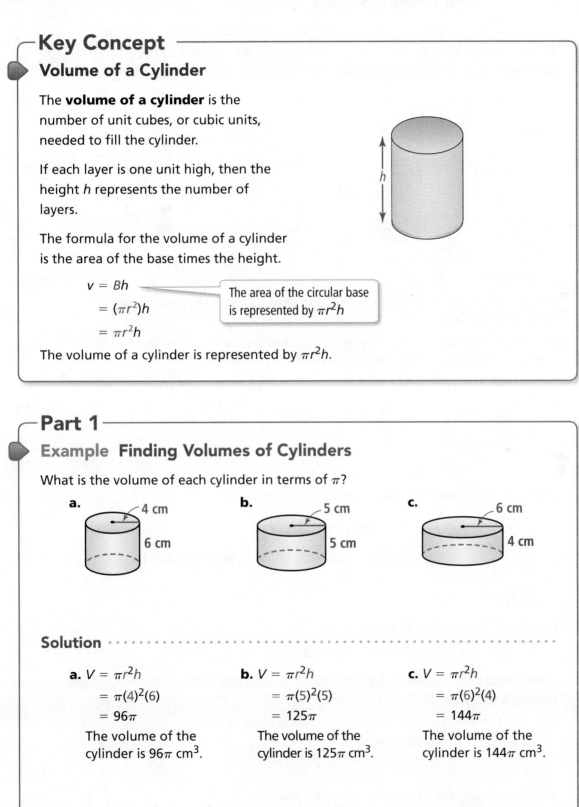

Part 1

Example Finding Volumes of Cylinders

What is the volume of each cylinder in terms of π?

a. 4 cm / 6 cm

b. 5 cm / 5 cm

c. 6 cm / 4 cm

Solution ·

a. $V = \pi r^2 h$
$\quad = \pi(4)^2(6)$
$\quad = 96\pi$

The volume of the
cylinder is 96π cm³.

b. $V = \pi r^2 h$
$\quad = \pi(5)^2(5)$
$\quad = 125\pi$

The volume of the
cylinder is 125π cm³.

c. $V = \pi r^2 h$
$\quad = \pi(6)^2(4)$
$\quad = 144\pi$

The volume of the
cylinder is 144π cm³.

Part 2

Example Calculating Volumes of Cylinders in Real-World Problems

For an art project, you plan to pour different colored sand into a vase with a volume of 47.5 in³. You have three cylindrical bottles of sand. Do you have enough sand to fill the vase? Explain. Use 3.14 for π.

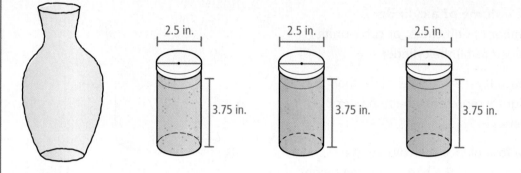

Solution

Find the volume of sand in the bottles and then compare that volume to the volume of the vase.

The amounts of sand in the three cylindrical bottles are identical. So you can find the volume of sand in one bottle and then multiply by three.

To calculate the volume of the sand in one bottle, first find the radius.

$$\text{radius} = \frac{\text{diameter}}{2}$$
$$= \frac{2.5}{2}$$
$$= 1.25$$

Then use the formula for the volume of a cylinder.

Substitute 1.25 for *r*, 3.75 for *h*, and 3.14 for π.

$$v = \pi r^2 h$$
$$\approx (3.14)(1.25)^2(3.75)$$

Multiply.

$$\approx 18.4$$

One bottle holds about 18.4 in.³ of sand.

3 bottles of sand $\approx 18.4 \cdot 3 = 55.2$

Three bottles hold about 55.2 in.³ of sand. Compare this to the volume of the vase you want to fill.

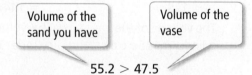

Volume of the sand you have

Volume of the vase

$$55.2 > 47.5$$

Yes, there is enough sand to fill the entire vase.

Part 3

Example Finding Radii of Cylinders Given the Volume and Height

A company is designing a can for a new green iced tea. The volume of the can will be 15 in.³. To the nearest tenth of an inch, what is the radius of the can? Use 3.14 for π.

4.8 in.

Solution

Use the formula for the volume of a cylinder.	$v = \pi r^2 h$
Substitute 15 for *V* and 4.8 for *h*.	$15 = \pi r^2 (4.8)$
Use 3.14 for π.	$15 \approx (3.14) r^2 (4.8)$
Simplify	$15 = 15.07 r^2$
Divide each side of the equation by 15.07.	$\dfrac{15}{15.07} = \dfrac{15.07 r^2}{15.07}$
Simplify.	$1.00 \approx r^2$
Find the positive square root of each side of the equation.	$\sqrt{1.00} = \sqrt{r^2}$
Simplify.	$1.0 = r$

The radius of the can is about 1.0 in.

1.

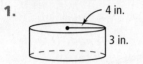

4 in.

3 in.

(This figure is not to scale.)

a. Find the volume of the cylinder. Write an exact answer in terms of π.

b. Find the volume of a cylinder with the same radius and double the height. Write an exact answer in terms of π.

2. A can of vegetables has a radius 2.3 in. and a height 5.5 in. Find the volume of the can. Use 3.14 for π. Round to the nearest tenth as needed.

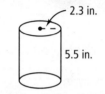

2.3 in.

5.5 in.

(This figure is not to scale.)

3. The volume of a cylinder is $1,029\pi$ cm³. The height of the cylinder is 21 cm. What is the radius of the cylinder? Simplify your answer.

4. A company is designing a new cylindrical water bottle. The volume of the bottle will be 103 cm³. The height of the water bottle is 8.1 cm. What is the radius of the water bottle? Use 3.14 for π. Round to the nearest tenth as needed.π

8.1 cm

5. You are building a sand castle and want to use a bucket that holds a volume of 885 in.³ and has height 11.7 in.

11.7 in.

a. What is the radius of the bucket? Use 3.14 for π.

b. If the height of the bucket is changed, but the volume stays the same, then how will the radius change? Explain.

6. a. Writing Find the volume of a cylinder with radius 10 m and height 8 m. Write an exact answer in terms of π.

b. How does the volume change when the height is tripled? When the radius is tripled? Explain.

7. Error Analysis The cylinder is filled with water. A student was asked to find the volume of water in the cylinder using 3.14 for π. He was asked to decide if the water will fill the rectangular container. He incorrectly said the volume of water in the cylinder is 45.9 in.³ and that the water will fill the rectangular container.

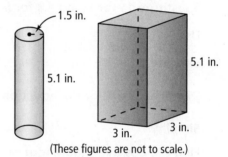

1.5 in.

5.1 in.

5.1 in.

3 in.

3 in.

(These figures are not to scale.)

a. Find the volume of water in the cylinder. Round to the nearest tenth as needed.

b. Will the water fill the rectangular container?

c. What mistake might the student have made?

8. a. Find the volume of a cylinder with diameter 8 ft and height 6 ft.

b. Find the volume of the cylinder with the height and radius quadrupled.

c. How many times greater is the volume of the larger cylinder than the smaller cylinder?

See your complete lesson at MyMathUniverse.com

9. Toy rubber balls are packaged in a cylinder that holds 3 balls. The diameter of each ball is 6.9 cm. Find the volume of the cylinder. Use 3.14 for π. Round to the nearest tenth as needed.

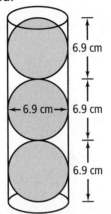

6.9 cm

←6.9 cm→ 6.9 cm

6.9 cm

10. The diameter of the cylinder is $(6x - 8)$ in. and the height of the cylinder is $(11x + 10)$ in. Find the volume of the cylinder when $x = 7$. Write an exact answer in terms of π.

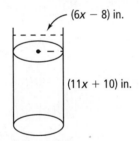

$(6x - 8)$ in.

$(11x + 10)$ in.

(This figure is not to scale.)

11. The volume of a cylinder is 368π m³ and the height of the cylinder is $(6x - 91)$ m. Find the radius of the cylinder when $(x = 19)$. Simplify your answer.

12. Think About the Process The diameter of a cylinder is 7 yd. The height is 12 yd.

   a. What is the first step to finding the volume of the cylinder?

   A. Use the diameter to find the radius of the cylinder.

   B. Use the diameter to find the area of the cylinder.

   C. Find the product of the diameter and the height.

   D. Find the sum of the diameter and the height.

   b. Find the volume of the cylinder.

13. Think About the Process A juice can is 13.1 cm high. A new can is 1.7 cm shorter than the original can. The new can has a diameter of 5.4 cm.

   a. What is a possible first step in finding the volume of the new can?

   b. What is the volume of the new can? Use 3.14 for π.

14. Challenge The inner cylinder of the bushing shown is hollow. What is the weight of the bushing if it is made of steel weighing 0.2835 pound per cubic inch? Use 3.14 for π. Do not round until the final answer. Then round to the nearest tenth as needed.

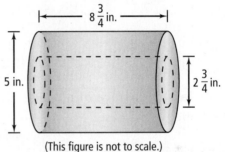

$8\frac{3}{4}$ in.

5 in.

$2\frac{3}{4}$ in.

(This figure is not to scale.)

15. Challenge An orange juice company is designing cylindrical containers for their juice. The containers are going to hold the same volume and have the same height as the prism shaped container. What is the radius of the cylindrical container? Use 3.14 for π. Round to the nearest tenth as needed.

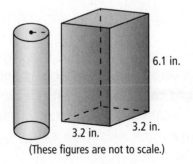

6.1 in.

3.2 in.   3.2 in.

(These figures are not to scale.)

See your complete lesson at MyMathUniverse.com

CCSS: 8.G.C.9

Vocabulary
base of a cone, cone, height of a cone, lateral area of a cone, lateral surface of a cone, right cone, slant height of a cone, surface area of a cone, vertex of a cone

Part 1

Intro

A **cone** is a three-dimensional figure with one circular base and one vertex.

The **base of a cone** is a circle with a radius *r*.

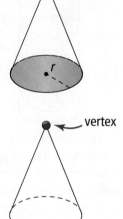

The **vertex of a cone** is the point farthest from the base.

vertex

The **lateral surface of a cone** is the curved surface not included in the base.

The **slant height of a cone** is the length of the lateral surface from base to vertex.

ℓ

The **height of a cone** *h* is the length of a segment from the vertex perpendicular to the plane of the base. In a **right cone**, the segment representing the height connects the vertex and the center of the base. In this Topic, you can assume that a cone is a right cone unless stated otherwise.

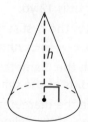

h

Part 1

Example Finding Lateral Areas of Cones

To the nearest square inch, how much paper does it take to make the cone-shaped gift box? Use 3.14 for π.

6 in.

1.5 in.

6 in.

1.5 in.

Solution ·

Surface area of cone = area of base + area of lateral surface

> The base of the cone is a circle.

Step 1 Find the area of the base.

Use the formula for area of a circle.	$A = \pi r^2$
Substitute.	$\approx 3.14(1.5)^2$
Simplify.	≈ 7.07

The area of the base is about 7.07 in.^{2}.

Step 2 Find the area of the lateral surface.

The lateral surface of the cone unfolds into a flat shape with a 90° angle. It occupies one-fourth of the circle with radius 6.

Use the formula for area of a circle.	Area $= \frac{1}{4} \cdot$ Area of circle
Substitute.	$= \frac{1}{4} \cdot \pi r^2$
Simplify.	$\approx \frac{1}{4} \cdot 3.14(6)^2$
	$= 28.26$

The area of the lateral surface is about 28.26 in.^{2}.

continued on next page >

Solution continued

Step 3 Find the surface area of the cone.

Surface area of cone = area of base + area of lateral surface

$$\approx 7.07 + 28.26$$

$$= 35.33$$

It takes about 35 in.^{2} of paper to make the cone-shaped gift box.

Key Concept

The **lateral area of a cone** is the area of its lateral surface. The formula is L.A. = $\pi r \ell$.

By flattening and slicing the lateral surface of the cone, you can find a formula for its area. Cutting the cone eight times, you will get a figure that looks somewhat like a parallelogram. However, the more cuts you make, the closer the resulting figure comes to actually being a parallelogram.

So you can use the formula for the area of a parallelogram to find the lateral area of the cone. The area of a parallelogram is base times height. The base is equal to πr and the height is ℓ. So the lateral area equals $\pi r \ell$.

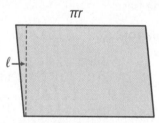

The **base area of a cone** is the area of a circle. $B = \pi r^2$

continued on next page >

Key Concept

continued

The **surface area (S.A.) of a cone** is the sum of the lateral area (L.A.) and the area of the base (*B*).

$$\text{S.A.} = \text{L.A.} + B$$
$$= \pi r \ell + \pi r^2$$

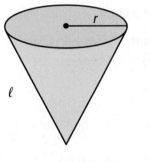

Part 2

Example Finding Surface Areas of Cones

Find the surface area of the cone-shaped lantern. The lantern has a base. Use 3.14 for π.

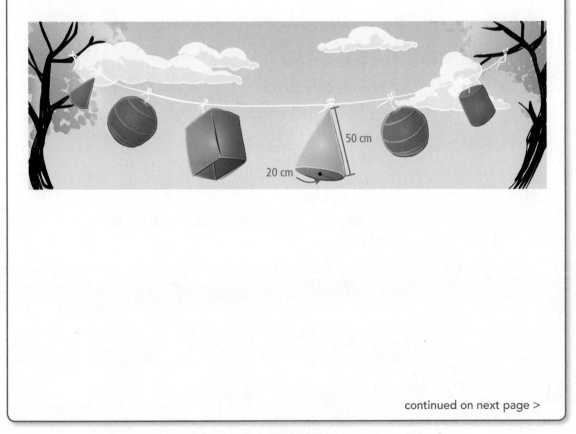

continued on next page >

Part 2

Example continued

Solution ·

Method 1 Use S.A. = L.A. + *B*.

Step 1 Find the lateral area.

> *ℓ* represents the slant height of the cone.

Use the formula for lateral area of a cone.   L.A. = $\pi r \ell$

Substitute 20 for *r* and 50 for *ℓ*. Use 3.14 for π.   ≈ 3.14(20)(50)

Multiply.   = 3,140

The lateral area of the lantern is about 3,140 cm².

Step 2 Find the area of the base.

Use the formula for area of a circle. $B = \pi r^2$

Substitute 20 for *r* and use 3.14 for π.   ≈ 3.14(20)²

Simplify.   = 1,256

The area of the base of the lantern is about 1,256 cm².

Step 3 Find the surface area.

Use the formula for surface area of a cone.   S.A. = L.A. + *B*

Substitute 3,140 for L.A. and 1,256 for *B*.   ≈ 3,140 + 1,256

Add.   = 4,396

The surface area of the cone-shaped lantern is about 4,396 cm².

continued on next page >

Part 2

Solution continued

Method 2 Use S.A. $= \pi r\ell + \pi r^2$.

$$\text{S.A.} = \pi r\ell + \pi r^2$$

Substitute 20 for *r* and
50 for ℓ. Use 3.14 for π.
$$\approx (3.14)(20)(50) + (3.14)(20)^2$$

Simplify.
$$= 4{,}396$$

The surface area of the cone-shaped lantern is about 4,396 cm².

Part 3

Example Solving Surface Area of Cones in Real-World Problems

A florist shop is designing a new cone-shaped arrangement box. To the nearest square inch, how much cardboard will be needed to make each box? Use 3.14 for π.

10 in.

15 in.

Solution ·

The amount of cardboard needed to make the box will be equal to the surface area of the box. Use S.A. $= \pi r\ell + \pi r^2$.

Step 1 Find the radius of the base.

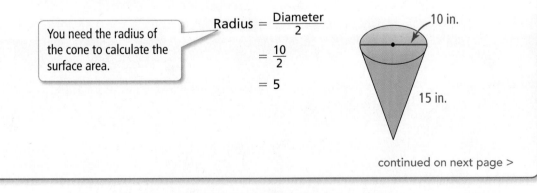

You need the radius of the cone to calculate the surface area.

$$\text{Radius} = \frac{\text{Diameter}}{2}$$

$$= \frac{10}{2}$$

$$= 5$$

10 in.

15 in.

continued on next page >

Part 3

Solution continued

    Step 2 Find the surface area of the cone.

Use the formula for surface area of a cone.	S.A. $= \pi r \ell + \pi r^2$
Substitute 5 for _r_ and 15 for ℓ. Use 3.14 for π.	$\approx (3.14)(5)(15) + (3.14)(5)^2$
Simplify.	$= 314$

About 314 in.^{2} of cardboard will be needed to make each box.

See your complete lesson at MyMathUniverse.com

1. Use a net to find the surface area of the cone to the nearest square centimeter. Use 3.14 for π. Round to the nearest whole number as needed.

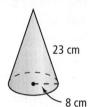

23 cm

8 cm

(The figure is not drawn to scale.)

2. You want to wrap a gift shaped like the cone shown. How many square centimeters of wrapping paper do you need to completely cover the cone? Use 3.14 for π. Round to the nearest whole number as needed.

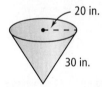

22 cm

6 cm

(The figure is not drawn to scale.)

3. Find the surface area of the cone. Use 3.14 for π. Round to the nearest whole number as needed.

20 in.

30 in.

(The figure is not drawn to scale.)

4.

47 cm

22 cm

(The figure is not drawn to scale.)

a. Find the surface area of the cone shown. Do not round until the final answer. Then round to the nearest whole number as needed.

b. Find the surface area of a cone with the same slant height and double the diameter. Use

3.14 for π. Do not round until the final answer. Then round to the nearest whole number as needed.

5. a. **Writing** Use a net to find the surface area of a cone with radius 15.5 m and slant height 16.5 m. Use 3.14 for π. Round to the nearest whole number as needed.

b. Is it possible to have another cone with the same surface area but different dimensions? Explain.

6.

12 cm

6 cm

(The figure is not drawn to scale.)

a. **Reasoning** What is the surface area of the cone? Use 3.14 for π. Do not round until the final answer. Then round to the nearest whole number as needed.

b. Suppose the diameter and the slant height of a cone are cut in half. How does this affect the surface area of the cone? Explain.

7. a. **Error Analysis** You and your friend are making a cone. The cone's radius must be 6 cm and its slant height must be 8 cm. Your friend incorrectly says the surface area is 151 cm². Find the correct surface area of the cone you want to make. Use 3.14 for π. Round to the nearest whole number as needed.

b. What was your friend's likely error?

8. **Stage Design** You are making a plastic cone for a school play. This cone has radius 5 cm and slant height 20 cm. How much plastic is needed to make the cone? Use a net to find the surface area. Use 3.14 for π. Round to the nearest whole number as needed.

See your complete lesson at MyMathUniverse.com

9. **Multiple Representations** Find the surface area of the cone. Use 3.14 for π. Draw a net and use it to verify the answer.

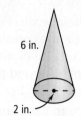

6 in.

2 in.

(The figure is not drawn to scale.)

10. Find the surface area of each cone. Use 3.14 for π. Which cone has the greater surface area?

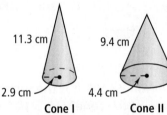

11.3 cm   9.4 cm

2.9 cm   4.4 cm

Cone I   **Cone II**

(The figures are not to scale.)

11. What is the surface area of the cone? Use 3.14 for π. Round your final answer to the nearest whole number as needed.

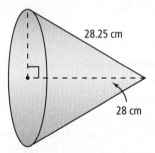

28.25 cm

28 cm

(The figure is not drawn to scale.)

12. **Think About the Process** The diameter of a cone is 33.6 cm. The slant height is 19.4 cm.

a. What is the first step in finding the surface area of the cone?
   A. Find the radius of the cone.
   B. Find the difference of the diameter and the slant height.
   C. Find the sum of the diameter and the slant height.
   D. Find the height of the cone.

b. Find the surface area of the cone. Use 3.14 for π.

13. **Think About the Process** Dona paints a cone for a school project. The diameter of the cone is 32.8 cm. The slant height is 18.5 cm. She uses one bottle of paint to paint 90 cm².

a. What is the first step in finding the surface area of the cone?
   A. Find the height of the cone.
   B. Find the sum of the diameter and the slant height.
   C. Find the difference of the diameter and the slant height.
   D. Find the radius of the cone.

b. How many bottles of paint does Dona need in order to paint the cone?

14. **Challenge** Donna paints ornaments for a school play. Each ornament is made up of two identical cones, as shown. She uses one bottle of paint to paint 200 cm².

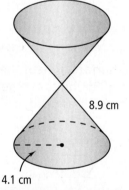

8.9 cm

4.1 cm

(The figure is not drawn to scale.)

a. What is the surface area of one ornament? Use 3.14 for π. Do not round until the final answer. Then round to one decimal place as needed.

b. How many bottles of paint does she need in order to paint 70 ornaments? Round up to the nearest whole number.

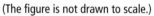

| # Volumes of Cones

CCSS: 8.G.C.9

Key Concept

The **volume of a cone** is the number of unit cubes, or cubic units, needed to fill the cone. The formula for the volume of a cone is $\frac{1}{3}$ the product of the base area and the height of the cone.

$$V = \frac{1}{3}Bh$$

$$V = \frac{1}{3}\pi r^2 h$$

> Since the base of a cone is always a circle, you can substitute πr^2 for B.

This cylinder and cone have the same height. They also have the same radius, so the area of their bases is the same. If you mark the cylinder in thirds, you can pour the contents of the cone into $\frac{1}{3}$ of the cylinder.

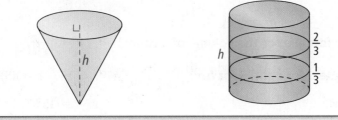

Part 1

Example Finding Volumes of Cones

What is the volume of each cone in terms of π?

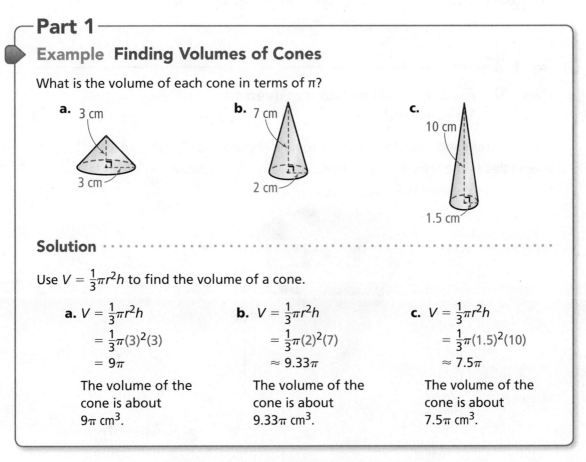

a. 3 cm
3 cm

b. 7 cm
2 cm

c. 10 cm
1.5 cm

Solution ·

Use $V = \frac{1}{3}\pi r^2 h$ to find the volume of a cone.

a. $V = \frac{1}{3}\pi r^2 h$

$= \frac{1}{3}\pi (3)^2 (3)$

$= 9\pi$

The volume of the cone is about 9π cm³.

b. $V = \frac{1}{3}\pi r^2 h$

$= \frac{1}{3}\pi (2)^2 (7)$

$\approx 9.33\pi$

The volume of the cone is about 9.33π cm³.

c. $V = \frac{1}{3}\pi r^2 h$

$= \frac{1}{3}\pi (1.5)^2 (10)$

$\approx 7.5\pi$

The volume of the cone is about 7.5π cm³.

See your complete lesson at MyMathUniverse.com

Part 2

Example Finding Volumes of Cones in Real-World Problems

You are making some bug repellant candles for an outdoor barbeque. What is the volume of wax needed for one of the candles? Use 3.14 for π.

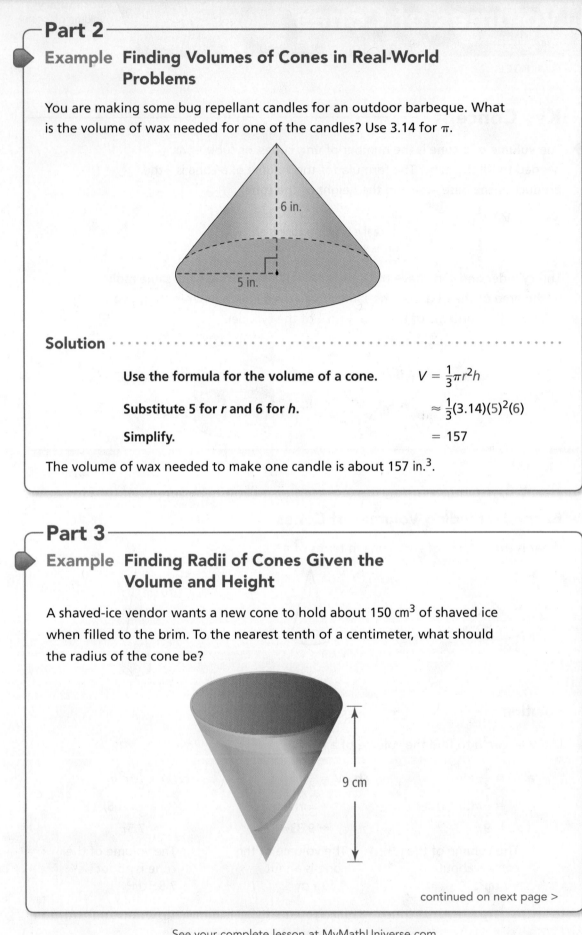

6 in.

5 in.

Solution

Use the formula for the volume of a cone.	$V = \frac{1}{3}\pi r^2 h$
Substitute 5 for *r* and 6 for *h*.	$\approx \frac{1}{3}(3.14)(5)^2(6)$
Simplify.	$= 157$

The volume of wax needed to make one candle is about 157 in.^{3}.

Part 3

Example Finding Radii of Cones Given the Volume and Height

A shaved-ice vendor wants a new cone to hold about 150 cm^3 of shaved ice when filled to the brim. To the nearest tenth of a centimeter, what should the radius of the cone be?

9 cm

continued on next page >

Part 3

Example continued

Solution ·

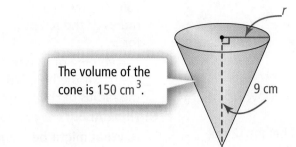

The volume of the cone is 150 cm^3.

9 cm

Use the formula of a cone to find the radius.

Use the volume formula.	$V = \frac{1}{3}\pi r^2 h$
Substitute 9 for *h*, 150 for *V* and 3.14 for π.	$150 \approx \frac{1}{3}(3.14)(r^2)(9)$
Multiply.	$150 = 9.42r^2$
Divide each side by 9.42.	$\dfrac{150}{9.42} = \dfrac{9.42r^2}{9.42}$
Simplify.	$15.92 \approx r^2$
Find the positive square root of each side.	$r = \sqrt{15.92}$
Simplify.	$r \approx 3.99$

The radius of the cone should be about 4.0 cm.

1. What is the exact volume of the figure? Write an exact answer in terms of π.

3 cm   4 cm

(The figure is not drawn to scale.)

2. Order the cones described below from least to greatest volume.

    Cone 1: radius 6 cm and height 12 cm

    Cone 2: radius 12 cm and height 6 cm

    Cone 3: radius 9 cm and height 8 cm

3. How many cubic meters of material are there in a conical pile of dirt that has radius 11 meters and height 6 meters? Use 3.14 for π. Round to the nearest hundredth as needed.

4. **Think About the Process**

  a. What is the radius of a cone with diameter d?

    A. The radius is d.

    B. The radius is $\frac{d}{2}$.

    C. The radius is $2d$.

    D. There is not enough information to find the radius of the cone.

  b. An ice cream cone is filled exactly level with the top of the cone. The cone has a 9-cm diameter and 9-cm depth. Approximately how much ice cream (in cm³) is in the cone? Use 3.14 for π.

5. A special stainless steel cone sits on top of a cable television antenna. The cost of the stainless steel is $8.00 per cubic centimeter. The cone has radius 12 cm and height 10 cm. What is the cost of the stainless steel needed to make this solid steel cone? Use 3.14 for π. Round to the nearest cent as needed.

6. The volume of the cone is 147π yd³. What is the radius of the cone?

9 yd

(The figure is not drawn to scale.)

7. An artist creates a cone-shaped sculpture for an art exhibit. If the sculpture is 7 feet tall and has total volume 109.9 cubic feet, what is the radius of the sculpture? Use 3.14 for π.

8. The volume of a cone-shaped hole is 49π ft³. If the hole is 3 ft deep, what is the radius of the hole?

9. **Think About the Process**

  a. What might be a good first step when solving the equation $V = \frac{1}{3}\pi r^2 h$ for r? Select all that apply.

    A. Divide each side of the equation by 3.

    B. Multiply each side of the equation by 3.

    C. Divide each side of the equation by h.

    D. Multiply each side of the equation by h.

  b. A prop for a movie is a cone with height 36 yd and volume $56\frac{1}{3}\pi$ yd³. Find the radius of the cone.

10.

9 m

5 m

(The figure is not drawn to scale.)

  a. **Writing** Find the exact volume of the cone. Write an exact answer in terms of π.

  b. Explain why an answer in terms of π is more accurate than an answer that uses 3.14 for π.

11. a. **Reasoning** A cone with radius 3 and height 11 has its radius quadrupled. How many times greater is the volume of the larger cone than the smaller cone?

  b. Explain how the volume of the cone would change if the radius were divided by four.

12. Error Analysis The volume of the cone is 64π cubic units. Your friend says that the radius of the cone is 16 units.

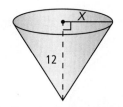

(The figure is not drawn to scale.)

a. What is the radius of the cone?

b. What error might your friend have made?

    A. Your friend found the diameter, not the radius.

    B. Your friend forgot to multiply by 2.

    C. Your friend forgot to take the square root of r^2.

    D. Your friend forgot to divide by 3.

13.

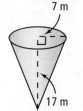

(The figure is not drawn to scale.)

a. Water Tank A water tank is shaped like the cone shown here. How much water can the tank hold? Use 3.14 for π. Round to the nearest hundredth as needed.

b. If water is drained from the tank to fill smaller tanks that each hold 200 m² of water, how many smaller tanks can be filled?

    A. 4   **B.** 3

    C. 5   **D.** 200

14.

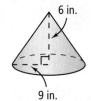

(The figure is not drawn to scale.)

a. Find the volume of the cone shown. Use 3.14 for π. Round to the nearest hundredth as needed.

b. Use the volume of the cone to find the volume of a cylinder with the same height and radius. Round to the nearest hundredth as needed.

15. The volume of a cone is 28.26 cm³. The radius and height of the cone are equal. What is the radius of the cone? Use 3.14 for π.

16. A cone-shaped vase has height 28 cm and radius 9 cm. An artist wants to fill the vase with colored sand. The sand comes in small packages, each of which is a cube with side length 2 cm. At most, how many packages of sand can the artist use without making the vase overflow? Use 3.14 for π.

17.

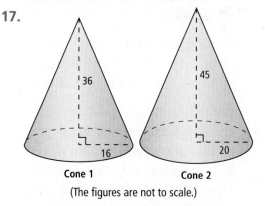

Cone 1   Cone 2

(The figures are not to scale.)

a. Challenge Find the exact volume of each cone. Write an exact answer in terms of π.

b. The cones shown are similar solids, which means their corresponding dimensions are proportional. Find the constant of proportionality for the volumes of the cones.

Surface Area of Spheres

Vocabulary
radius of a sphere, sphere, surface area of a sphere

CCSS: 8.G.C.9

Key Concept

A **sphere** is the set of all points in space that are the same distance from a center point.

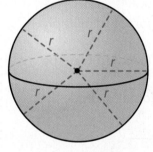

The **radius of a sphere** *r* is a segment that has one endpoint at the center and the other endpoint on the sphere. *Radius* can also mean the length of this segment.

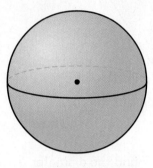

The **surface area of a sphere** is equal to the lateral area of a cylinder that has the same radius *r* and a height 2*r*.

Starting with a sphere, you can build a cylinder around it with the same radius *r* and a height of two radii, or 2*r*.

Imagine wrapping the lateral surface of the cylinder with string. That same amount of string would completely cover the original sphere. So the surface area of the sphere is the same as the lateral area of the cylinder.

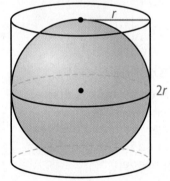

L.A. $= 2\pi rh$

$\quad\;\; = 2\pi r(2r)$ ← The height of this cylinder is 2*r*.

$\quad\;\; = 4\pi r^2$

Surface Area of a Sphere $= 4\pi r^2$

Part 1

Example Finding Surface Areas of Spheres Given the Radius

To the nearest square centimeter, what is the surface area of the bubble? Use 3.14 for π.

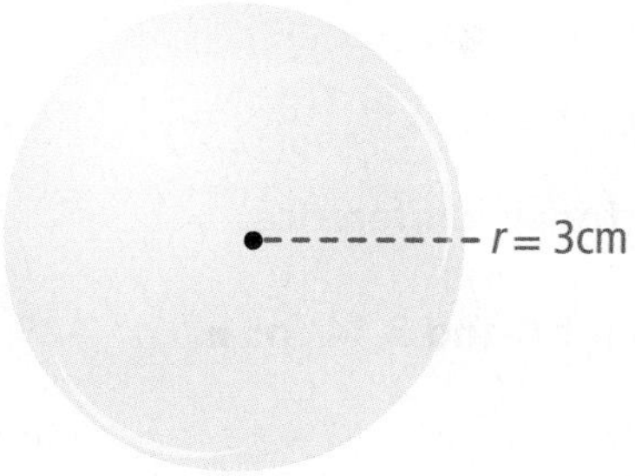

$r = 3\text{cm}$

Solution

Use the formula for the surface area of a sphere.	$\text{S.A.} = 4\pi r^2$
Substitute 3.14 for π and 3 for r.	$\approx 4(3.14)(3)^2$
Simplify.	$= 113.04$

The surface area of the bubble is about 113 cm^2.

Part 2

Example Finding Surface Areas of Spheres Given Circumference

To the nearest square foot, what is the surface area of the giant cheese ball? Use 3.14 for π.

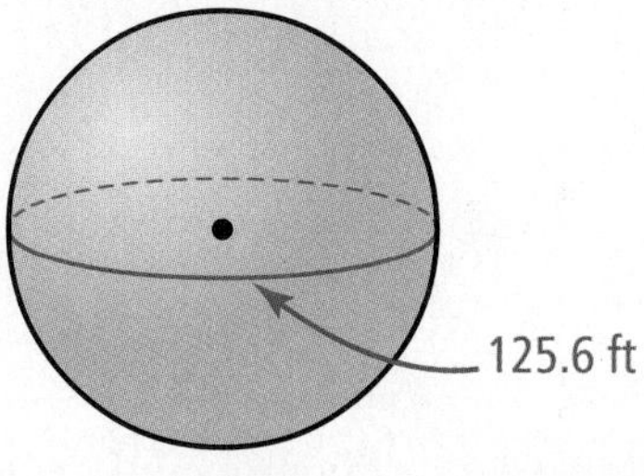

125.6 ft

continued on next page >

Solution ·

Use the circumference to find the radius, and then use the radius to find the surface area.

Step 1 Find the radius of the cheese ball.

Use the formula for circumference.	$C = 2\pi r$
Substitute 125.6 for C and 3.14 for π.	$125.6 \approx 2(3.14)r$
Multiply.	$125.6 = 6.28r$
Divide each side by 6.28.	$\dfrac{125.6}{6.28} = \dfrac{6.28r}{6.28}$
Simplify.	$20 = r$

The radius of the giant cheese ball is about 20 ft.

Step 2 Find the surface area.

Use the formula for the surface area of a sphere.	$\text{S.A.} = 4\pi r^2$
Substitute 3.14 for π and 20 for r.	$\approx 4(3.14)(20)^2$
Simplify.	$= 5{,}024$

The surface area of the giant cheese ball is about 5,024 ft².

Part 3

Example Solving for Radii of Spheres Given Surface Area

A static electricity ball has a surface area of 314 in.². How far does a bolt of static electricity have to travel from the center of the ball to the glass?

Solution ·

Find the radius of the sphere to determine how far the bolt of static electricity has to travel.

Use the formula for the surface area of a sphere.	$S.A. = 4\pi r^2$
Substitute 314 for S.A. and 3.14 for π.	$314 \approx 4(3.14)r^2$
Multiply.	$314 = 12.56r^2$
Divide each side by 12.56.	$\dfrac{314}{12.56} = \dfrac{12.56r^2}{12.56}$
Simplify.	$25 = r^2$
Find the square root of each side.	$\sqrt{25} = r$
Simplify.	$5 = r$

A bolt of static electricity has to travel about 5 in. from the center of the ball to the glass.

1. What is the surface area of a sphere with radius r of 6 cm? Use 3.14 for π. Write an integer or decimal rounded to the nearest hundredth as needed.

2. Find the surface area of the ball shown. Use 3.14 for π. Write an integer or decimal rounded to the nearest hundredth as needed.

Radius is 9 cm.

3. If the circumference of a spherical object is 37.68 cm, what is the surface area of the object? Use 3.14 for π. Round to the nearest whole number as needed.

4. A theme park has a ride that is located in a sphere. The ride goes around the widest circle of the sphere which has a circumference of 514.96 yd. What is the surface area of the sphere? Use 3.14 for π. Write an integer or decimal rounded to the nearest hundredth as needed.

5. If the surface area of a sphere is 4,534.16 cm², what is the radius of the sphere? Use 3.14 for π.

6. An art museum has a glass sphere on the front lawn with a surface area of 143,799.44 cm². Management wants to add a light to the center of the glass sphere. To support the light, they need to add a pole that runs from the bottom of the sphere to the center. How long does the pole need to be? Use 3.14 for π.

7. A class goes to the science museum. There is an exhibit which has a giant sphere that shows different weather patterns. The surface area of the sphere is 35,281.04 ft². What is the radius of the sphere? Use 3.14 for π.

8. **Writing** An artist creates a large spherical object out of paper mache for an art exhibit. The radius of the object is 17 in.

   a. What is the surface area of the object? Use 3.14 for π. Write an integer or decimal rounded to the nearest hundredth as needed.

   b. Explain why a person might need to know the surface area of a sphere.

9. a. **Reasoning** What is the radius of a sphere which has a surface area of 9,244 ft²? Use 3.14 for π. Write an integer or decimal rounded to the nearest hundredth as needed.

   b. Explain how you can check if the radius is correct.

10. **Error Analysis** Jakub is asked to find the surface area of a sphere which has a radius of 16 in. He says the surface area is 200.96 in².

    a. What is the surface area of the sphere? Use 3.14 for π. Write an integer or decimal rounded to the nearest hundredth as needed.

    b. What is Jakub's likely error?

       A. Jakub did not square the radius when solving.

       B. Jakub did not multiply by four when solving.

       C. Jakub did not multiply by 3.14.

11. **Water Tank** An architect wants to build a water tank in the shape of a sphere. The water tank will have a circumference of 665.68 in. The material he wants to use costs $0.79 per square inch. How much would it cost to cover the entire surface of the tank with this material? Use 3.14 for π. Round to the nearest dollar as needed.

12. a. **Mental Math** If the radius r of a sphere is $\sqrt{\frac{8}{3.14}}$ yd, what is the surface area? Use 3.14 for π.

    b. Explain why you can use mental math.

13. Think About the Process A sphere has a diameter of 52 ft.

   a. What should be the first step to find the surface area of the sphere?

     A. Find the circumference of the sphere.

     B. Find the radius of the sphere.

     C. Use the measure of the diameter in the formula for the surface area.

     D. Find the volume of the sphere.

   b. What is the surface area? Use 3.14 for π.

14. A scientist discovers a new moon. He calculates that the diameter of the moon is 298 km. What is the surface area of the new moon if it is spherical? Use 3.14 for π. Round to the nearest whole number as needed.

15. A farmer picks a spherical piece of fruit. The farmer measures the diameter to be 10.6 cm. What is the surface area of the fruit? Use 3.14 for π.

16. Find the radius of a sphere with a surface area of 16,430 m². Use 3.14 for π. Write an integer or decimal rounded to the nearest hundredth as needed.

17. Think About the Process

   a. If a sphere has a circumference of 69.08 in., what formula should you use to find the radius?

     A. $C = \pi r^2$ **B.** $C = 2\pi r$

     C. $C = \frac{4}{3}\pi r^3$ **D.** $C = 4\pi r^2$

   b. What is the surface area of the sphere?

18. Challenge A welder is making a metal sphere for a craft show. The circumference will be 718 cm. The welder has 30% of the sphere covered in a metal that is tinted red.

   a. What is the surface area of the metal sphere? Use 3.14 for π. Round the final answer to the nearest integer as needed. Round all intermediate values to the nearest hundredth as needed.

   b. What is the area of the section of the sphere that is tinted red?

19. Challenge The approximate surface areas of four spherical planets are shown in the table. **(Figure 1)**

   a. Find the distance between the center of each planet and its surface. Use 3.14 for π. Round to the nearest kilometer as needed.

   b. Compare the radii and surface areas of the planets. Do you notice a pattern? Explain.

(Figure 1)

Surface Areas

	Planet A	Planet B	Planet C	Planet D
Surface Area (km²)	3.60×10^7	1.44×10^8	3.24×10^8	5.76×10^8

| # Volumes of Spheres

CCSS: 8.G.C.9

Key Concept

The volume of a sphere is the number of unit cubes, or cubic units, needed to fill the sphere.

You can find the formula for the volume of a sphere by comparing it with the volume of a cylinder with a height and diameter equal to the diameter of the sphere.

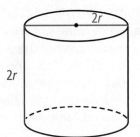

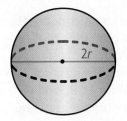

Fill the cylinder with water up to the $\frac{1}{3}$ mark.

Drop the sphere in the cylinder. When the sphere is completely submerged, the water level reaches the top of the cylinder.

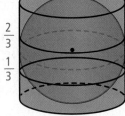

Use the formula $V = \pi r^2 h$ to find the volume of the cylinder.

$$V = \pi r^2 h$$
$$= \pi r^2 (2r)$$
$$= 2\pi r^3$$

> In this cylinder, the height is equal to $2r$.

The formula for the volume of this cylinder is $V = 2\pi r^3$.

The sphere filled two-thirds of the space in the cylinder.

Volume of the sphere $= \frac{2}{3}$ (Volume of the cylinder)

$$= \frac{2}{3}(2\pi r^3)$$
$$= \frac{4}{3}\pi r^3$$

See your complete lesson at MyMathUniverse.com

Part 1

Example Finding Volumes of Spheres

To the nearest cubic foot, how much space is contained inside the water-walking ball? Use 3.14 for π.

3 ft.

Solution

Use the formula for the volume of a sphere.	$V = \left(\dfrac{4}{3}\right)\pi r^3$
Substitute 3.14 for π and 3 for r.	$\approx \left(\dfrac{4}{3}\right)(3.14)(3)^3$
Simplify.	$= 113.04$

There is about 113 ft^3 of space inside the water-walking ball.

Part 2

Example Calculating the Space Inside Spheres

When it spins, the quarter forms what appears to be a sphere. To the nearest hundredth of a cubic inch, how much space does the spinning quarter occupy? Use 3.14 for π.

|← 0.995 in. →|

continued on next page >

Part 2

Example continued

Solution ·

Step 1 Find the radius.

$$Radius = \frac{Diameter}{2}$$

$$= \frac{0.995}{2}$$

$$= 0.4975$$

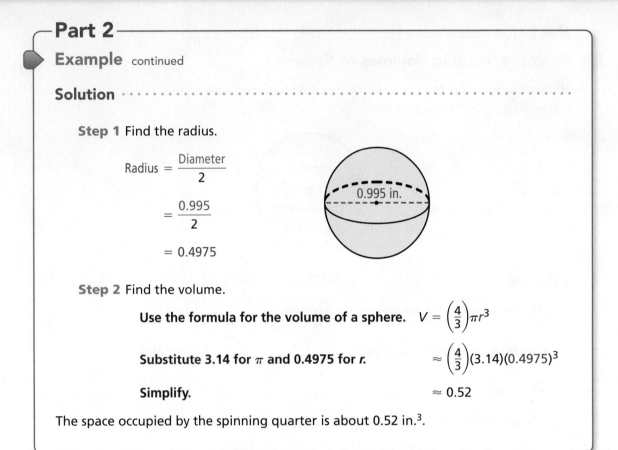

0.995 in.

Step 2 Find the volume.

Use the formula for the volume of a sphere. $V = \left(\frac{4}{3}\right)\pi r^3$

Substitute 3.14 for π and 0.4975 for r. $\approx \left(\frac{4}{3}\right)(3.14)(0.4975)^3$

Simplify. ≈ 0.52

The space occupied by the spinning quarter is about 0.52 in.³.

Part 3

Example Finding Radii of Spheres Given the Volume

An agate geode is spherical and has a volume of about 904 cm³. Geodes are often found in gem shops sliced in half like the one shown. What is the radius of the geode to the nearest centimeter? Use 3.14 for π.

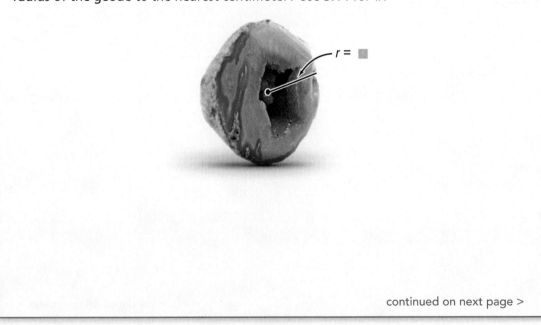

$r = \blacksquare$

continued on next page >

Part 3

Example continued

Solution ·

Use the formula for the volume of a sphere.

$$V = \left(\frac{4}{3}\right)\pi r^3$$

Substitute 3.14 for π and 0.4975 for r.

$$904 \approx \left(\frac{4}{3}\right)(3.14)r^3$$

Multiply.

$$904 \approx 4.19 r^3$$

Divide each side by 4.19.

$$\frac{904}{4.19} \approx \frac{4.19 r^3}{4.19}$$

Simplify.

$$215.75 \approx r^3$$

Find the cube root of each side.

$$\sqrt[3]{215.75} \approx r$$

Simplify.

$$6.00 \approx r$$

The radius of the geode is about 6 cm.

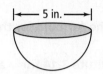
1. A solid plastic ball is a sphere with radius 8 in. How much plastic does it take to make one ball? Use 3.14 for π. Round to the nearest hundredth as needed.

2. Find the volume of the sphere to the nearest cubic foot. Use 3.14 for π.

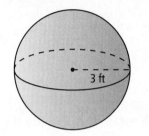

3 ft

3. Find the volume of the figure. Use 3.14 as the value of π. Round to the nearest whole number.

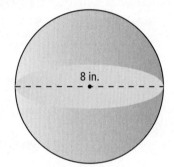

8 in.

4. A spherical boulder is 20 ft in diameter and weighs almost 8 tons. Find the volume. Use 3.14 for π. Round to the nearest whole number as needed.

5. A sphere has a diameter of 0.968 inches.
   a. What is the volume of the sphere?
   b. How does the volume of this sphere compare to the volume of a sphere with radius 0.968 inches? Use 3.14 for π.

6. The volume of a rubber ball is $5,461\frac{1}{3}\pi$ cm³. What is the radius of the ball?

7. The volume of a sphere is 7,234.56 cm³. To the nearest centimeter, what is the radius of the sphere? Use 3.14 for π.

8. The volume of a soap bubble is 1,375.4 mm³. Find the radius and diameter of the soap bubble. Use 3.14 for π.

9. **Think About the Process** A bowl is in the shape of a hemisphere (half a sphere) with a diameter of 5 in.

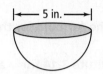

|← 5 in. →|

a. How can you find the radius if you know the diameter of the sphere?
   A. $d = 2\pi r$
   B. $d = 2r$
   C. $r = 2d$
   D. $r = \pi d$

b. Find the volume of the bowl. Use 3.14 for π and round to the nearest whole number as needed.

10.

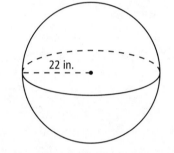

22 in.

a. **Writing** What is the volume of the sphere? Use 3.14 for π. Round to the nearest hundredth as needed.

b. Describe how the volume of the sphere changes if the radius is increased by 1.

11. a. **Reasoning** The volume of a sphere is 356.64 in.³. To the nearest tenth, what is the radius of the sphere? Use 3.14 for π.

b. How can you check that your answer is correct? Explain.

See your complete lesson at MyMathUniverse.com

12. Error Analysis Your friend says that the volume of this sphere is 659.25 m³.

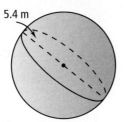

5.4 m

a. Find the correct volume, using 3.14 for π. Write a whole number or a decimal. Round to the nearest hundredth as needed.

b. What mistake might your friend have made?

  A. Your friend forgot to cube the radius.

  B. Your friend calculated using the diameter, not the radius.

  C. Your friend multiplied the diameter by 2, instead of dividing by 2, to find the radius.

  D. Your friend squared the radius instead of cubing it.

13. Plastic Factory A certain machine in a factory fills a spherical mold with plastic. If the diameter of the mold is 26.2 inches, how many cubic inches of plastic will it take to fill the mold? Use 3.14 for π. Round to the nearest hundredth as needed.

14. Estimation A spherical container has radius 12 cm.

a. What is the volume of the container? Use 3.14 for π. Round to the nearest hundredth as needed.

b. If 300 cm³ of water flow into the container in one minute, about how many minutes will it take to fill the container? Round to the nearest whole number as needed.

15. Find the volume of a sphere with a surface area of 144π yd². Round to the nearest whole number as needed.

16. A sphere has volume 1,837.85 cm³.

a. What is the radius of the sphere? Use 3.14 for π. Round to the nearest tenth as needed.

b. A second sphere has radius half as long as this radius. What is the volume of the second sphere? Round to the nearest hundredth as needed.

17. Think About the Process A soap bubble has radius 5.1 cm.

a. What is the first operation you should perform to find how much air is inside the bubble?

  A. Multiply r by 4.

  B. Find the value of r^3.

  C. Divide r by 3.

  D. Multiply r by $\frac{4}{3}$.

b. How much air is inside the bubble? Use 3.14 for π.

18. Challenge A bowl is in the shape of a hemisphere (half a sphere) with diameter 13 inches. Find the volume of the bowl. Use 3.14 for π. Simplify your answer. Round to the nearest whole number as needed.

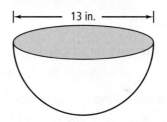

           13 in.

19. Challenge A spherical balloon has an 8-in. diameter when it is fully inflated. Half of the air is let out of the balloon. Assume that the balloon remains a sphere.

a. Find the volume of the fully-inflated balloon. Write an exact answer, using pi as needed. Use integers or fractions for any numbers in the expression.

b. Find the volume of the half-inflated balloon.

c. What is the radius of the half-inflated balloon? Round to the nearest whole number as needed.

See your complete lesson at MyMathUniverse.com

CCSS: 8.G.C.9

Part 1

Example **Finding Surface Areas of Composite 3-D Figures**

The party favors have the shape of 2 identical cones attached at their bases. The base radius is 2 in. To the nearest square inch, how much paper do you need to cover each party favor?

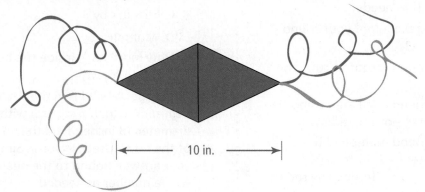

|← 10 in. →|

Solution

Find the amount of paper used to cover the party favor by calculating the lateral area of one cone and doubling it.

Step 1 Find the slant height of one cone.

Since the double cone is 10 in. long, the height of one cone is 5 in.

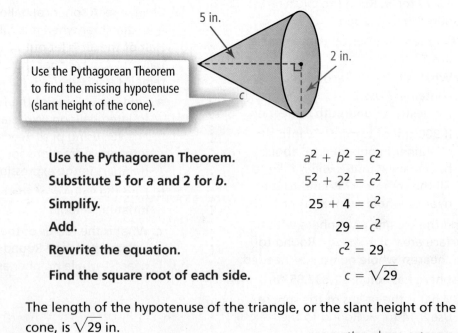

5 in.

2 in.

Use the Pythagorean Theorem to find the missing hypotenuse (slant height of the cone).

c

Use the Pythagorean Theorem.	$a^2 + b^2 = c^2$
Substitute 5 for *a* and 2 for *b*.	$5^2 + 2^2 = c^2$
Simplify.	$25 + 4 = c^2$
Add.	$29 = c^2$
Rewrite the equation.	$c^2 = 29$
Find the square root of each side.	$c = \sqrt{29}$

The length of the hypotenuse of the triangle, or the slant height of the cone, is $\sqrt{29}$ in.

continued on next page >

Part 1

Solution continued

Step 2 Find the lateral area of the party favor.

First find the lateral area of one cone.

Use the formula for the lateral area of a cone.	L.A. = $\pi r \ell$
Substitute 3.14 for π, 2 for r and $\sqrt{29}$ for ℓ.	$\approx (3.14)(2)(\sqrt{29})$
Multiply.	≈ 33.82

The surface area of the party favor is twice the lateral area of the cone.

Total surface area = 2 · L.A.

Substitute 33.82 for L.A.	= 2(33.82)
Multiply.	= 67.64

The amount of paper needed to cover the party favor is about 68 in.^{2}.

Part 2

Example Finding Volumes of Composite 3-D Figures

You are installing a cylindrical basin to collect rainwater from the gutter. The bottom of the cylinder resembles the lower part of a cone. To the nearest tenth of a cubic foot, how much rainwater can the basin hold? Use 3.14 for π.

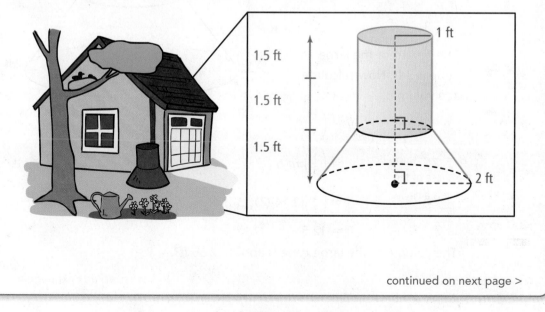

continued on next page >

Solution ·

> **Know**
>
> Dimensions of the cylinder, cone, and partial cone that form the shape of the basin

> **Need**
>
> The volume of the cone part and the cylinder part

> **Plan**
>
> Find the volume of the partial cone by finding the volume of the larger cone, then subtracting the volume of the smaller cone. Find the volume of the cylinder. Add the volume of the partial cone and the volume of the cylinder to find the total volume of the basin.

First, find the volume of the partial cone. (Steps 1–3)

Step 1 Find the volume of the larger cone.

The radius of the large cone is 2 ft.

The height of the large cone is the height of the bottom half plus the height of the top half

$h = 1.5 + 1.5$

$ = 3$

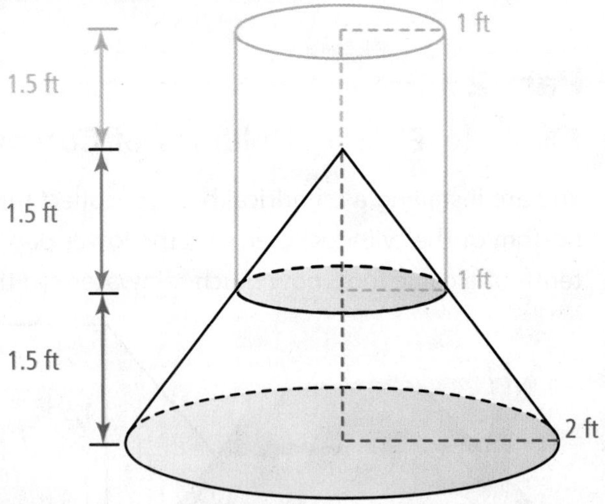

The height of the large cone is 3 ft. Now calculate the volume.

$$V = \left(\frac{1}{3}\right) Bh$$

$B = \pi r^2$ since the base of the cone is a circle.

$$= \left(\frac{1}{3}\right)\pi r^2 h$$

$$\approx \left(\frac{1}{3}\right)(3.14)(2)^2(3)$$

$$= 12.56$$

The volume of the large cone is about 12.56 ft³.

continued on next page >

Solution continued

Step 2 Find the volume of the smaller cone.

The smaller cone has a height of 1.5 ft and a radius of 1 ft.

$$V = \left(\frac{1}{3}\right)Bh$$

$$= \left(\frac{1}{3}\right)\pi r^2 h$$

$$\approx \left(\frac{1}{3}\right)(3.14)(1)^2(1.5)$$

$$= 1.57$$

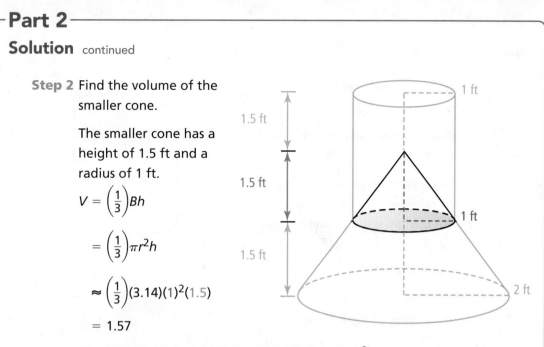

The volume of the smaller cone is about 1.57 ft³.

Step 3 Calculate the volume of the partial cone.

Volume of partial cone = Volume of larger cone − Volume of smaller cone

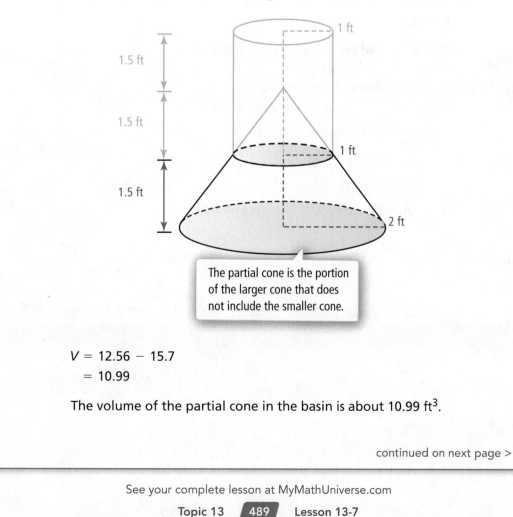

The partial cone is the portion of the larger cone that does not include the smaller cone.

$$V = 12.56 - 15.7$$

$$= 10.99$$

The volume of the partial cone in the basin is about 10.99 ft³.

continued on next page >

Solution continued

Step 4 Find the volume of the cylinder.

The radius of the cylinder is 1 ft.

To find the height of the cylinder, add the height of the bottom half and the height of the top half.

$h = 1.5 + 1.5$

$\quad = 3$

The height of the cylinder is 3 ft.

$V = Bh$

$\quad = \pi r^2 h$

$\quad \approx (3.14)(1)^2(3)$

$\quad = 9.42$

The volume of the cylinder is about 9.42 ft^3.

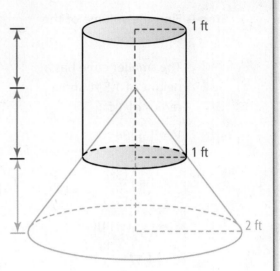

Step 5 Find the volume of the rain basin.

$$\frac{\text{Volume of}}{\text{basin}} = \frac{\text{volume of}}{\text{partial cone}} + \frac{\text{volume of}}{\text{cylinder}}$$

$$= 10.99 + 9.42$$

$$= 20.41$$

The volume of the water basin is about 20.4 ft^3.

1. Find the surface area of the solid. Use 3.14 for π. Do not round until the final answer. Then round to the nearest whole number as needed.

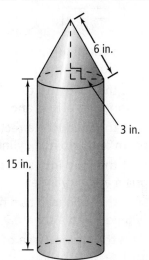

2. Find the volume of the figure. Use 3.14 for π. Round to the nearest whole number as needed.

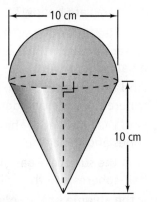

3. a. Find the surface area of the solid. Use 3.14 for π. Do not round until the final answer. Then round to the nearest whole number as needed.

b. Explain how adding a half-sphere to the other side of the cylinder would change the surface area.

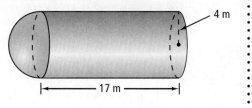

4. Find the surface area of the solid. Use 3.14 for π.

5. A student was asked to find the volume of the solid where the inner cylinder is hollow. She incorrectly said the volume is 2,034.72 in.^{3}.

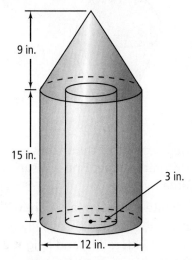

a. Find the volume of the solid. Use 3.14 for π. Round to the nearest whole number as needed.

b. What mistake might the student have made?

A. She did not subtract the volume of the smaller cylinder.

B. She found the surface area instead of the volume.

C. She found the volume of a sphere instead of a cone.

D. She found the volume of a rectangular prism instead of a cylinder.

6. The figure shows a peg used in a board game. Find the amount of plastic needed to create one of these pegs. Use 3.14 for π. Round to the nearest whole number as needed.

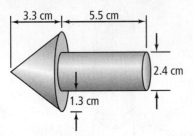

7. a. Find the surface area of the solid. Use 3.14 for π. Do not round until the final answer. Then round to the nearest whole number as needed.

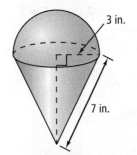

b. Replace one of the shapes with a different shape. Find the surface area.

8. A satellite consists of a sphere with a radius $r = 18$ m and six equally spaced cylinders with radii $\frac{r}{2}$ and height 20 m extending from the sphere.

a. Find the volume of the satellite. Use 3.14 for π. Round to the nearest whole number as needed.

b. Draw a picture of the satellite.

9. A septic tank has the shape shown below. How many gallons does it hold? Use 3.14 for π. Note that $1 \text{ ft}^3 \approx 7.48$ gal.

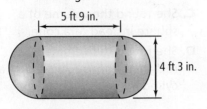

10. Think About the Process

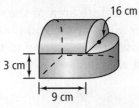

a. How can you split up the solid to find the surface area?

A. Split the solid into two rectangular prisms and a cone.

B. Split the solid into a rectangular prism and two half-cylinders.

C. Split the solid into a rectangular prism and a cylinder.

D. Split the solid into two half-cylinders and a sphere.

b. What is the surface area of the solid? Use 3.14 for π.

11. Think About the Process

a. What is the first step to find the volume of this solid where the half-spheres are hollow?

A. Find the difference of the surface areas of the cylinder and a half sphere.

B. Find the volumes of the half-spheres and the cylinder.

C. Find the volumes of the half-cones and the cylinder.

D. Find the surface areas of the half-spheres and the cylinder.

b. Find the volume of the solid. Use 3.14 for π.

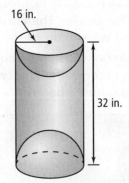

Interpreting a Scatter Plot

CCSS: 8.SP.A.1

Key Concept

A **scatter plot** is a graph that uses points to display the relationship between two different sets of data. Each point can be represented by an ordered pair.

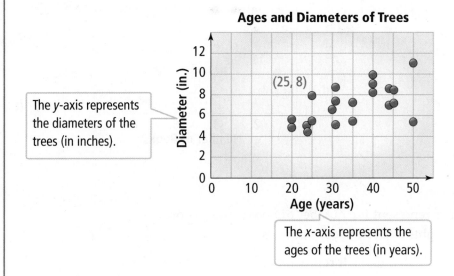

Ages and Diameters of Trees

The *y*-axis represents the diameters of the trees (in inches).

(25, 8)

The *x*-axis represents the ages of the trees (in years).

This scatter plot shows the relationship between the ages and diameters of various trees.

Consider the point (25, 8). This point represents a tree that is 25 years old and has a diameter of 8 inches.

The data might have been collected in a table. Each point represents the age and diameter of a tree.

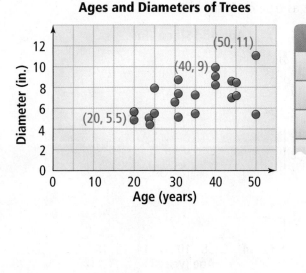

Ages and Diameters of Trees

(50, 11)

(40, 9)

(20, 5.5)

Tree	Age (years)	Diameter (in.)
A	20	5.5
B	40	9
C	50	11

Part 1

Example Understanding Points on Scatter Plots

What does the highlighted point on the scatter plot represent?

Book Bag Weights

Solution ·

The *x*-coordinates represent the number of books. The *y*-coordinates represent the weights of book bags in pounds.

The point on the graph is (5, 6). It represents a book bag that contains 5 books and weighs 6 pounds.

Part 2

Example Interpreting Scatter Plots

The scatter plot shows the ages and sleep times of several people. Use the scatter plot to classify each statement as *true* or *false*.

a. Two people slept for 7 hours.

b. Five people over the age of 12 were in the group.

c. Everyone in the group slept for at least six hours.

Age and Sleep Time

continued on next page >

Part 2

Solution

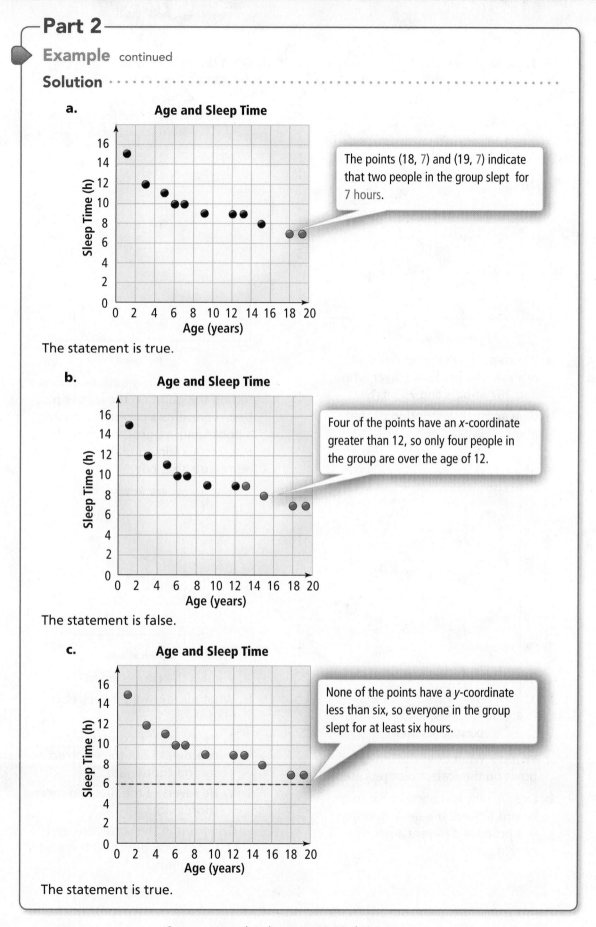

a.

Age and Sleep Time

The points (18, 7) and (19, 7) indicate that two people in the group slept for 7 hours.

The statement is true.

b.

Age and Sleep Time

Four of the points have an *x*-coordinate greater than 12, so only four people in the group are over the age of 12.

The statement is false.

c.

Age and Sleep Time

None of the points have a *y*-coordinate less than six, so everyone in the group slept for at least six hours.

The statement is true.

1. Multiple Representations

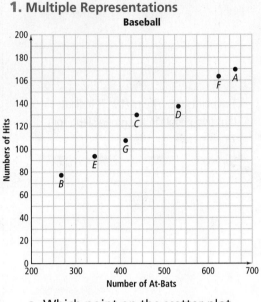

Baseball

a. Which point on the scatter plot represents a baseball player who had 267 at-bats and 76 hits?

b. Give another description of that point.

2.

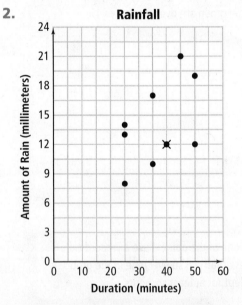

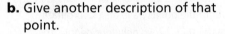

Rainfall

a. Writing What does the indicated point on the scatter plot represent?

b. Explain why it is possible for two storms to have the same duration but produce different amounts of rain.

3. What do the indicated points on the scatter plot represent?

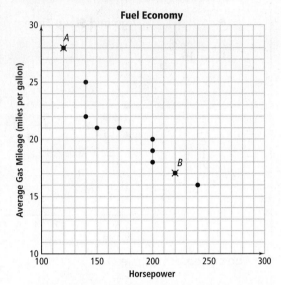

Fuel Economy

4. Error Analysis On a quiz, Beck needed to find the point on the scatter plot that represents a bag that contains 4 books and weighs 3 pounds. He incorrectly claimed that point *F* represents that bag.

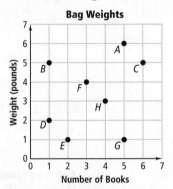

Bag Weights

a. What is the correct point?

b. What mistake might Beck have made?

A. He found the correct first coordinate but the incorrect second coordinate.

B. He reversed the first and second coordinates.

C. He found the correct second coordinate but the incorrect first coordinate.

5. Think About the Process The scatter plot shows ten gymnasts' scores in two events.

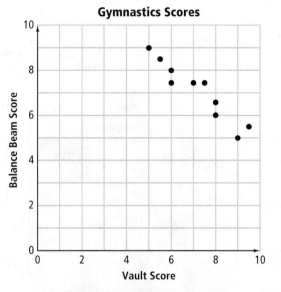

Gymnastics Scores

1. Six of the vault scores were at least 7.
2. Eight of the balance beam scores were less than 8.
3. There were four gymnasts whose combined scores were 14.

a. What should you do first to decide whether statement 3 is true?

b. Select each statement that is true.

6. Think About the Process Ten athletes ran two races of the same length. The scatter plot shows their times.

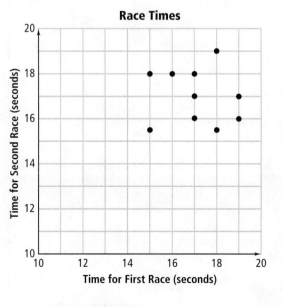

Race Times

1. Seven of the times for the first race were at least 17 seconds.
2. Three of the times for the second race were less than 16 seconds.
3. There were four athletes who did better in the second race than in the first.

a. What should you do first to decide whether statement 3 is false?

b. Select each statement that is false.

7.

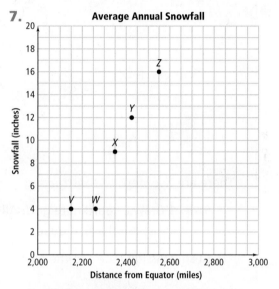

Average Annual Snowfall

a. **Challenge** Find each point on the scatter plot that represents a city that is at least 2,400 miles from the equator and whose annual snowfall is at least 12 inches.

b. Use the scatter plot to describe what the average annual temperature might be for each city.

CCSS: 8.SP.A.1

Key Concept

Scuba divers wear wet suits to maintain a comfortable body temperature as they dive. The table shows the temperature of the water and the thickness of a comfortable wet suit.

Temperature (°F)	Suit Thickness (mm)
76	1.6
69	3
64	5
49	6.5
33	9.5
80	3
70	6.5
65	9.5
45	9.5
60	6.5

There are five steps to constructing a scatter plot of the data.

Step 1 Draw a coordinate grid. All of the data are positive, so you can just use the first quadrant of the coordinate plane.

Step 2 Assign labels to the axes.

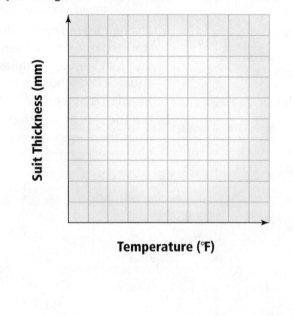

continued on next page >

Key Concept

continued

Step 3 Determine a scale for the horizontal axis.

The temperatures listed range from 33°F to 80°F, so consider a range of 0°F to 100°F.

Temperature (°F)	Suit Thickness (mm)
76	1.6
69	3
64	5
49	6.5
33	9.5
80	3
70	6.5
65	9.5
45	9.5
60	6.5

Set the increment so that you can make sense of the data once they have been graphed. Use an increment of 10°F.

Step 4 Determine a scale for the vertical axis.

Temperature (°F)	Suit Thickness (mm)
76	1.6
69	3
64	5
49	6.5
33	9.5
80	3
70	6.5
65	9.5
45	9.5
60	6.5

The scuba suit thicknesses listed range from 1.6 mm to 9.5 mm, so consider a range of 0 mm to 10 mm.

Use an increment of 1 mm.

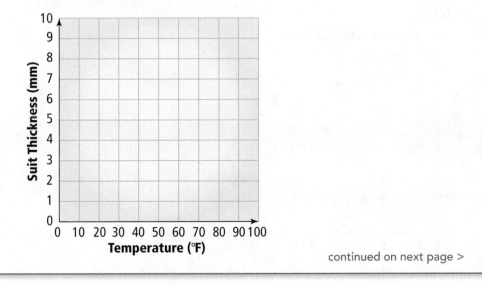

continued on next page >

Key Concept

continued

Step 5 Graph each ordered pair.

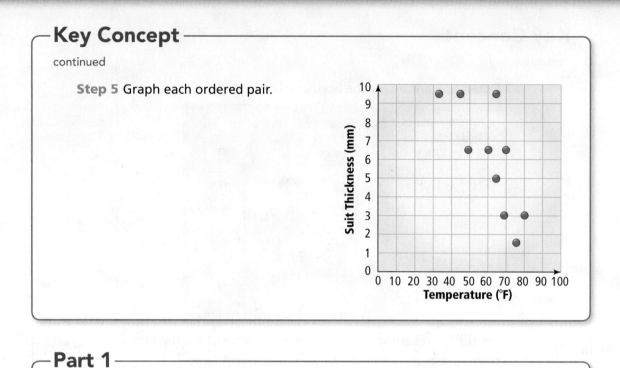

Part 1

Example Making Scatter Plots with Whole Number Values

The table shows nutritional values per serving for various foods. Make a scatter plot to represent the data.

Food	Fiber (g)	Protein (g)
Apple	5	1
Oatmeal	3	3
Kale	3	2
Chicken	0	9
Soy Yogurt	1	6
Broccoli	9	7
Squash	0	2
Carrots	0	0
7-Grain Bread	2	3
Brown rice	4	5

Solution

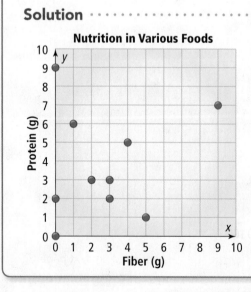

See your complete lesson at MyMathUniverse.com

Part 2

Example Making Scatter Plots with Decimal Values

The table shows the average movie ticket prices for several years. Make a scatter plot to represent the data.

Year	Average Ticket Price ($)
2005	6.41
2006	6.55
2007	6.88
2008	7.18
2009	7.50
2010	7.89

Solution ·

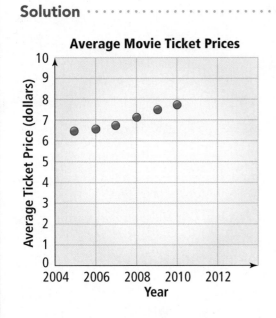

Part 3

Example Making Scatter Plots with the Graphing Tool

The table shows the route length and the number of stations for several major U.S. subway systems. Make a scatter plot to represent the data.

Length (mi)	No. of Stations
229	468
106.3	86
107.5	144
38	51
104	44
47.6	38

Solution ·

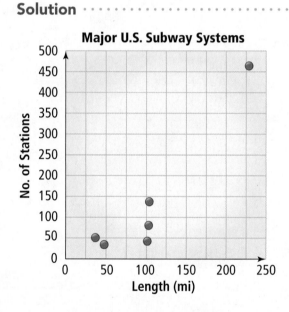

1. The table shows the average price of a pair of jeans and the number of pairs of jeans sold. Draw a scatter plot which represents the data.

Jeans Sales				
Average Price ($)	21	28	36	40
Number Sold	128	114	82	65

2. The table shows the hour of the day and the number of people at a park in the morning. Draw a scatter plot which represents the data.

Park Attendance					
Hour	7	8	9	10	11
Number of People	16	19	31	59	43

3. **Writing** The table shows the number of reported rainstorms in two different regions of a country.

Rainstorms						
Region A	1	3	5	7	9	11
Region B	6	9	11	14	16	19

a. Draw a scatter plot which represents the data.

b. Explain how a scatter plot shows the relationship between the data points.

4. **Open-Ended** The table shows the price and the number of items sold.

Items Sold

Price ($)	Number
10	42
15	39
20	14
25	17
30	18
35	14

a. Draw a scatter plot which represents the data.

b. Give a situation and decide what kind of items the data could represent.

5. **Reasoning** The table shows the total yearly revenue for a company in billions of dollars.

Total Revenue						
Year	2001	2002	2003	2004	2005	2006
Billions of Dollars	2.3	3.5	3.2	4.5	5.2	4.3

a. Draw a scatter plot which represents the data.

b. What characteristics of a data set should you consider in making a scatter plot?

6. The table shows the year and the monthly salary for a worker at a local store. **(Figure 1)**

a. Draw a scatter plot which represents the data.

b. Do you prefer to display the data in a table or in a scatter plot? Explain.

7. **Think About the Process** The table shows the Calories and fat content for a chicken sandwich at certain restaurants.

Chicken Sandwiches						
Restaurant	A	B	C	D	E	F
Number of Calories	370	440	520	690	720	910
Number of Fat Grams	4	13	23	34	26	51

a. How should you plot each point to complete the scatter plot?

b. Draw a scatter plot which represents the data.

(Figure 1)

Monthly Salary									
Year	2002	2003	2004	2005	2006	2007	2008	2009	2010
Salary ($)	1,300	1,500	1,700	2,000	2,000	2,100	2,400	2,700	2,700

See your complete lesson at MyMathUniverse.com

8. Error Analysis The table shows the number of painters and sculptors enrolled in various art schools. Jashar makes the scatter plot to represent the data.

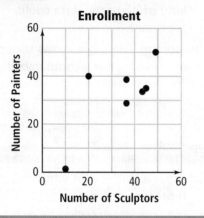

Enrollment

Enrollment							
Number of Painters	35	43	48	35	10	44	20
Number of Sculptors	28	33	50	37	3	34	42

a. Draw a scatter plot which represents the data.

b. What was Jashar's likely error?

   A. He used an incorrect scale.

   B. He switched the axes labels.

   C. He plotted the points incorrectly.

   D. He assigned labels incorrectly.

9. The table shows the time spent studying, in hours, and the test scores for two students.

Student A						
Time	1.5	3	5.75	10.5	12.25	15.5
Score	62	67	77	97	95	91

Student B						
Time	5.25	6	9.5	12	12.25	15.5
Score	83	81	91	97	93	96

a. Draw a scatter plot which represents the data for Student A.

b. Draw a scatter plot which represents the data for Student B.

c. What are the similarities between the scatter plots? What are the differences?

10. Think About the Process The table shows the temperature, in degrees Fahrenheit, and the number of kids wearing shorts. You draw the first quadrant of the coordinate plane and decide to label the temperature on the horizontal axis and the number of kids on the vertical axis.

Kids Wearing Shorts

Temperature	Number of Kids
64	4
72	10
84	19
75	9
89	24

a. What is the next step?

   A. Graph each ordered pair.

   B. Decide on the scale for the axes.

   C. Label the axes.

   D. Interpret the data.

b. Draw a scatter plot which represents the data.

11. The table shows the height and grade point average (GPA) for the students in a class. Draw a scatter plot which represents the data.

Student Data						
Height (in.)	59	62	64	65	67	68
GPA	3.23	3.26	3.29	2.75	2.82	3.83
Height (in.)	68	69	70	71	73	74
GPA	1.19	2.28	3.97	3.55	3.18	2.17

See your complete lesson at MyMathUniverse.com

Vocabulary
cluster, gap, outlier

CCSS: 8.SP.A.1

Key Concept

The following are features of scatter plots.

Cluster A cluster is a group of points that lie close together.

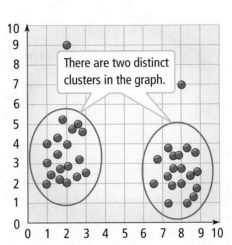

There are two distinct clusters in the graph.

Gap A gap is an area on the graph that contains no data points.

The gap falls between *x*-values 3 and 6.5.

Outlier An outlier is a piece of data that does not seem to fit with the rest of the data set.

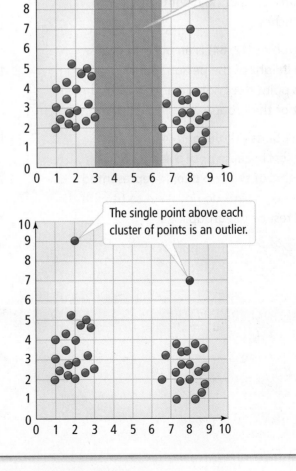

The single point above each cluster of points is an outlier.

Part 1

Example Identifying Clusters and Outliers from Scatter Plots

The graph represents the ages and heights of several people in a classroom. Identify the cluster and outliers in the graph. Explain your reasoning.

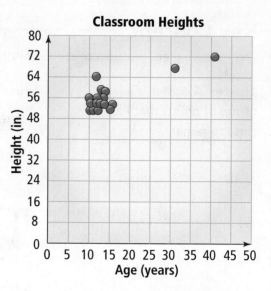

Solution

There is a cluster between the ages of 10 and 15 and the heights of 49 and 60 inches.

The point (12, 64) is an outlier because the height of the person represented by this point does not seem to fit with the rest of the group.

The points (31, 66) and (41, 72) are outliers because both the ages and heights of the two people represented by these points do not seem to fit with the rest of the group.

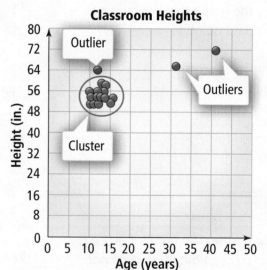

Part 2

Example Constructing and Analyzing Scatter Plots

For each person in your classroom, plot a point to represent the person's age and the number of languages the person speaks to form a scatterplot. Then describe any features of the scatter plot that represent the data for your class.

Solution ·

Answers may vary. Sample:

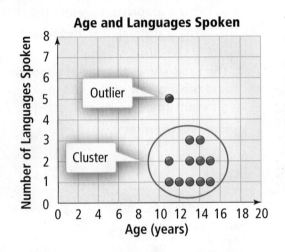

There is a cluster between ages 10 and 16, where most of the people in your classroom speak between 1 and 3 languages.

The point (11, 5) is an outlier because the person represented by this point speaks 5 languages, which is more than the rest of the group.

1. Which statement describes the cluster in the graph?

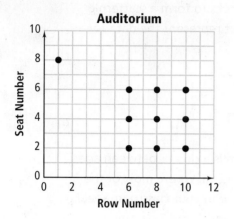

Auditorium

A. There is a cluster between row 6 and row 8 and between seat 2 and seat 4.

B. There is a cluster between row 6 and row 10 and between seat 2 and seat 6.

C. There is a cluster between row 8 and row 10 and between seat 4 and seat 6.

D. There are no clusters in the graph.

2. Consider the scatter plot shown. Which point is an outlier? Write an ordered pair.

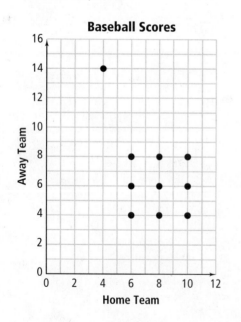

3. The table shows the day of a month and the temperature in degrees Celsius in different cities.

Temperature in Different Cities for Different Days of a Month							
City	1	2	3	4	5	6	7
Temperature	23	25	22	25	23	24	23
Day of Month	5	8	8	11	10	6	21

a. Draw a graph to represent the data.

b. Write a statement to describe the cluster.

4. The table shows the day of a month and the amount of the rain in different cities.

Amount of Rain in Different Cities for Different Days of a Month							
City	1	2	3	4	5	6	7
Day of Month	5	8	6	11	10	6	26
Amount of Rain (in mm)	27	29	26	29	27	28	27

a. Which graph represents the data?

b. Identify the outlier in the graph. Write an ordered pair.

5. The graph represents the number of students graduating from colleges and how much they earn in the first year in thousands of dollars.

Which statement below describes any clusters in the graph?

6. **Writing** The graph represents the price and the number of books sold in book stores.

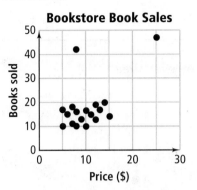

Bookstore Book Sales

a. Which statement describes the cluster?

b. How does a graph show the relationship between the data points? Explain.

7. **Reasoning** The graph represents the price and the number of items sold.

a. Identify the outlier in the graph. Write an ordered pair.

b. How do you know that a point is not an outlier? Explain.

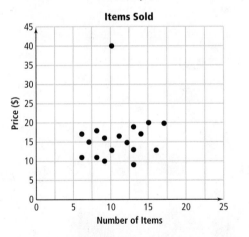

8. The graph represents the month of the year and the number of people staying in hotels. What is/are the cluster(s) in the graph?

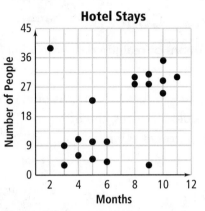

Hotel Stays

9. **Think About the Process** The table shows the years of experience and the monthly salary in thousands of dollars for people working at stores. **(Figure 1)**

a. How should you plot each point to complete the scatter plot?

b. Which scatter plot below represents the data?

c. Which statement below describes any clusters?

10. **Think About the Process** The table shows the hour of the day and the number of people at parks in a particular town. **(Figure 2)**

a. In what quadrant of the coordinate plane should you graph the scatter plot?

b. Which scatter plot represents the data?

c. Identify the outliers in the graph.

(Figure 1)

Monthly Salary							
Number of Years	2	4	5	5	6	6	7	7
Salary (in thousands)	1.0	3.75	1.0	1.5	1.25	1.75	1.5	1.25

(Figure 2)

Park Attendance							
Hour of Day	7	9	8	8	9	9	10	11
Number of People	12	26	8	10	8	10	12	30

CCSS: 8.SP.A.1

Key Concept

Graphs of real-life data rarely fall in straight lines. However, their arrangement may suggest associations or trends.

Positive Association As one set of values increases, the other set tends to increase as well.

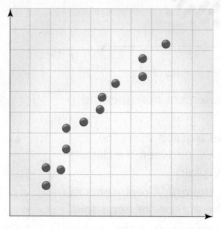

Negative Association As one set of values increases, the other set tends to decrease.

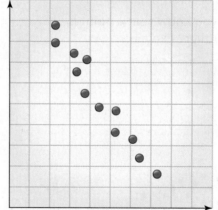

No Association There is no apparent relationship among the data.

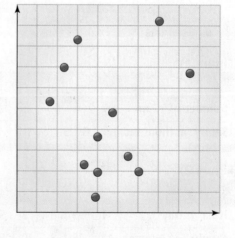

See your complete lesson at MyMathUniverse.com

Part 1

Example Making Predictions from Scatter Plots

Biologists recorded the lengths and weights of several wild alligators.

a. Make a scatter plot to represent the data.

b. Does an association exist between the length and the weight of an alligator? Explain.

c. Predict the weight of an alligator that is 58 inches long.

Alligator	Length (in.)	Weight (lb)
A	12	0.15
B	18	0.42
C	24	0.68
D	30	3.5
E	36	8.6
F	42	13.0
G	48	17.7
H	54	28.0
I	60	39.6
J	66	45.4
K	72	49.6

Solution ···

a. Let the horizontal axis represent length, in inches. Let the vertical axis represent weight, in pounds.

b. As the length of an alligator increases, so does its weight. So the scatter plot shows a positive association.

c. By looking at the pattern in the graph, you can predict that an alligator that is 58 inches long would weigh between 30 and 40 pounds.

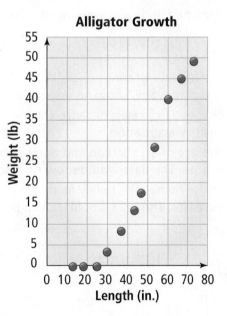

See your complete lesson at MyMathUniverse.com

Part 2

Intro

In many cases, you can analyze two data sets before you graph them and determine whether a scatter plot of the data would show an association.

Consider the possible relationship between the distance a student lives from school and the time it takes the student to get to school.

The farther a student lives from school, the longer it will take the student to get to school. So you would expect to see a positive association if you were to make a scatter plot.

Example Identifying Associations Between Categories of Data

Determine whether a scatter plot of data for each pair of categories would show a *positive*, a *negative*, or *no* association. Explain your reasoning.

a. number of songs on a CD and cost of a CD
b. speed and distance traveled
c. size of a TV screen and number of channels a TV receives
d. size of a family and amount of water bill

Solution

a. The number of songs on a CD usually does not affect the cost of the CD. The data would show no association.

b. As speed increases, distance traveled increases. The data would show a positive association.

c. The size of a TV screen and number of channels a TV receives are not related. The data would show no association.

d. As the number of family members increases, the amount of water used increases. The data would show a positive association.

Key Concept

There are several other associations that are easily visible using a scatter plot.

A linear association is formed when data points fall in a straight line.

Positive Linear Association

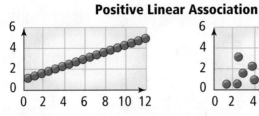

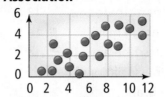

Negative Linear Association

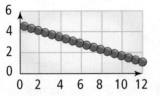

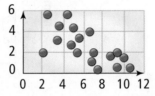

A nonlinear association is formed when the data points do not fall in a straight line.

Nonlinear Association

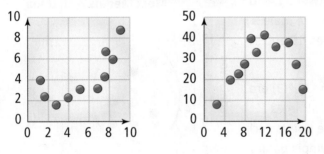

Part 3

Example Describing Clusters, Outliers, and Associations in Graphs

The graph shows the number of medals won and the number of Olympic games participated in by top medal-winning male Olympic athletes. Describe any clusters, outliers, or associations that you see in the graph.

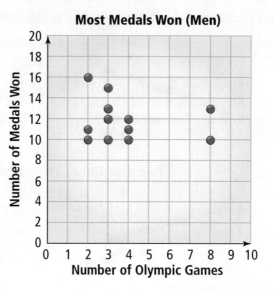

Most Medals Won (Men)

Solution

There is a cluster between 2 and 4 Olympic games, where male athletes won between 10 and 16 medals.

The points (8, 10) and (8, 13) are outliers because the athletes represented by these points each participated in 8 Olympic games, which is more than the rest of the group.

There is no association.

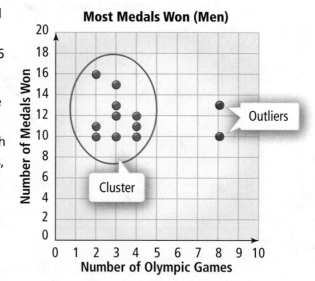

Most Medals Won (Men)

Outliers

Cluster

See your complete lesson at MyMathUniverse.com

1. Does the scatter plot show a positive, a negative, or no association?

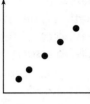

2. What type of association exists for these data?

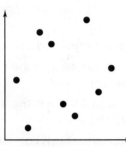

3. Determine whether a scatter plot of data for the following would show a positive, a negative, or no association.

time working and money earned

4. Which of these pairs of categories would produce a scatter plot that has no association?

A. age of a tadpole and the length of its tail

B. time working and money earned

C. amount of exercise and income

5. Does the scatter plot show a linear association, a nonlinear association, or no association?

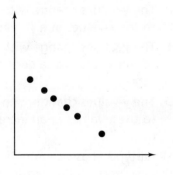

6. Open-Ended

a. Which of these pairs of categories would produce a scatter plot that has no association?

A. Cost of gas and a taxi driver's profit

B. Temperature and cooling costs

C. Fuel efficiency and the amount of traffic

b. Are there any pairs of categories that could produce scatter plots that show positive and negative associations? Explain.

7. a. Writing Determine whether a scatter plot of the data for the following would show a positive, a negative, or no association.

treadmill running time and calories burned

b. Describe a situation that would have a positive, negative, and no association.

8. a. Reasoning Which of these pairs of categories would produce a scatter plot that has a negative association?

A. amount of exercise and income

B. age of a car and reliability of a car

C. time exercising and calories burned

b. Explain your reasoning.

9. Research A sociologist is studying how sleep affects the amount of money a person spends. A scatter plot was made showing the results of the study. What type of association exists between the amount of sleep and money spent?

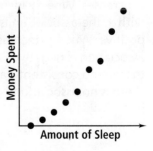

See your complete lesson at MyMathUniverse.com

10. Think About the Process

(1,1)   (2,10)   (3,7)   (4,5)   (5,8)
(6,6)   (7,5)   (8,9)   (9,10)

a. Which graph is the scatter plot of the data shown?

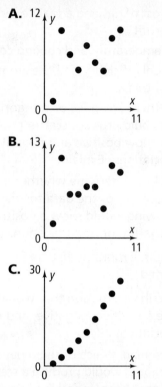

A.

B.

C.

b. How is a scatter plot useful in determining the type of association for a set of data?

A. The scatter plot shows the pattern of how *y* changes as *x* increases. When *y* increases with *x*, the association is negative. When *y* decreases, the association is positive. When there is no consistent pattern, there is no association.

B. The scatter plot shows the pattern of how *y* changes as *x* increases. When *y* increases with *x*, the association is positive. When *y* decreases, the association is negative. When there is no consistent pattern, there is no association.

C. The scatter plot shows the pattern of how *x* changes as *y* increases. When *y* increases with *x*, the association is positive. When *y* decreases, the association is negative. When there is no consistent pattern, there is no association.

c. What type of association does the scatter plot show?

11. a. Open-Ended Which of these pairs of categories would produce a scatter plot that has a negative association?

A. temperature and size of a glacier

B. temperature and the number of cookouts

C. temperature and the ability to play chess

b. Describe situations connected with age and sketch a scatter plot for each one. Make sure all possible associations are illustrated.

12. Think About the Process

a. How do you know if a scatter plot shows a linear association?

A. The *y*-values change with respect to the *x*-values at a constant rate.

B. The *y*-values change with respect to the *x*-values at a varying rate.

C. The *y*-values change with respect to the *x*-values at a decreasing rate.

D. The *y*-values change with respect to the *x*-values at an increasing rate.

b. What type of association, if any, is represented by the scatter plot above?

CCSS: 8.SP.A.2

Key Concept

When two sets of data have a positive or negative linear association, you can use a special line, called a trend line, to show the association more clearly.

A **trend line** is a line on a scatter plot, drawn near the points, that approximates the association between the data sets.

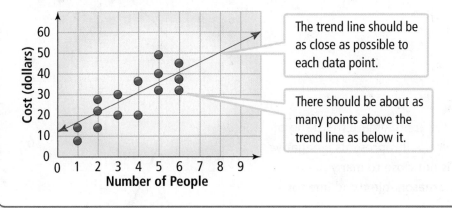

The trend line should be as close as possible to each data point.

There should be about as many points above the trend line as below it.

Part 1

Example Choosing Reasonable Trend Lines

Which of the lines shown are reasonable trend lines for the scatter plot? Explain your reasoning.

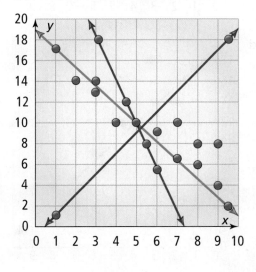

continued on next page >

Solution

This line does not approximate the trend of the data well. It represents a positive association, while the data show a downward trend. So this line is not a reasonable trend line for these data.

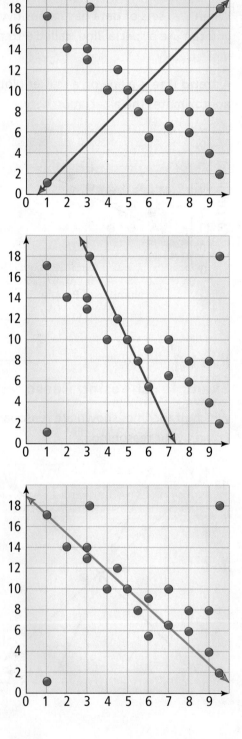

This line does not approximate the trend of the data well. While it represents a negative association, it is not close to many points. So this line is not a reasonable trend line for these data.

This line represents a negative association and is close to many points. So it approximates the trend of the data well and is a reasonable trend line for these data.

Part 2

Intro

There are four steps to writing an equation of a trend line.

Step 1 Identify two points on the trend line. Choose points that will be easy to use, such as whole-number values.

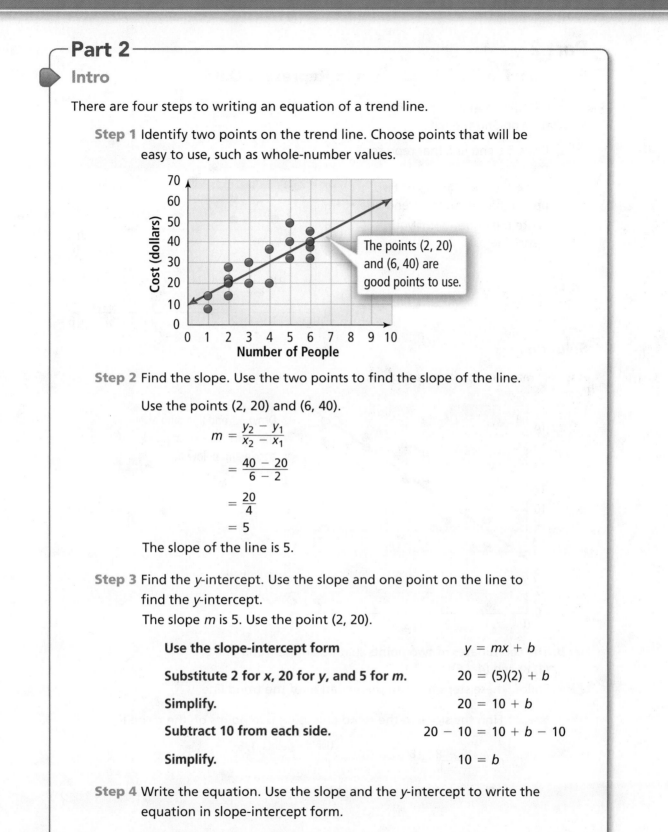

The points (2, 20) and (6, 40) are good points to use.

Step 2 Find the slope. Use the two points to find the slope of the line.

Use the points (2, 20) and (6, 40).

$$m = \frac{y_2 - y_1}{x_2 - x_1}$$

$$= \frac{40 - 20}{6 - 2}$$

$$= \frac{20}{4}$$

$$= 5$$

The slope of the line is 5.

Step 3 Find the *y*-intercept. Use the slope and one point on the line to find the *y*-intercept.

The slope *m* is 5. Use the point (2, 20).

Use the slope-intercept form	$y = mx + b$
Substitute 2 for *x*, 20 for *y*, and 5 for *m*.	$20 = (5)(2) + b$
Simplify.	$20 = 10 + b$
Subtract 10 from each side.	$20 - 10 = 10 + b - 10$
Simplify.	$10 = b$

Step 4 Write the equation. Use the slope and the *y*-intercept to write the equation in slope-intercept form.

Substitute 5 for *m* and 10 for *b* in $y = mx + b$.

$$y = mx + b$$

$$y = 5x + 10$$

The equation of the trend line is $y = 5x + 10$.

Part 2

Example Finding Trend Lines to Represent Data

The scatter plot suggests a linear association among the data.

  a. Draw a trend line that represents the data.

  b. Write the coordinates of two points that lie on the trend line.

  c. Write the equation of your trend line.

Solution

Answers may vary. Samples are given.

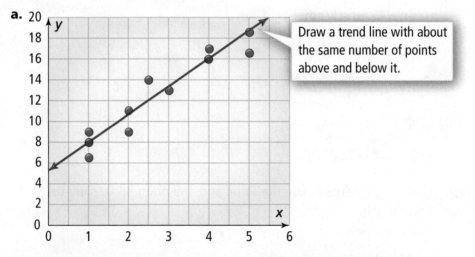

a.

Draw a trend line with about the same number of points above and below it.

  b. The coordinates of two points that lie on the trend line are (1, 8) and (4, 16).

  c. Follow these steps to write the equation of the trend line.

  Step 1 Find the slope of the trend line using two points on the trend line.

$$m = \frac{16 - 8}{4 - 1} = \frac{8}{3}$$

Use the points (1, 8) and (4, 16).

continued on next page >

Part 2

Solution continued

Step 2 Use the slope and one of the points to find the *y*-intercept.

$$y = mx + b$$

$$16 = \frac{8}{3}(4) + b$$ — Use the points (4, 16).

$$16 = \frac{32}{3} + b$$

$$16 - \frac{32}{3} = \frac{32}{3} - \frac{32}{3} + b$$

$$\frac{48}{3} - \frac{32}{3} = b$$

$$\frac{16}{3} = b$$

Step 3 Write the equation of the trend line.

$$y = mx + b$$

$$y = \frac{8}{3}x + \frac{16}{3}$$ — Substitute $\frac{8}{3}$ for *m* and $\frac{16}{3}$ for *b*.

The equation of the trend line is $y = \frac{8}{3}x + \frac{16}{3}$.

Part 3

Example Finding Trend Lines Using the Graphing Tool

The scatter plot suggests a linear association among the data.

a. Draw a trend line to represent the data.

b. Find the equation of your trend line.

Column A	Column B
1	5
2	11.75
3	15.5
4	16.3
5	20.1
6	22.2
7	25.2
8	26.5
9	29.0

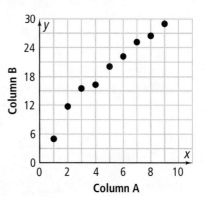

continued on next page >

Solution

Answers may vary. Samples are given.

a.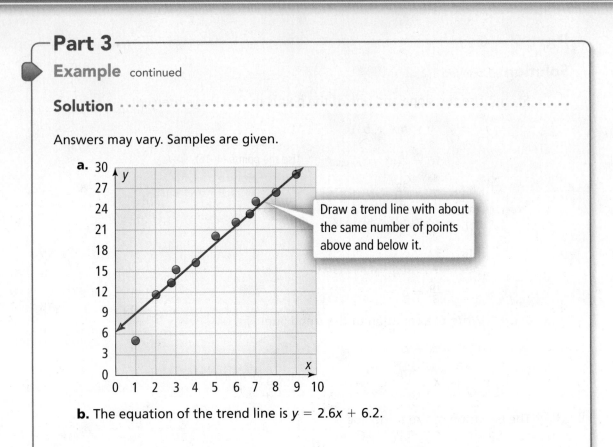

Draw a trend line with about the same number of points above and below it.

b. The equation of the trend line is $y = 2.6x + 6.2$.

1. Which of the lines shown is a reasonable trend line for the scatter plot?

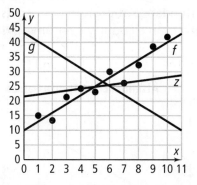

2. The scatter plot suggests a linear association between respiration and heart rates for adult males. Find an approximate equation for the trend line drawn for the data.

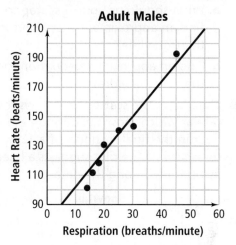

Adult Males

3. Estimation The scatter plot suggests a linear trend in the population of a certain city over time. Two points that lie on the trend line drawn are (18,31) and (82,72). Estimate an equation for the trend line that is drawn for the data.

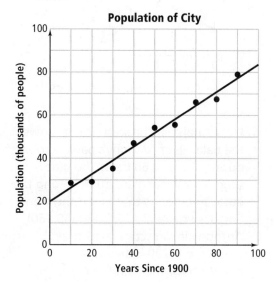

Population of City

4. Mental Math The scatter plot shows Leanna's elevation above sea level during her hike from the base to the top of a mountain. The plot suggests a linear association among the data. Two points that lie on the trend line drawn are (30,1070) and (75,1680).

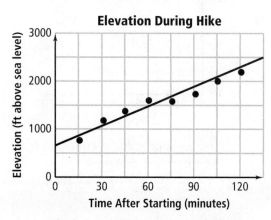

Elevation During Hike

a. Find an approximate equation for the trend line drawn.

b. Use mental math to find a similar equation if the base was 100 ft higher above sea level.

5. The scatter plot suggests a linear association among the data. Find an approximate equation for the trend line drawn for the data.

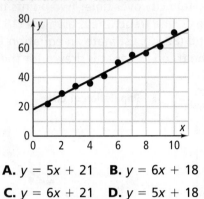

A. $y = 5x + 21$ **B.** $y = 6x + 18$

C. $y = 6x + 21$ **D.** $y = 5x + 18$

6. Error Analysis The scatter plot shows the balance of Anthony's bank account during the past 60 days. The plot suggests a linear association among the data. Two points that lie on the trend line drawn are (10,264) and (50,160). Anthony incorrectly claims that $y = -\frac{5}{13}x + 290$ is an approximate equation for the trend line.

Anthony's Bank Account

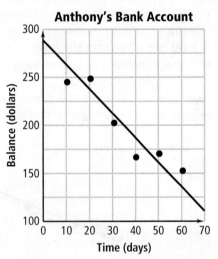

a. Find an approximate equation for the trend line drawn.

b. What error might Anthony have made?

   A. He swapped the numerator and the denominator for the slope.

   B. He used the incorrect sign for the slope.

   C. He used the incorrect sign for the y-intercept.

D. He swapped the x- and y-coordinates while finding the y-intercept.

7. Think About the Process The scatter plot suggests a linear trend in the attendance at professional sports games in a country over time. Two points that lie on the trend line drawn for the data are (2,154) and (14,222).

Attendance at Sports Games

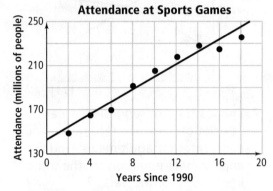

a. What should be your first step to find an approximate equation for the trend line?

b. Find an approximate equation for the trend line drawn.

8. Challenge The scatter plot shows the rate at which snow fell during each hour in the final six hours of a 12-hour snow storm. The plot suggests a linear association among the data.

Snowfall

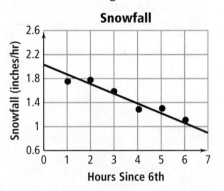

a. Find an approximate equation for the trend line drawn.

b. Describe a method to estimate the total amount of snow that fell during the final six hours. Then use your method to estimate the total amount.

Using the Equation of a Linear Model

CCSS: 8.SP.A.3, Also 8.SP.A.2

Part 1

Intro

You can adjust the representation of data so that the numbers are easier to work with, especially to find the equation of a trend line. Consider this movie ticket data.

Let the year 2000 equal Year 0. Then the year 2001 would be Year 2 and so on.

It will be easier to find an equation of the trend line using the second table.

Year	Total Revenue (in billions of dollars)
2000	7.7
2001	8.4
2003	9.2
2004	9.4
2007	9.7
2008	9.6
2009	10.6
2010	10.6

Year	Total Revenue (in billions of dollars)
0	7.7
1	8.4
3	9.2
4	9.4
7	9.7
8	9.6
9	10.6
10	10.6

Example Comparing Estimates from Trend Lines to Data

The scatter plot shows worldwide movie ticket revenues (in billions of dollars) for the top-grossing movie for several years. The scatter plot suggests a linear association.

Years Since 2000	Total Revenues
0	7.7
1	8.4
3	9.2
4	9.4
7	9.7
8	9.6
9	10.6
10	10.6

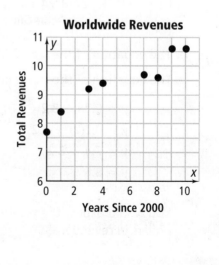

Worldwide Revenues

continued on next page >

See your complete lesson at MyMathUniverse.com

Example continued

   a. Find a trend line to represent the data.

   b. Find an equation for your trend line.

Now use the equation of your trend line to estimate the following.

   c. About how much would you expect the top-grossing movie for 2002 to make in total revenue?

   d. In what year would you expect the total revenue for the top-grossing movie to be about $9.5 billion?

   e. How does your answer to part d compare to the data collected for total revenues?

Solution

Answers may vary. Samples are given.

a.

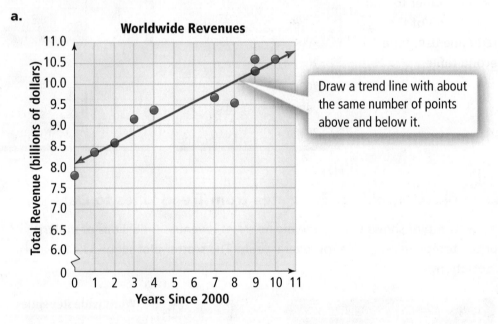

Worldwide Revenues

Draw a trend line with about the same number of points above and below it.

b. The equation of the trend line is $y = 0.2x + 8.2$.

c. The equation of the trend line that you found in part (b) is $y = 0.2x + 8.2$.

$$y = 0.2x + 8.2$$
$$y = 0.2(2) + 8.2$$
$$y = 0.4 + 8.2$$
$$y = 8.6$$

The units on the horizontal axis are "Years Since 2000." So to find the ticket cost, substitute 2 for x, not 2002.

You would expect the top-grossing movie in 2002 to make about $8.6 billion dollars in revenue.

continued on next page >

Part 1

Solution continued

d. Use the equation of the trend line to find the *x*-value when the *y*-value is 9.5.

Write the equation of the trend line.	$y = 0.2x + 8.2$
Substitute 9.5 for *y*.	$9.5 = 0.2x + 8.2$
Subtract 8.2 from each side.	$9.5 - 8.2 = 0.2x + 8.2 - 8.2$
Simplify.	$1.3 = 0.2x$
Divide each side by 0.2.	$\dfrac{1.3}{0.2} = \dfrac{0.2x}{0.2}$
Simplify.	$6.5 = x$

The units on the horizontal axis are "Years Since 2000," which are whole numbers, so round 6.5 to 7. Then add 7 to 2000 to find the year. So you would expect the top-grossing movie to have about $9.5 billion in total revenue in 2007.

e. Based on the linear model, the total revenue for 2007 would be $9.5 billion. The data provided for 2007 was actually $9.7 billion. So the trend line is not exact, but it is a reasonable model to estimate revenues.

Part 2

Example Using Trend Lines to Predict and Estimate

The scatter plot shows the average ticket prices for movies for several years. The scatter plot suggests a linear association.

Years Since 2000	Total Revenues
2	5.81
3	6.03
4	6.21
5	6.41
6	6.55
7	6.88
8	7.18
9	7.50
10	7.89

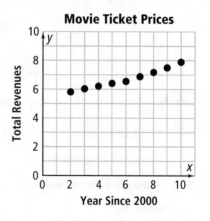

a. Find a trend line to represent the data.

b. Find an equation for your trend line.

Use the equation for your trend line to estimate the following.

c. How much will a movie ticket cost in 2020?

d. When did the average movie ticket cost $6.50?

continued on next page >

Part 2

Example continued

Solution

Answers may vary. Samples are given.

a.

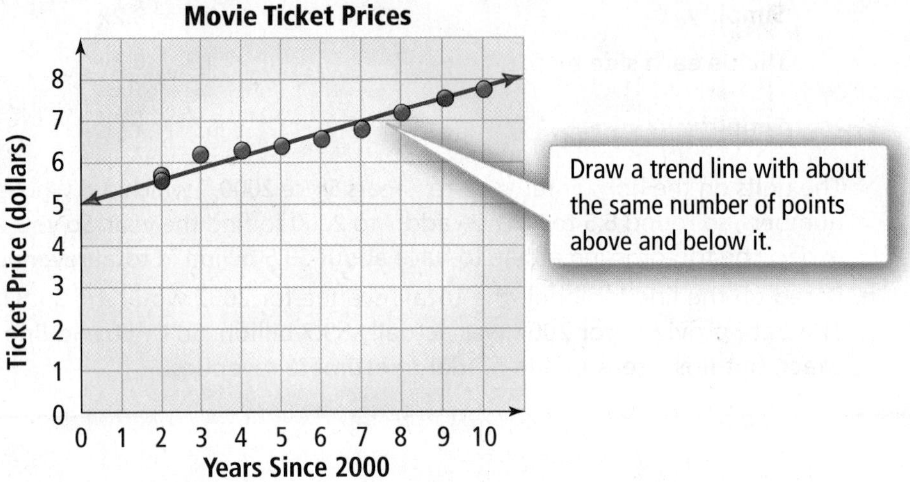

Movie Ticket Prices
Ticket Price (dollars)
8
7
6
5
4
3
2
1
0
0 1 2 3 4 5 6 7 8 9 10
Years Since 2000
Draw a trend line with about the same number of points above and below it.

b. The equation of the trend line is $y = 0.3x + 5$

c. The equation of the trend line that you found in part (b) is $y = 0.3x + 5$.

$y = 0.3x + 5$

$y = 0.3(20) + 5$

$y = 6 + 5$

$y = 11$

The units on the horizontal axis are "Years Since 2000." So to find the ticket cost for the year 2020, use 20, not 2020.

You would expect that in 2020 a movie ticket would cost $11.00.

d. Use the equation of the trend line to find the *x*-value when the *y*-value is 6.5.

Write the equation of the trend line.	$y = 0.3x + 5$
Substitute 6.5 for *y*.	$6.5 = 0.3x + 5$
Subtract 5 from each side.	$6.5 - 5 = 0.3x + 5 - 5$
Simplify.	$1.5 = 0.3x$
Divide each side by 0.3.	$\frac{1.5}{0.3} = \frac{0.3x}{0.3}$
Simplify.	$5 = x$

The units on the horizontal axis are "Years Since 2000." To find the year, add 5 to 2000. So you would expect that a movie ticket cost about $6.50 in 2005.

1. The scatter plot shows the annual profit for a certain airline (in millions of dollars) for years between 2000 and 2010. The equation of the trend line shown is $y = 0.4x + 4.1$, where x represents the year and y represents the profit. Use the equation to estimate the profit in 2002. Write an integer or a decimal.

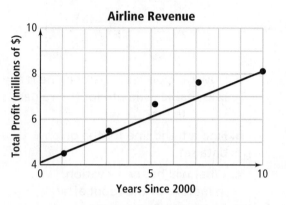

Airline Revenue

2. The data table shows the price of a certain stock on the first day of several months in one year. The equation of the trend line shown is $y = 0.2x + 13$, where x represents the month and y represents the price of the stock. In which month was the price of the stock about $14.80?

Stock Price

Month	Price ($)
January	13.20
March	12.76
May	14.54
July	14.28
December	15.40

3. **Reasoning** The data table shows the temperature inside an oven over the course of several minutes. The equation of the trend line shown is $y = 18.5x + 92$, where x represents the number of minutes and y represents the temperature in degrees Fahrenheit.

Oven Temperatures

Minutes	Temp (°F)
1	110.5
3	148.05
5	184.93
7	221.85
10	277.0

a. After about how many minutes was the temperature 203°F?

b. Could you use the data table to get a good estimate for the number of minutes? Explain.

4. **Hiking** The scatter plot shows a hiker's elevation above sea level during a hike from the base to the top of a mountain. The equation of a trend line for the hiker's elevation is $y = 8.77x + 686$, where x represents the number of minutes and y represents the hiker's elevation in feet. Use the equation of the trend line to estimate the hiker's elevation after 145 minutes. Round to the nearest whole number as needed.

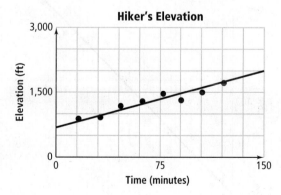

Hiker's Elevation

See your complete lesson at MyMathUniverse.com

5. **Estimation** The scatter plot shows the temperature in degrees Fahrenheit outside a house recorded every hour for 10 hours. The equation of the trend line shown is $y = -0.2x + 64.1$, where x represents the number of hours and y represents the temperature.

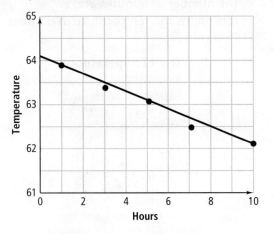

a. Based on the graph, what is true about the temperature after 6 hours?

b. Based on the equation, what is the temperature estimated to be after 6 hours?

6. **Mental Math** The graph shows the number of gallons of water in a large tank as it is being filled. The equation of the trend line shown is $y = 20x + 13$, where x represents the number of minutes that have passed and y represents the number of gallons of water. Use the equation to estimate how long it will take to fill the tank with 373 gallons of water.

Tank Volume

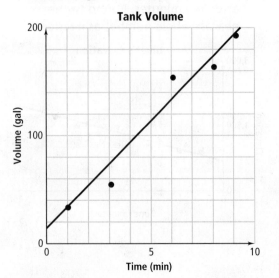

7. **Think About the Process** A robot explores a certain planet. The table shows the robot's elevation, y, after exploring for x minutes.

Robot's Elevation

Time (min)	Elevation (m)
1	−16.1
3	−9.1
4	1.6
7	16.8
8	25.2

a. How can you tell if a trend line is a reasonable estimate for the values in a data set?

b. Find a trend line for the given data set.

c. What will be the elevation, in meters, of the robot after 22 minutes?

8. **Challenge** The average price of two items between the years 2000 and 2010 is shown in the data table. The trend line for Object P is $y = 1.1x + 10.11$.

Cost of Objects

Year	Object P Cost ($)	Object Q Cost ($)
2001	11.21	18.38
2004	13.23	19.62
2007	17.18	19.77
2008	19.72	18.82
2010	21.11	19.28

a. What is a trend line for the cost of Object Q?

b. During which year did each object cost $18.78?

See your complete lesson at MyMathUniverse.com

Vocabulary
median-median line, summary point

CCSS: 8.SP.A.2

Part 1

▶ **Example** **Comparing Trend Lines With and Without Outliers**

The table and scatter plot show the length of certain models of cars and the miles per gallon they average when driven in the city. The scatter plot suggests a linear association.

Length (in.)	City (mpg)
194	18
183	22
194	21
191	21
198	20
196	18
200	19
188	24
197	17
200	17
191	22
190	24
193	18
200	18
196	17
190	22
197	18
215	1
212	17
192	23
189	22
185	24
197	22
188	22
190	20

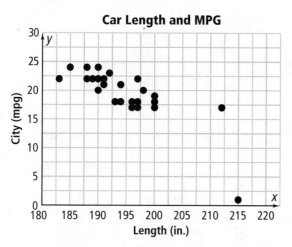

Car Length and MPG

a. Draw a trend line and find its equation.

b. Remove the outliers, (212, 17) and (215, 17), from the table. Draw a new trend line for the adjusted data set. Then find the equation for this trend line.

c. How do the outliers affect the position of a trend line? Explain your reasoning by examining the slope of each line.

continued on next page >

Solution

Answers may vary. Sample:

a.

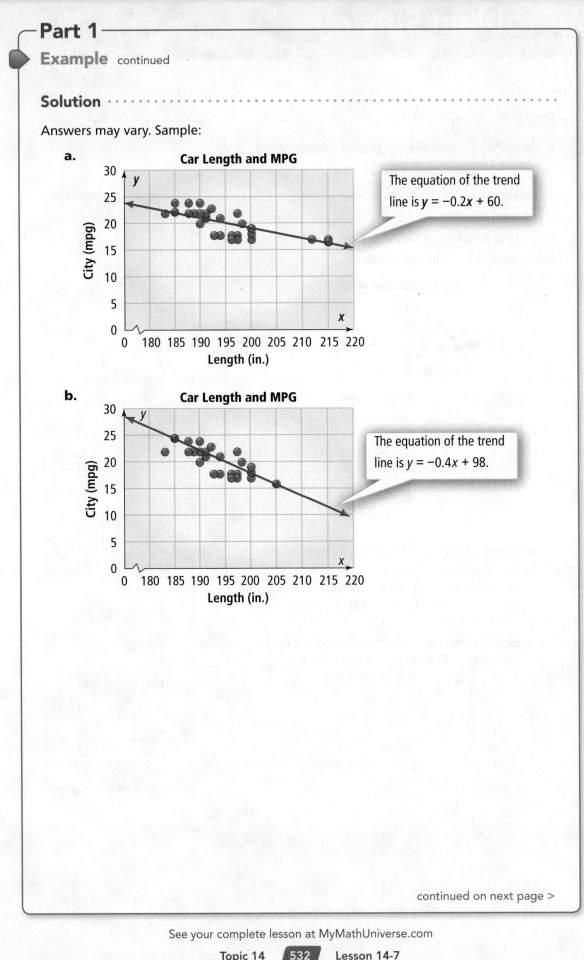

Car Length and MPG

The equation of the trend line is $y = -0.2x + 60$.

b.

Car Length and MPG

The equation of the trend line is $y = -0.4x + 98$.

continued on next page >

Solution continued

c. The outliers have an impact on both the slopes and *y*-intercepts of the trend lines. Although both lines have negative slopes, the slope of the line that includes the outliers is different from the one without the outliers. The line that excludes the outliers is steeper than the line that includes the outliers. This would indicate that the mileage for city driving decreases more quickly as the length of the car increases when the data for cars with unusual performances are removed from the scatter plot.

Includes outliers:

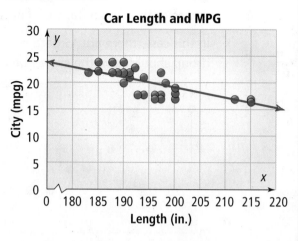

Excludes outliers:

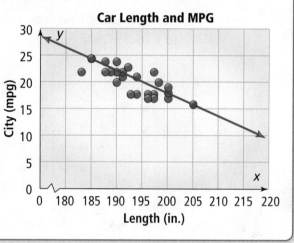

Key Concept

The **median-median line** or **median trend line** is a more formal way of finding a trend line for a scatter plot that suggests a linear association. There are five steps to this process.

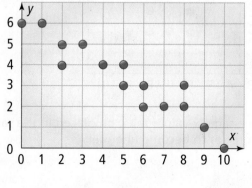

continued on next page >

Key Concept

continued

Step 1 Separate the points into three groups of equal size according to the values of the horizontal coordinates.

In this case, there are 15 data points. So each group has 5 points. Each group should have the same number of points.

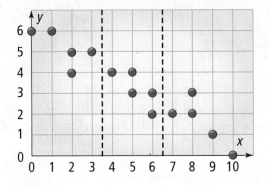

Sometimes there is 1 extra point. If there is one extra point, it should be added to the middle group.

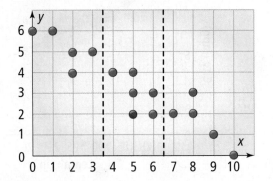

Sometimes there are 2 extra points. If there are two extra points, add one to each of the two outer groups.

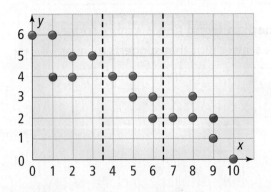

Points with the same *x*-values must be placed in the same group, even if it causes the groups to become unequal.

continued on next page >

Key Concept

continued

Step 2 Find the summary point for each group.

First Group

(0, 6) (1, 6) (2, 4) (2, 5) (3, 5)

x-coordinates	y-coordinates
0	4
1	5
2	5
2	6
3	6

Summary Point: (2, 5)

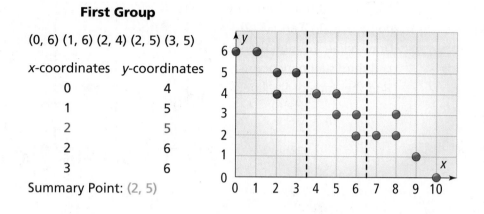

Second Group

(4, 4) (5, 4) (5, 3) (6, 2) (6, 3)

x-coordinates	y-coordinates
4	2
5	3
5	3
6	4
6	4

Summary Point: (5, 3)

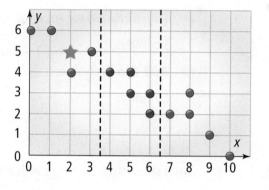

Third Group

(7, 2) (8, 2) (8, 3) (9, 1) (10, 0)

x-coordinates	y-coordinates
7	0
8	1
8	2
9	2
10	3

Summary Point: (8, 2)

continued on next page >

Step 3 Find the equation of a line using the two outer summary points.

The first and third summary points are (2, 5) and (8, 2). Draw a line through the first and third summary points. Find the slope of the line.

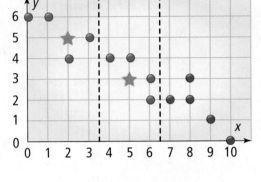

$$m = \frac{2 - 5}{8 - 2}$$

$$= \frac{-3}{6}$$

$$= -\frac{1}{2}$$

Now use the slope and one point to find the value of the y-intercept.

Write slope-intercept form.	$y = mx + b$
Substitute $-\frac{1}{2}$ for m, 2 for x, and 5 for y.	$5 = -\frac{1}{2}(2) + b$
Simplify.	$5 = -1 + b$
Add 1 to each side.	$5 + 1 = -1 + 1 + b$
Simplify.	$6 = b$

$$m = -\frac{1}{2}, \ 6 = b$$

Now substitute $-\frac{1}{2}$ for m and 6 for b in the slope-intercept form.

$$y = -\frac{1}{2}x + 6$$

Step 4 Translate the line using the middle summary point.

The middle summary point does not lie on the line that passes through the other two summary points. So you can use the middle summary point and the line that passes through the other two summary points to find the median-median trend line.

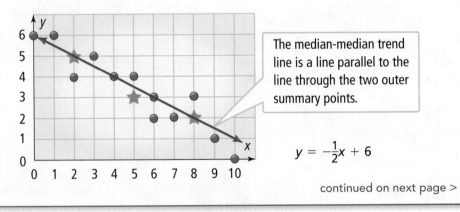

The median-median trend line is a line parallel to the line through the two outer summary points.

$$y = -\frac{1}{2}x + 6$$

continued on next page >

continued

The coordinates of the middle summary point are (5, 3). Find the y-coordinate of the point that lies on the line from Step 3 with the same x-coordinate as the middle summary point.

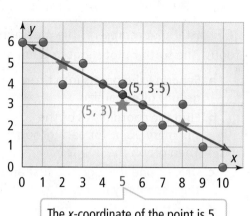

(5, 3.5)

(5, 3)

The x-coordinate of the point is 5.

Write the equation. $y = -\frac{1}{2}x + 6$

Substitute 5 for x. $y = -\frac{1}{2}(5) + 6$

Simplify. $y = -\frac{5}{2} + 6$

Simplify. $y = \frac{7}{2}$, or 3.5

Find the vertical distance between the middle summary point and the line by subtracting the y-values.

$$3.5 - 3 = 0.5$$

Since the middle summary point represents $\frac{1}{3}$ of the data, find $\frac{1}{3}$ of the vertical distance from the middle summary point to the line that passes through the other two summary points.

$$\frac{1}{3} \times 0.5 \approx 0.2 \text{ unit}$$

The median-median trend line is parallel to the line through the outer summary points. You can translate this line vertically 0.2 unit toward the middle summary point to find the median-median trend line.

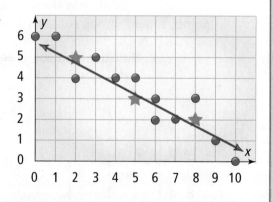

Step 5 Find the equation of the median-median trend line.

$$y = -\frac{1}{2}x + 6$$

$$y = -\frac{1}{2}x + (6 - 0.2)$$

So the equation of the median-median trend line is $y = -\frac{1}{2}x + 5.8$.

See your complete lesson at MyMathUniverse.com

Part 2

Example Finding Median-Median Trend Lines

The scatter plot represents the nutritional values per serving for various foods. The scatter plot suggests a linear association.

a. Separate the points into three groups of equal size.

b. Find the coordinates of the summary point for each group. Then graph the points.

c. Draw a line through the first and third summary points.

d. Find the equation of the line through the first and third summary points.

e. Find the vertical distance from the line through the first and third summary points to the middle summary point.

f. Find one third of the distance from the line to the middle summary point.

g. Write the equation of the median-median trend line.

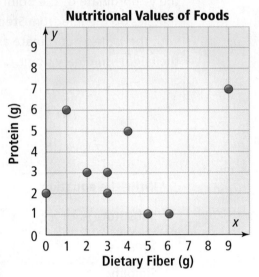

Nutritional Values of Foods

Use the equation of your median-median trend line to estimate the following.

h. How many grams of protein would you expect in a serving of food that has 7 grams of dietary fiber?

Solution

a. Separate the points into three groups of equal size. There are 9 data points, so each group contains 3 points.

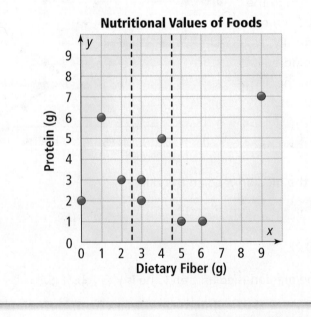

Nutritional Values of Foods

continued on next page >

See your complete lesson at MyMathUniverse.com

Solution continued

    b. Find the coordinates of the summary point for each group, using the median
        x-coordinate and *y*-coordinate.

First Group:

(0, 2), (1, 6), (2, 3)

Summary Point: (1, 3)

x-coordinates	y-coordinates
0	2
1	3
2	6

Second Group:

(3, 2), (3, 3), (4, 5)

Summary Point: (3, 3)

x-coordinates	y-coordinates
3	2
3	3
4	5

Third Group:

(5, 1), (6, 1), (9, 7)

Summary Point: (6, 1)

x-coordinates	y-coordinates
5	1
6	1
9	7

Then plot the summary points.

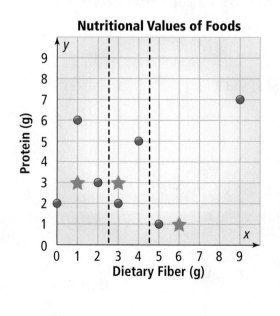

Nutritional Values of Foods

continued on next page >

c. Draw a line through the first and third summary points.

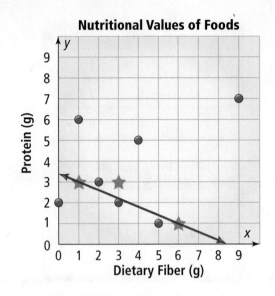

Nutritional Values of Foods

d. Find the equation of the line through the first and third summary points.
The first and third summary points have coordinates (1, 3) and (6, 1).
Find the slope of the line through the two points.

$$m = \frac{1-3}{6-1}$$

$$= \frac{-2}{5}$$

$$= -\frac{2}{5}$$

Use the slope and one point to find the value of *b* in $y = mx + b$.
Use $m = -\frac{2}{5}$ and (1, 3).

Write the slope-intercept form.	$y = mx + b$
Substitute $-\frac{2}{5}$ for *m*, 1 for *x*, and 3 for *y*.	$3 = -\frac{2}{5}(1) + b$
Add $\frac{2}{5}$ to both sides.	$3 + \frac{2}{5} = -\frac{2}{5} + \frac{2}{5} + b$
Simplify.	$\frac{17}{5} = b$

Substitute $-\frac{2}{5}$ for *m* and $\frac{17}{5}$ for *b* in $y = mx + b$.

$$y = mx + b$$

$$y = -\frac{2}{5}x + \frac{17}{5}$$

The equation of the line is $y = -\frac{2}{5}x + \frac{17}{5}$.

continued on next page >

Solution continued

e. Find the vertical distance from the line through the first and third summary points to the middle summary point.

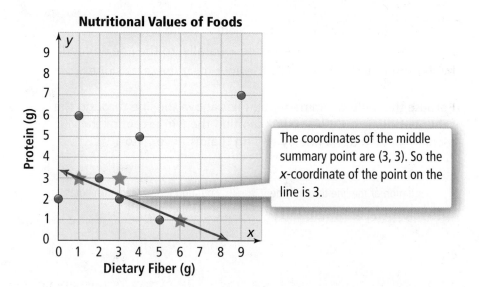

Nutritional Values of Foods

The coordinates of the middle summary point are (3, 3). So the *x*-coordinate of the point on the line is 3.

Use the equation of the line that passes through the other two summary points to find the *y*-value of the point on the line that has the same *x*-coordinate as the middle summary point.

Write the equation.	$y = -\frac{2}{5}x + \frac{17}{5}$
Substitute 3 for *x*.	$y = -\frac{2}{5}(3) + \frac{17}{5}$
Simplify.	$y = -\frac{6}{5} + \frac{17}{5}$
Simplify.	$y = \frac{11}{5}$

The point $\left(3, \frac{11}{5}\right)$ is the point on the line that passes through the two outer summary points that has the same *x*-coordinate as the middle summary point.

Now find the vertical distance between the middle summary point and the line by subtracting the *y*-values.

The middle summary point is (3, 3). The point on the line is $\left(3, \frac{11}{5}\right)$.

$$3 - \frac{11}{5} = \frac{4}{5}$$

The vertical distance between the middle summary point and the line that passes through the two outer summary points is $\frac{4}{5}$ unit.

continued on next page >

Solution continued

f. Find one third of the distance from the line to the middle summary point.

$$\frac{1}{3} \times \frac{4}{5} = \frac{4}{15} \text{ unit}$$

g. Write the equation of the median-median trend line.

Since the median-median trend line is parallel to the line defined by the equation $y = -\frac{2}{5}x + \frac{17}{5}$, the lines have the same slope.

Because the middle summary point lies above the line through the other two summary points, you can find the y-intercept of the median-median trend line by adding the distance $\frac{4}{15}$ to $\frac{17}{5}$.

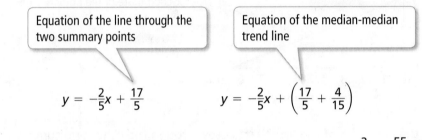

Equation of the line through the two summary points

Equation of the median-median trend line

$$y = -\frac{2}{5}x + \frac{17}{5} \qquad\qquad y = -\frac{2}{5}x + \left(\frac{17}{5} + \frac{4}{15}\right)$$

So, the equation of the median-median trend line is $y = -\frac{2}{5}x + \frac{55}{15}$.

h. Substitute 7 for x in the median-median trend line equation and solve for y.

Write the equation.	$y = -\frac{2}{5}x + \frac{55}{15}$
Substitute 7 for x.	$y = -\frac{2}{5}(7) + \frac{55}{15}$
Simplify.	$y = -\frac{14}{5} + \frac{55}{15}$
Simplify.	$y = \frac{13}{15}$

You would expect a serving of food that has 7 grams of dietary fiber to contain $\frac{13}{15}$ gram of protein.

1. Think About the Process The scatter plot shows data that suggest a linear association.

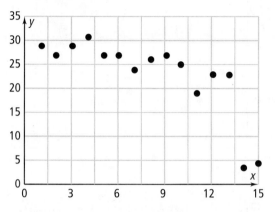

a. Find an equation for the trend line using the points (3,29) and (13,15).

    A. $y = 33.2x - 1.4$

    B. $y = -1.4x + 33.2$

    C. $y = -0.6x + 29.2$

    D. $y = -1.4x + 33.7$

b. How can you decide which points are the outliers?

c. Find the outliers.

d. Remove the outliers. Find a trend line for the adjusted data using the points (2,28) and (12,22).

e. How do the outliers affect the position of the trend line?

2. The scatter plot shows data for the circumference and height of a variety of tree. The plot suggests a linear association. The summary points are (50,30), (125,37), and (200,99).

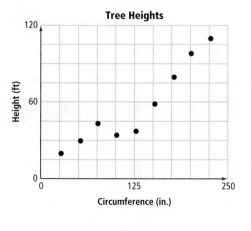

a. Find the median-median trend line.

A.

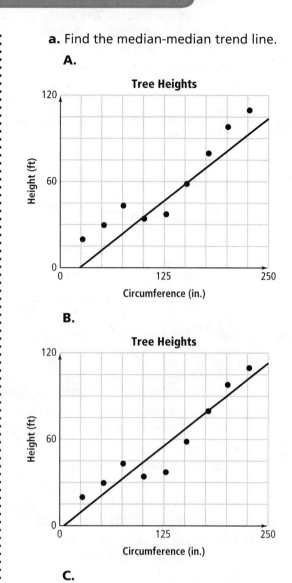

B.

C.

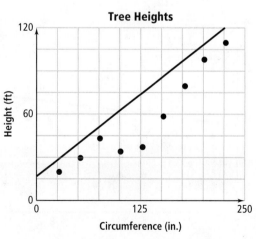

b. Estimate the height of a tree that has circumference 80 in.

3. **Think About the Process** The scatter plot shows data that suggest a linear association. The line through the first and third summary points has been drawn for you.

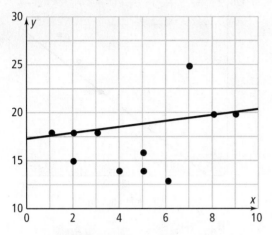

a. What is the next step to find the median-median trend line?

A. Write the equation of the median-median trend line.

B. Separate the points into three groups of equal size.

C. Find the equation of the line through the first and third summary points.

D. Find the coordinates for the summary point for each group.

b. Which graph below shows the median-median trend line?

A.

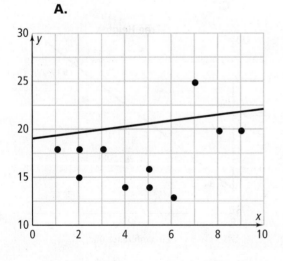

B.

C.

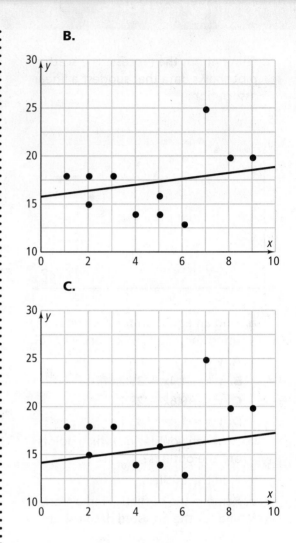

Bivariate Categorical Data

Vocabulary
bivariate
categorical data,
bivariate data,
categorical data,
measurement data

CCSS: 8.SP.A.4

Part 1

Intro

When you collect data, you record characteristics of the population, such as height or gender. These characteristics are called variables.

Some variables, like *Height* are *measurement variables* because they have values that are measures, such as 64 in.

Other variables, like *Gender,* are *categorical variables* because they have values that are categories, such as "Male" or "Female".

Measurement data consists of data that are measures.

Categorical data consists of data that fall into categories.

Example Identifying Categorical and Measurement Data

Indicate whether each variable has values that are *categorical data* or *measurement data*.

    a. City population   **b.** Tree species

    c. Eye color   **d.** Zip code

    e. Commute time

Solution

    a. City population is a measurement of the number of people in the city. This variable has values that are measurement data.

    b. Data about tree species will fall into categories such as "Oak," "Pine," and "Palm." This variable has values that are categorical data.

    c. Data about eye color will fall into categories such as "Blue," "Green," "Brown," and "Hazel." This variable has values that are categorical data.

    d. Data about zip codes will fall into categories. Zip codes are numbers, but not measurements. They indicate regions of the United States. This variable has values that are categorical data.

    e. Commute time is a measurement of how many minutes a commute takes. This variable has values that are measurement data.

Key Concept

Previously you have studied two-variable measurement data. Another term for two-variable data is **bivariate data**.

Bivariate categorical data pairs categorical data collected about two variables of the same population.

Suppose you collect data from a group of people about their gender and whether they own a pet. You are collecting bivariate categorical data. The data for each person will fall into one of the following groups.

Male with pet	Female with pet
Male without pet	Female without pet

Part 2

Example Collecting Bivariate Categorical Data

Tell which survey(s) you can use to collect bivariate categorical data about the students in your school.

Survey 1
- Are you male or female?
- How did you get to school today?

Survey 2
- How many minutes does it take you to get to school?
- How many inches tall are you?

Survey 3
- Did you watch a movie last weekend?
- Did you play a game last weekend?
- Did you do homework last weekend?

Solution

Survey 1 asks two questions, so it will collect bivariate data. The data for the first question will fall into categories "Male" and "Female." The data for the second question will fall into categories such as "Bus," "Foot," and "Car." Each question asks for categorical data. Survey 1 will collect bivariate categorical data.

Survey 2 asks two questions, so it will collect bivariate data. Each question asks for a measurement, so each question will collect measurement data. Survey 2 will collect bivariate data about the population, but not bivariate categorical data.

Survey 3 asks three questions, so it will collect data about three variables. It will not collect bivariate categorical data.

Part 3

Designing Surveys for Bivariate Categorical Data

You want to see if there is an association between dogs being purebred and needing surgery during the last year.

Design a survey to collect bivariate categorical data. Identify the variables, the categories, and the groups in which the data will fall.

Solution ·

Answers may vary. Sample:

You can ask the following questions:

> Is your dog purebred?
> Did your dog need surgery during the last year?

The variables are *Purebred*? and *Needed Surgery*?

> The *Purebred?* data will fall into the categories "Yes" or "No."
> The *Needed Surgery?* data will fall into the categories "Yes" or "No."

The data you collect will fall into the following groups:

> Purebred dog that needed surgery,
> Purebred dog that did not need surgery,
> Not a purebred dog that needed surgery, and
> Not a purebred dog that did not need surgery.

1. Which of the given variables have values that are categorical data? Select all that apply.

   A. country

   B. music genre

   C. circumference

   D. boiling temperature

2. Which of the given variables have values that are measurement data? Select all that apply.

   A. revolutions per minutes

   B. volume

   C. gender

   D. book genre

3. Brian wonders if there is an association between someone's favorite meal of the day and whether he or she plays a sport. He designs a survey to collect bivariate categorical data from students in his school. The questions to ask and the variables are given.

   Questions:

   What is your favorite meal of the day?

   Do you play a sport?

   Variables:

   Favorite Meal?

   Play Sport?

   a. Identify the categories for the "Favorite Meal?" variable. Select all that apply.

   A. "Breakfast"   **B.** "Dinner"

   C. "Snack"   **D.** "Lunch"

   b. Identify the categories for the "Play Sport?" variable.

   c. Identify the groups for the data. Select all that apply.

   A. Person who prefers lunch and does not play a sport

   B. Person who prefers dinner and plays a sport

   C. Person who prefers lunch and plays a sport

   D. Person who prefers dinner and does not play a sport

   E. Person who prefers breakfast and does not play a sport

   F. Person who prefers breakfast and plays a sport

4. **Think About the Process** A town has been having an annual car race since 1913. The results for the first few races, as well as some recent races, are shown in **Figure 1**.

   a. How can you identify the variables that have values that are categorical data?

   A. Find the variables that have values that fall into categories.

   B. Find the variables that have values that are words.

   C. Find the variables that have values that fall into one of two categories.

   D. Find the variables that have values that are measures.

   E. Find the variables that have values that are numbers.

   b. Determine the variables that have values that are categorical data.

(Figure 1)

Car Race Results

Year	Winner	Car	Time (hr)	Margin (s)	Car #
1913	Jen Dorian	Brand Z	6.6866	3	71
1914	Carla Turkleton	Brand W	6.5688	2	63
...					
2002	Perry Cox	Brand X	3.1196	2	26
2003	Robert Kelso	Brand X	2.7171	3	82

See your complete lesson at MyMathUniverse.com

5. **Think About the Process** The manager of a pet store hands out these surveys to random customers.

Survey 1:

How much time did you spend in the store?
How far do you live from the store?

Survey 2:

Did you pay with cash or a credit card?
What is your zip code?

Survey 3:

Did you use any coupons?
Did you purchase any pet food?

Survey 4:

What did you purchase?
How long did you wait in line?

How long does it take you to drive here?

a. How can you identify the surveys that collect bivariate categorical data?

A. Find the surveys that ask two questions.

B. Find the surveys that ask two questions, where the responses for each question have values that are words.

C. Find the surveys that ask two questions, where the responses for each question have values that fall into categories.

D. Find the surveys where the responses for each question have values that fall into one of two categories.

b. Which survey(s) do not collect bivariate categorical data? Select all that apply.

A. Survey 2   B. Survey 1
C. Survey 4   D. Survey 3

6. Jimmy wonders if there is an association between someone's favorite day of the week and whether they eat oatmeal. He decides to survey the students in his school. Design a survey to collect bivariate categorical data.

a. What is the most appropriate set of questions to ask?

A. Do you like Saturdays? How often do you eat oatmeal?

B. Do you play baseball on Saturdays? How often do you eat oatmeal?

C. Do you like Saturdays? Do you eat oatmeal?

D. Do you like Saturdays? Do you eat oatmeal often?

E. What is your favorite day of the week? Do you eat oatmeal often?

F. What is your favorite day of the week? Do you eat oatmeal?

b. What are the variables?

A. Like Saturdays? Eat Oatmeal Often?

B. Baseball on Saturdays? Eat Oatmeal?

C. Favorite Day? Eat Oatmeal Often?

D. Like Saturdays? Oatmeal Frequency?

E. Baseball on Saturdays? Oatmeal Frequency?

F. Favorite Day? Eat Oatmeal?

Constructing Two-Way Frequency Tables

Vocabulary
two-way frequency table, two-way table

CCSS: 8.SP.A.4

Key Concept

A **two-way table** shows bivariate categorical data for a population. A **two-way frequency table** displays the counts of the data in each group.

Variables Show the data for one variable in the rows. Show the data for the other variable in the columns.

The categories for the row variable are shown to the right of the variable. In this table, the row variable categories are "Home" and "Away."

The categories for the column variable are shown below the column variable. In this table, the column variable categories are "Yes" and "No."

Fan of Team		Watched game?		
		Yes	**No**	**Total**
	Home	42	18	60
	Away	33	7	40
	Total	75	25	100

Column variable

Row variable

Frequencies Each cell in the table shows the count of the data that falls into that group.

This table shows the following groups: Home team fan who watched the game, Home team fan who did not watch the game, Away team fan who watched the game, and Away team fan who did not watch the game.

Fan of Team		Watched game?		
		Yes	**No**	**Total**
	Home	42	18	60
	Away	33	7	40
	Total	75	25	100

42 Home team fans watched the game.

60 Home team fans were surveyed.

100 people were surveyed.

25 people did not watch the game.

continued on next page >

Key Concept

continued

Row and Column Sums The frequencies in each row sum to the row totals.
The frequencies in each column sum to the column totals.

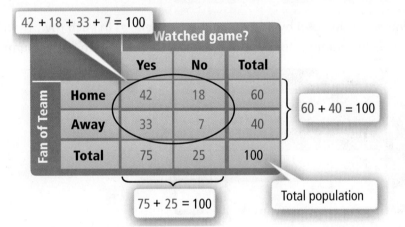

	Watched game?		
Fan of Team	**Yes**	**No**	**Total**
Home	42	18	60
Away	33	7	40
Total	75	25	100

42 + 18 = 60

33 + 7 = 40

42 + 33 = 75

18 + 7 = 25

Total Sums The frequencies for the groups, the row totals, and the column totals each sum to the total population.

42 + 18 + 33 + 7 = 100

	Watched game?		
Fan of Team	**Yes**	**No**	**Total**
Home	42	18	60
Away	33	7	40
Total	75	25	100

60 + 40 = 100

75 + 25 = 100

Total population

Part 1

Example Putting Data in Two-Way Frequency Tables

You ask 60 of your neighbors whether they donate to charity. There are 30 women who give to charity and 15 who do not. There are 10 men who give to charity and 5 who do not.

Complete a two-way frequency table to show the results of the survey.

Solution

Step 1 Write the frequencies in the appropriate cells.

		Gender		
		Male	**Female**	**Total**
Donates?	**Yes**	10	30	▪
	No	5	15	▪
	Total	▪	▪	▪

Step 2 Find each row total by adding up the frequencies in each row. Then find each column total by adding up the frequencies in each column.

		Gender		
		Male	**Female**	**Total**
Donates?	**Yes**	10	30	40
	No	5	15	20
	Total	15	45	

$10 + 30 = 40$

$5 + 15 = 20$

$10 + 5 = 15$ $30 + 15 = 45$

Step 3 Find the total population by adding up the group frequencies, the row totals, or the column totals.

		Gender		
		Male	**Female**	**Total**
Donates?	**Yes**	10	30	40
	No	5	15	20
	Total	15	45	60

$15 + 45 = 60$

$40 + 20 = 60$

Part 2

Example Completing Two-Way Frequency Tables

A survey was taken at a university. Students responded to the statement, "The school needs a new student center." Complete the two-way frequency table.

		Class				
		Freshman	Sophomore	Junior	Senior	Total
Response	**Agree**	▪	336	264	168	1,200
	Disagree	288	144	▪	120	▪
	No Opinion	192	▪	24	96	432
	Total	▪	600	504	▪	▪

Solution

Find how many of the freshmen agreed. The sum of the "Agree" responses should equal 1,200.

$$x + 336 + 264 + 168 = 1,200$$
$$x + 768 = 1,200$$
$$x = 432$$

Now find the total number of freshman responses.

$$432 + 288 + 192 = x$$
$$912 = x$$

Now find how many sophomores responded, "No opinion." 120 sophomores responded, "No opinion."

And find how many juniors disagreed. 216 juniors disagreed.

Find the total number of seniors surveyed. 384 seniors were surveyed.

And find the total number of students who disagreed. 768 students disagreed.

Finally, find the total number of students who were surveyed. 2,400 students were surveyed.

		Class				
		Freshman	Sophomore	Junior	Senior	Total
Response	**Agree**	432	336	264	168	1,200
	Disagree	288	144	216	120	768
	No Opinion	192	120	24	96	432
	Total	912	600	504	384	2,400

Part 3

Example Constructing Two-Way Frequency Tables

You and a friend survey people about whether they recycle and if curbside pick-up is available in their community. Construct a single two-way frequency table to show all of the results of both surveys.

Survey #1

Recycle?

Pick-up?		Yes	No
	Yes	卌 卌 卌 卌 卌 丨	卌 丨丨丨丨
	No	卌	卌 卌

Survey #2

Pick-up?

Recycle?		Yes	No
	Yes	卌 卌 卌 卌 卌 卌	卌 丨丨丨丨
	No	丨丨丨	卌 丨

Solution

First, find the total number of responses in each group.

Recycles and has curbside pick-up:	$26 + 29 = 55$
Recycles and does not have curbside pick-up:	$5 + 9 = 14$
Does not recycle and has curbside pick-up:	$9 + 3 = 12$
Does not recycle and does not have curbside pick-up:	$10 + 6 = 16$

Then construct the two-way frequency table. There are two possible tables.

		Pick-up?		
		Yes	**No**	**Total**
Recycle?	**Yes**	55	14	69
	No	12	16	28
	Total	67	30	97

		Recycle?		
		Yes	**No**	**Total**
Pick-up?	**Yes**	55	12	67
	No	14	16	30
	Total	69	28	97

1. You ask 60 of your classmates how they get to school. There are 20 girls who walk to school and 10 who do not. There are 5 boys who walk to school and 25 who do not. Complete the two-way frequency table to show the results of the survey.

Walks to School?	Gender		
	Girls	Boys	Total
Yes	■	■	■
No	■	■	■
Total	■	■	■

2. You ask 170 of your classmates how often they send a letter in the mail. Complete the two-way frequency table to show the results of the survey.

	How Often do You Send a Letter?				
Gender	Weekly	Monthly	Yearly	Never	Total
Girls	■	20	15	■	90
Boys	15	10	■	■	■
Total	40	■	40	60	170

3. Mental Math You ask 55 of your classmates if they wear glasses. Complete the two-way frequency table to show the results of the survey.

Wear Glasses?	Gender		
	Girls	Boys	Total
Yes	■	10	■
No	25	■	30
Total	■	■	55

4. Multiple Representations You and a friend survey people about whether they are right-handed or left-handed and if they prefer to use pencils or pens.

Which Hand?	Writing Preference	
	Pen	Pencil
Right-Handed	‖‖‖ ‖‖‖	‖‖‖ ‖
Left-Handed	‖‖‖	‖‖‖ ‖

Writing Preference	Which Hand?	
	Right-Handed	Left-Handed
Pen	‖‖‖ ‖‖‖ ‖‖‖	‖‖‖ ‖‖
Pencil	‖‖‖ ‖‖‖ ‖‖	‖‖‖ ‖‖‖ ‖‖

a. Construct a single two-way frequency table to show all of the results of the surveys.

Which Hand?	Writing Preference		
	Pen	Pencil	Total
Right-Handed	■	■	■
Left-Handed	■	■	■
Total	■	■	■

b. Construct a single, two-way frequency table with Writing Preference as the row variable.

5. At one point last year, the local animal shelter had only cats and dogs. There were 74 animals in all. Of the cats, 25 were male and 14 were female. Of the dogs, 23 were male and 12 were female.

a. Construct a two-way frequency table of the data.

Gender	Type of Animal		
	Cat	Dog	Total
Male	■	■	■
Female	■	■	■
Total	■	■	■

b. Construct a two-way frequency table to show the type of animal as the row variable instead of the column variable.

See your complete lesson at MyMathUniverse.com

6. You ask 96 of your classmates what their favorite season is. Complete the two-way frequency table to show the results of the survey.

Favorite Season	Gender		
	Girls	Boys	Total
Fall	■	8	■
Spring	14	■	24
Summer	■	12	20
Winter	21	■	37
Total	■	■	96

7. Think About the Process A researcher tracks data about the outgoing mail in a large office. Suppose you want to complete the two-way frequency table to show the researcher's results.

a. Which cell values can you find first? Select all that apply.

A. You can find the number of overnight packages.

B. You can find the number of regular letters.

C. You can find the total number of overnight deliveries.

D. You can find the total number of regular deliveries.

E. You can find the total number of letters.

b. Complete the two-way frequency table to show the results of the survey.

Kind of Mail	Type of Delivery		
	Regular	Overnight	Total
Letter	■	5	■
Package	25	■	35
Total	■	■	55

8. Think About the Process Two different classes were asked, "Which color do you prefer, red or blue?"

Preferred Color	Gender	
	Boys	Girls
Blue	⊞⊞	⊞⊞⊞⊞ ⊞⊞⊞⊞
Red	l	⊞⊞

Gender	Preferred Color	
	Blue	Red
Boys	⊞⊞⊞ ⊞⊞ llll	⊞⊞⊞ ⊞⊞ ll
Girls	⊞⊞	⊞⊞ lll

a. What is the first step to combine the two tables?

A. Find the total number of people.

B. Find the total number of people who liked blue.

C. Find the total number of responses for each group.

D. Find the total number of people who are boys.

b. Construct a single two-way frequency table to show all of the results.

Preferred Color	Gender		
	Boys	Girls	Total
Blue	■	■	■
Red	■	■	■
Total	■	■	■

Interpreting Two-Way Frequency Tables

CCSS: 8.SP.A.4

Part 1

Example Reading Two-Way Frequency Tables

Students were asked, "How did you get to school today?" The two-way frequency table shows the results of the survey.

a. How many students walked to school?

b. How many middle school students rode a bicycle to school?

c. How many high school students were surveyed?

d. How many students were surveyed?

Transportation	Type of School			
	Middle	High	College	Total
Walked	30	40	12	82
Bus	17	41	9	67
Car	22	8	33	63
Bicycle	18	25	20	63
Total	87	114	74	275

Solution

Transportation	Type of School			
	Middle	High	College	Total
Walked	30	40	12	82
Bus	17	41	9	67
Car	22	8	33	63
Bicycle	18	25	20	63
Total	87	114	74	275

82 students walked to school.

275 students were surveyed.

18 middle school students rode a bicycle to school.

114 high school students were surveyed.

a. 82 students walked to school.

b. 18 middle school students rode a bicycle to school.

c. 114 high school students were surveyed.

d. 275 students were surveyed.

Example Interpreting Two-Way Frequency Tables

The table shows the results of a survey about the color of car people own. Tell whether each statement is *true* or *false*.

a. More men than women own black cars.

b. Black is the most popular color overall.

c. Fewer people own a blue car than any other color of car.

		Gender		
		Male	Female	Total
Color	Red	12	15	27
	Blue	8	4	12
	White	25	33	58
	Black	39	14	53
	Total	84	66	150

Solution

a. The statement is true.

		Gender		
		Male	Female	Total
Color	Red	12	15	27
	Blue	8	4	12
	White	25	33	58
	Black	39	14	53
	Total	84	66	150

39 men own black cars.

14 women own black cars.

b. The statement is false.

		Gender		
		Male	Female	Total
Color	Red	12	15	27
	Blue	8	4	12
	White	25	33	58
	Black	39	14	53
	Total	84	66	150

58 people own white cars.

53 people own black cars.

continued on next page >

Part 2

Solution continued

c. The statement is true.

	Gender			
		Male	**Female**	**Total**
Color	**Red**	12	15	27
	Blue	8	4	12
	White	25	33	58
	Black	39	14	53
	Total	84	66	150

27 people own a red car.

12 people own a blue car.

58 people own a white car.

53 people own black cars.

Part 3

Example Analyzing Two-Way Frequency Tables

Your friend's family is having a family reunion. Your friend needs to choose a movie to show. Your friend surveys family members about their favorite type of movie.

		Movie Type			
		Action	**Drama**	**Comedy**	**Total**
Age	**Child**	14	6	19	39
	Adult	10	16	7	33
	Total	24	22	26	72

Your friend thinks a comedy would be best because *Comedy* was the most frequent response. Do you agree? Explain.

Solution

Answers may vary. Sample:

Comedy was the most frequent overall response, but it was the least frequent response among the adults. Almost all of the people who chose *Comedy* were children. Although the children would be happy with a comedy, the adults would not.

Action was the second most frequent overall response, and the second most frequent response among both the children and the adults. Almost the same number of children picked Action as picked *Comedy*.

You could show an action movie because that type of movie was the second choice of both the children and the adults.

1. The two-way frequency table shows the results of a survey at a school. Students responded to the question "Do you play any sports?" Decide if the following statement is true or false.
More boys than girls do not play sports.

Sports

Gender	Play Sports?		
	Yes	No	Total
Boys	23	19	42
Girls	20	25	45
Total	43	44	87

2. Students at a local high school responded to the question "Do you have a part-time job?" The two-way frequency table shows the results. How many juniors and seniors have a job?

High School Students

Class	Part-time job?		
	Yes	No	Total
Freshman	17	29	46
Sophomore	17	24	41
Junior	18	20	38
Senior	18	15	33
Total	70	88	158

3. A new radio station wants to know which type of music people in the area like the most. The table shows the results of a survey of people in the area.

Survey Results

Type of Music	Gender		
	Women	Men	Total
Pop	35	42	77
Rock	61	46	107
Jazz	52	43	95
Country	44	41	85
Alternative	36	53	89
Total	228	225	453

What type of music should the station play to get the most women to listen? To get the most men to listen?

4. **Reasoning** A company is deciding in which stores it wants to sell its products. The results of a survey of customers at each store who bought similar products are shown in the table.

Survey Results

Store	Product			
	A	B	C	Total
Store 1	43	33	28	104
Store 2	30	39	25	94
Total	73	72	53	198

a. If the company can choose two products to sell at one store, which store and products do you think they should choose?

b. Describe a situation where another choice of store and/or products would be better. Explain.

5. **Estimation** A recent survey asked employees, "Do you prefer desktop computers or laptop computers?" The results are shown in the table.

Computer Preference

Computer Type	Office Location			
	1	2	3	Total
Desktop	23	17	24	64
Laptop	16	18	16	50
Total	39	35	40	114

a. Classify the statement as true or false: More employees prefer desktops over laptops.

b. If the number of people at each office doubled, estimate the number of people who would prefer desktops and the number who would prefer laptops. Do you think this estimate is reasonable? Explain.

See your complete lesson at MyMathUniverse.com

6. Students at a local school were asked, "About how many hours do you spend on homework each week?" The two-way frequency table in **Figure 1** shows the results of the survey.

   a. How many students spend between 1 and 2 hours on homework each week?

   b. How many students were surveyed?

7. **Think About the Process** The two-way frequency table in **Figure 2** shows the number of toys sold in one day in three countries for different types of stores.

   a. What values do you need to compare to decide if the statement "Country A sold more toys online than Country B" is true or false? Select all that apply.

   A. 9,643   B. 0

   C. 323   D. 161

   E. 24,266   F. 7,847

   G. 6,776   H. 484

   b. Is the statement true or false?

8. **Think About the Process** To decide where to go on a field trip, the principal polls the students at a school. The table shows the survey results. The principal wants to go where the greatest number of students would like to go.

   Field Trip

	Location			
Grade	Zoo	Lake	Museum	Total
Seventh	35	26	39	100
Eighth	31	43	33	107
Total	66	69	72	207

   a. How should the principal use the table to make the decision?

   A. Compare the values that correspond to each location for each grade.

   B. Compare the values in the total row.

   C. Compare the values in the total column.

   D. Compare the values in the total row and total column.

   b. Where should the principal decide to go?

(Figure 1)

Homework

	Number of Hours					
Grade	Less than 1	1–2	3–4	5–6	More than 6	Total
Sixth	16	50	42	20	7	135
Seventh	21	45	46	25	15	152
Eighth	11	49	60	55	17	192
Total	48	144	148	100	39	479

(Figure 2)

Toy Sales

	Type of Store				
Country	Toy Chain Store	Department Store	Catalog	Online	Total
Country A	6,509	943	1,868	323	9,643
Country B	5,114	2,056	516	161	7,847
Country C	4,291	2,231	254	0	6,776
Total	15,914	5,230	2,638	484	24,266

See your complete lesson at MyMathUniverse.com

Constructing Two-Way Relative Frequency Tables

Vocabulary
two-way relative
frequency table

CCSS: 8.SP.A.4

Part 1

Intro

A **two-way relative frequency table** shows the ratio of the number of data in each group to the population. The ratio can be expressed as a fraction, decimal, or percent. In this Topic all relative frequency tables show percents.

You can construct three different types of two-way relative frequency tables from a two-way frequency table.

You can construct a total relative frequency table with respect to the total population. To construct this type of table, divide the frequency count in each cell by the total population.

Frequency Table

Team Fan	Watched game?		
	Yes	**No**	**Total**
Home	42	18	60
Away	33	7	40
Total	75	25	100

Total Relative Frequency Table

Team Fan	Watched game?		
	Yes	**No**	**Total**
Home	42%	18%	60%
Away	33%	7%	40%
Total	75%	25%	100%

To find the percentage of people surveyed who are Home team fans and watched the game, divide the number of Home team fans who watched the game, 42, by the total number of people surveyed, 100. So 42% of the people surveyed are Home team fans who watched the game.

Use the same process to complete the rest of the table.

Example Completing Total Relative Frequency Tables

The frequency table shows data from a survey about eye color and handedness. Complete a relative frequency table to show the distribution of the data with respect to the total population surveyed.

Frequency Table

Eye Color	Handedness		
	Left	**Right**	**Total**
Brown	6	36	42
Blue	7	26	33
Other	6	33	39
Total	19	95	114

continued on next page >

Part 1

Example continued

Solution ··

Find the percent of the people surveyed that are in each group. To do this, divide each frequency by 114, and then multiply by 100.

Total Relative Frequency Table

$\frac{6}{114} \cdot 100 \approx 5.3\%$

$\frac{36}{114} \cdot 100 \approx 31.6\%$

		Handedness		
		Left	**Right**	**Total**
Eye color	**Brown**	5.3%	31.6%	36.9%
	Blue	6.1%	22.8%	28.9%
	Other	5.3%	28.9%	34.2%
	Total	16.7%	83.3%	100%

Part 2

Intro

You can also find the relative frequencies with respect to the row variable. To make this type of table, you treat each row category as a separate population. That is, you divide the frequency of each group by the row total, *not* by the total population.

Frequency Table

		Watched game?		
		Yes	**No**	**Total**
Team Fan	**Home**	42	18	60
	Away	33	7	40
	Total	75	25	100

Row Relative Frequency Table

		Watched game?		
		Yes	**No**	**Total**
Team Fan	**Home**	70%	30%	100%
	Away	82.5%	17.5%	100%
	Total	75%	25%	100%

42 of the 60 Home team fans watched the game. So 70% of the Home team fans surveyed watched the game.

18 of the 60 Home team fans did not watch the game. So 30% of the Home team fans surveyed did not watch the game.

continued on next page >

Part 2

33 of the 40 Away team fans watched the game. So 82.5% of the Away team fans surveyed watched the game.

7 of the 40 Away team fans did not watch the game. So 17.5% of the Away team fans surveyed did not watch the game.

Of the 100 people surveyed, 75 watched the game. So 75% of the people surveyed watched the game.

25 of the 100 people surveyed did not watch the game. So 25% of the people surveyed did not watch the game.

Note that the percents in each row sum to 100%, but the percents in each column do not.

Example Completing Row Relative Frequency Tables

Use the results of the survey to complete a relative frequency table showing how handedness was distributed with respect to eye color.

Frequency Table

		Handedness		
		Left	**Right**	**Total**
Eye Color	**Brown**	6	36	42
	Blue	7	26	33
	Other	6	33	39
	Total	19	95	114

Solution ·

Frequency Table

		Handedness		
		Left	**Right**	**Total**
Eye Color	**Brown**	6	36	42
	Blue	7	26	33
	Other	6	33	39
	Total	19	95	114

Find what percent each number is of 42.

Find what percent each number is of 33.

Find what percent each number is of 39.

Find what percent each number is of 114.

continued on next page >

Part 2

Solution continued

Row Relative Frequency Table

$\frac{6}{42} \cdot 100 \approx 14.3\%$

$\frac{36}{42} \cdot 100 \approx 85.7\%$

$\frac{42}{42} \cdot 100 = 100\%$

	Handedness		
Eye Color	**Left**	**Right**	**Total**
Brown	14.3%	85.7%	100%
Blue	21.2%	78.8%	100%
Other	15.4%	84.6%	100%
Total	16.7%	83.3%	100%

Part 3

Intro

You can also find the relative frequencies with respect to the column variable. To make this type of table, you treat each column category as a separate population. That is, you divide the frequency of each group by the column total, *not* by the total population.

Frequency Table

	Watched game?		
Team Fan	**Yes**	**No**	**Total**
Home	42	18	60
Away	33	7	40
Total	75	25	100

Column Relative Frequency Table

	Watched game?		
Team Fan	**Yes**	**No**	**Total**
Home	56%	72%	60%
Away	44%	28%	40%
Total	100%	100%	100%

42 of the 75 people who watched the game are Home team fans. So 56% of people surveyed who watched the game are Home team fans.

33 of the 75 people who watched the game are Away team fans. So 44% of people surveyed who watched the game are Away team fans.

18 of the 25 people who did not watch the game are Home team fans. So 72% of people surveyed who did not watch the game are Home team fans.

7 of the 25 people who did not watch the game are Away team fans. So 28% of people surveyed who did not watch the game are Away team fans.

continued on next page >

Part 3

Intro continued

60 of the 100 people surveyed are home team fans. So 60% of people surveyed are Home team fans.

40 of the 100 people surveyed are Away team fans. So 40% of people surveyed are Away team fans.

Notice that the percents in each column sum to 100%, but the percents in each row do not.

Example Completing Column Relative Frequency Tables

Use the results of the survey to complete a relative frequency table showing how eye color was distributed with respect to right- and left-handedness.

Frequency Table

		Handedness		
		Left	Right	Total
Eye Color	Brown	6	36	42
	Blue	7	26	33
	Other	6	33	39
	Total	19	95	114

Solution

Frequency Table

Find what percent each number is of 19.

Find what percent each number is of 95.

Find what percent each number is of 114.

		Handedness		
		Left	Right	Total
Eye Color	Brown	6	36	42
	Blue	7	26	33
	Other	6	33	39
	Total	19	95	114

continued on next page >

Part 3

Solution continued

Column Relative Frequency Table

$\frac{6}{19} \cdot 100 \approx 31.6\%$

$\frac{7}{19} \cdot 100 \approx 36.8\%$

$\frac{6}{19} \cdot 100 \approx 31.6\%$

Eye Color	Handedness		
	Left	**Right**	**Total**
Brown	31.6%	37.9%	36.8%
Blue	36.8%	27.4%	28.9%
Other	31.6%	34.7%	34.2%
Total	100%	100%	100%

Key Concept

A total relative frequency table shows the percent of the total population that falls into each group.

The sum of the percents of the groups is 100%.

Total Relative Frequency Table

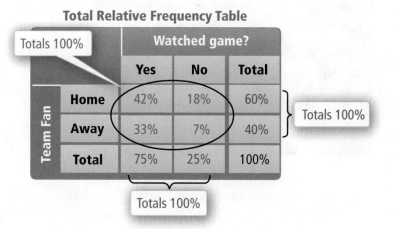

Totals 100%

Team Fan	Watched game?		
	Yes	**No**	**Total**
Home	42%	18%	60%
Away	33%	7%	40%
Total	75%	25%	100%

Totals 100%

Totals 100%

continued on next page >

Key Concept

A row relative frequency table shows the percent of each row population that falls into each column category.

The sum of the percents in each row is 100%.

Row Relative Frequency Table

		Watched game?		
		Yes	No	Total
Team Fan	Home	70%	30%	100%
	Away	82.5%	17.5%	100%
	Total	75%	25%	100%

Each row totals 100%

A column relative frequency table shows the percent of each column population that falls into each row category.

The sum of the percents of each column is 100%.

Column Relative Frequency Table

		Watched game?		
		Yes	No	Total
Team Fan	Home	56%	72%	60%
	Away	44%	28%	40%
	Total	100%	100%	100%

Each column totals 100%

1. A stock broker compiled data about 40 popular stocks. She made this frequency table to show how their changes in 2010 compared to their changes in 2009. Complete the relative frequency table to show the distribution of the data with respect to all 40 stocks.

Frequency Table

Change in 2010	Change in 2009		
	Positive Change	Negative Change	Total
Positive Change	7	9	16
Negative Change	10	14	24
Total	17	23	40

Total Relative Frequency Table

Change in 2010	Change in 2009		
	Positive Change	Negative Change	Total
Positive Change	■%	■%	■%
Negative Change	■%	■%	■%
Total	■%	■%	100%

2. The frequency table shows data about winning teams in several sports. Complete a relative frequency table to show the distribution of the data with respect to sport.

Frequency Table

Sport	Which Team Won?		
	Home	Visiting	Total
Hockey	54	43	97
Football	47	42	89
Soccer	46	42	88
Baseball	63	63	126
Total	210	190	400

Complete the following table

Row Relative Frequency Table

Sport	Which Team Won?		
	Home	Visiting	Total
Hockey	■%	■%	100%
Football	■%	■%	100%
Soccer	■%	■%	100%
Baseball	■%	■%	100%
Total	■%	■%	100%

3. Estimation A researcher asked each person in a large group, "In what month were you born?" The frequency table shows the results of the survey. Round the numbers in the table to the nearest multiple of 10. Then use those rounded values to complete a relative frequency table showing the distribution of the data with respect to gender.

Frequency Table

Month of Birth	Gender		
	Men	Women	Total
January-June	22	8	30
July-December	21	29	50
Total	43	37	80

Complete the following table.

Column Relative Frequency Table

Month of Birth	Gender		
	Men	Women	Total
January-June	■%	■%	■%
July-December	■%	■%	■%
Total	100%	100%	100%

4. Think About the Process The frequency table shows data about the outgoing mail in a large office. Suppose you want to complete a relative frequency table to show the distribution of the data with respect to all the outgoing mail.

Frequency Table

Kind of Mail	Type of Delivery		
	Regular	Overnight	Total
Letter	25	7	32
Package	28	10	38
Total	53	17	70

a. By what should you divide the frequency count in each cell to do this?

b. Complete the relative frequency table.

Total Relative Frequency Table

Kind of Mail	Type of Delivery		
	Regular	Overnight	Total
Letter	%	%	%
Package	%	%	%
Total	%	%	100%

5. Middle school students were asked, "Do you enjoy playing sports?" The frequency table shows some of the results of the survey.

Total Relative Frequency Table

Grade	Enjoy Playing Sports?		
	Yes	No	Total
6th	■	■	51
7th	27	20	■
8th	■	31	52
Total	68	82	150

a. Complete the frequency table.

Frequency Table

Grade	Enjoy Playing Sports?		
	Yes	No	Total
6th	■	■	51
7th	27	20	■
8th	■	31	52
Total	68	82	150

b. Complete the relative frequency table to show the distribution of the data with respect to all 150 students. Round to the nearest tenth as needed.

Frequency Table

Grade	Enjoy Playing Sports?		
	Yes	No	Total
6th	■%	■%	■%
7th	■%	■%	■%
8th	■%	■%	■%
Total	■%	■%	100%

6. Think About the Process A researcher asked 85 students, "Do you prefer math or history?" The frequency table shows all of the results of the survey except one.

Frequency Table

Subject	Boys	Girls	Total
Math	22	16	38
History	20	■	47
Total	42	43	85

a. How could you find the missing number? Select all that apply.

A. Subtract 20 from 43.

B. Subtract 20 from 47.

C. Subtract 16 from 43.

D. Subtract 16 from 47.

b. Complete the relative frequency table.

Row Relative Frequency Table

Subject	Boys	Girls	Total
Math	%	%	100%
History	%	%	100%
Total	%	%	100%

Interpreting Two-Way Relative Frequency Tables

CCSS: 8.SP.A.4

Part 1

Example Interpreting Total Relative Frequency Tables

The frequency table shows the results of a trial that tested a new headache medicine. The relative frequency table shows the percents with respect to the total population.

Frequency Table

Pill	Improvement?	Yes	No	Total
	Medicine	64	36	100
	Placebo	20	80	100
	Total	84	116	200

Total Relative Frequency Table

Pill	Improvement?	Yes	No	Total
	Medicine	32%	18%	50%
	Placebo	10%	40%	50%
	Total	42%	58%	100%

a. What percent of the participants in the study were given the medicine and saw improvement?

b. Was the number of participants given the medicine the same as the number of participants given the placebo? How do you know?

Solution

a. 32% of the participants in the study were given the medicine and saw improvement.

Total Relative Frequency Table

Pill	Improvement?	Yes	No	Total
	Medicine	32%	18%	50%
	Placebo	10%	40%	50%
	Total	42%	58%	100%

b. Yes; 50% of the participants were given the medicine and 50% of the participants were given the placebo.

Total Relative Frequency Table

Pill	Improvement?	Yes	No	Total
	Medicine	32%	18%	50%
	Placebo	10%	40%	50%
	Total	42%	58%	100%

See your complete lesson at MyMathUniverse.com

Part 2

Example Interpreting Row Relative Frequency Tables

You can also calculate relative frequencies for each row. These percents can help you see if there is an association between the two variables.

The row relative frequency table shows the relative frequencies calculated with respect to the type of pill.

Frequency Table

Pill		Improvement?		
		Yes	No	Total
	Medicine	64	36	100
	Placebo	20	80	100
	Total	84	116	200

Row Relative Frequency Table

Pill		Improvement?		
		Yes	No	Total
	Medicine	64%	36%	100%
	Placebo	20%	80%	100%
	Total	42%	58%	100%

a. What percent of the people given a pill reported an improvement?

b. Is there evidence that the medicine is more effective than the placebo? Explain.

Solution

a. 42% of the people given a pill reported an improvement.

Row Relative Frequency Table

Pill		Improvement?		
		Yes	No	Total
	Medicine	64%	36%	100%
	Placebo	20%	80%	100%
	Total	42%	58%	100%

b. Yes, there is evidence that the medicine is more effective than the placebo. 64% of the people given the medicine reported an improvement, but only 20% of the people given the placebo reported an improvement.

Row Relative Frequency Table

Pill		Improvement?		
		Yes	No	Total
	Medicine	64%	36%	100%
	Placebo	20%	80%	100%
	Total	42%	58%	100%

Part 3

Example Interpreting Column Relative Frequency Tables

You can also calculate relative frequencies for each column. These percents can also help you see if there is an association between the two variables.

The column relative frequency table shows the relative frequencies calculated with respect to improvement.

Frequency Table

		Improvement?		
		Yes	No	Total
Pill	**Medicine**	64	36	100
	Placebo	20	80	100
	Total	84	116	200

Column Relative Frequency Table

		Improvement?		
		Yes	No	Total
Pill	**Medicine**	76.2%	31.0%	50%
	Placebo	23.8%	69.0%	50%
	Total	100%	100%	100%

a. What percent of those who saw an improvement were given the medicine?

b. Is there any evidence that improvement was related to the type of pill? Explain.

Solution

a. 76.2% of those who saw an improvement were given the medicine.

b. Compare the percent of people who reported improvement *and* were given the medicine to the percent of people who were given the medicine. If the type of pill did *not* influence improvement, you would expect the percents to be about equal.

Column Relative Frequency Table

		Improvement?		
		Yes	No	Total
Pill	**Medicine**	76.2%	31.0%	50%
	Placebo	23.8%	69.0%	50%
	Total	100%	100%	100%

About 76.2% of the people who reported improvement were given the medicine. 50% of *all* of the people were given the medicine.

Since 76.2% > 50%, there is evidence that the improvement was related to the type of pill.

continued on next page >

Part 3

Solution continued

You are looking for evidence that the medicine is effective. Which table do you think is more helpful? Explain.

Column Relative Frequency Table

		Improvement?		
		Yes	**No**	**Total**
Pill	**Medicine**	76.2%	31.0%	50%
	Placebo	23.8%	69.0%	50%
	Total	100%	100%	100%

Row Relative Frequency Table

		Improvement?		
		Yes	**No**	**Total**
Pill	**Medicine**	64%	36%	100%
	Placebo	20%	80%	100%
	Total	42%	58%	100%

Solution

Answers may vary. Sample:

The row relative frequency table shows the percents with respect to the type of pill. You are interested in seeing if the medicine is more effective than the placebo. So it is more important to look at the results with respect to the type of pill than the results with respect to improvement. The row relative frequency table is more helpful.

1. Men and women are asked what type of car they own. The relative frequency table shows the relative frequencies with respect to the total population asked. What percent of people own a 2-door car?

Total Relative Frequency Table

Gender	Type of Car		
	2-door	4-door	Total
Men	32%	18%	50%
Women	22%	28%	50%
Total	54%	46%	100%

2. Two train stations recorded the number of on-time and delayed departures. The relative frequency table shows the relative frequencies with respect to the type of departure.

Column Relative Frequency Table

Station	Train Departures		
	On-time	Delayed	Total
X	54.2%	46.6%	51.2%
Y	45.8%	53.4%	48.8%
Total	100%	100%	100%

a. What percent of delayed departures are from station Y?

b. What percent of the total departures are from station Y?

3. **Think About the Process** Adults and children were asked if they watch sports. The relative frequency table shows the relative frequencies with respect to the total population asked.

Total Relative Frequency Table

Age	Watch Sports?		
	Yes	No	Total
Adults	26.4%	23.6%	50%
Kids	12.3%	37.7%	50%
Total	38.7%	61.3%	100%

a. Where do you look to find what percent are kids who watch sports?

b. What percent of the population are kids who watch sports?

4. After the first day of training, some students on the soccer team were asked if they saw improvement in their skills. The relative frequency table shows the relative frequencies with respect to the total number of students surveyed. Which class had the lesser percent of students who did not see improvement?

Total Relative Frequency Table

Class	Improvement?		
	Yes	No	Total
Freshmen	45%	5%	50%
Sophomore	47%	3%	50%
Total	92%	8%	100%

A. Freshmen

B. Sophomore

5. Students in two grades were asked what type of book they prefer. The relative frequency table shows the relative frequencies with respect to the total population asked.

Total Relative Frequency Table

Grade	Type of Book		
	Fiction	Non-Fiction	Total
Grade 7	34%	16%	50%
Grade 8	41%	9%	50%
Total	75%	25%	100%

a. What percent are seventh graders who prefer fiction?

b. What percent are eighth graders who prefer non-fiction?

6. The relative frequency table shows the relative frequencies of students who ride a bus to school with respect to the response.

Column Relative Frequency Table

Grade	Ride a Bus?		
	Yes	No	Total
Grade 7	47%	46%	46.5%
Grade 8	53%	54%	53.5%
Total	100%	100%	100%

a. What percent of students who do not ride a bus are seventh graders?

b. If there are 300 students who do not ride a bus, how many are seventh graders?

7. Think About the Process Students were asked if they have siblings. The relative frequency table shows the relative frequencies with respect to gender.

Row Relative Frequency Table

Gender	Have Siblings?		
	Yes	No	Total
Boys	88.7%	11.3%	100%
Girls	90.5%	9.5%	100%
Total	89.6%	10.4%	100%

a. Where do you look to find the percent of boys that do not have siblings?

A. Look in the "Girls" row and the "Yes" column to find the percent of boys that do not have siblings.

B. Look in the "Boys" row and the "Yes" column to find the percent of boys that do not have siblings.

C. Look in the "Boys" row and the "No" column to find the percent of boys that do not have siblings.

D. Look in the "Boys" row and the "Total" column to find the percent of boys that do not have siblings.

b. What percent of boys do not have siblings?

8. Challenge You ask your classmates "Do you prefer to use pencils or pens?" The relative frequency table shows the relative frequencies with respect to the type of writing tool.

Column Relative Frequency Table

Pencils or Pens?	Gender		
	Boys	Girls	Total
Pens	70.7%	10.2%	34.4%
Pencils	29.3%	89.8%	65.6%
Total	100%	100%	100%

a. Compare the percent for boys. Compare the percent for girls.

A greater percent of boys prefer ▇.
A greater percent of girls prefer ▇.

b. Is there evidence of an association between gender and type of writing tool preferred?

A. No, because the percent of boys who prefer pens is the same as the percent of girls who prefer pens.

B. Yes, because the percent of boys who prefer pens is different than the percent of girls who prefer pens.

C. Yes, because the percent of boys who prefer pens is the same as the percent of girls who prefer pens.

D. No, because the percent of boys who prefer pens is different than the percent of girls who prefer pens.

Choosing a Measure of Frequency

CCSS: 8.SP.A.4

Part 1

Example Choosing Frequency Tables as Appropriate

The athletic department surveys students as they leave a game. You want to know if more male students than female students have season tickets. Which table will be more helpful in finding that information? Explain your choice.

Frequency Table

		Season Ticket?		
		Yes	No	Total
Gender	Male	120	30	150
	Female	80	20	100
	Total	200	50	250

Row Relative Frequency Table

		Season Ticket?		
		Yes	No	Total
Gender	Male	80%	20%	100%
	Female	80%	20%	100%
	Total	80%	20%	100%

Solution

You want to compare the number of male students with season tickets and the number of female students with season tickets. Since you are interested in frequencies, not percents, the frequency table is more helpful.

Part 2

Example Choosing Total Relative Frequency Tables as Appropriate

You surveyed train riders on a Monday morning. The frequency table shows the results.

What type of relative frequency table shows the percent of the people surveyed who were arriving commuters? What percent of the people surveyed were arriving commuters?

Frequency Table

		Type of Rider		
		Commuter	Vacationer	Total
Train	Arriving	80	36	116
	Departing	40	44	84
	Total	120	80	200

continued on next page >

See your complete lesson at MyMathUniverse.com

Part 2

Example continued

Solution ·

You want to find the percent of *all* of the people surveyed who were arriving commuters. A total relative frequency table shows percents with respect to all of the people surveyed, so construct a total relative frequency table.

Total Relative Frequency Table

		Type of Rider		
		Commuter	**Vacationer**	**Total**
Train	**Arriving**	40%	18%	58%
	Departing	20%	22%	42%
	Total	60%	40%	100%

Of all the people surveyed, 40% were commuters who were arriving.

Part 3

Example Choosing Row Relative Frequency Tables as Appropriate

A pet groomer wants to see if the type of pet a client has influences the grooming period. The groomer's data are shown in the table.

Based on the groomer's data, is there evidence of an association between the type of pet and the grooming period? Explain.

		Time Between Visits			
		Week	**Month**	**Year**	**Total**
Type of Pet	**Dog**	78	410	165	653
	Cat	51	266	105	422
	Total	129	676	270	1,075

continued on next page >

Example continued

Solution

To see if the type of pet influences the time between visits, the groomer should compare the relative frequencies with respect to the type of pet. The groomer should use a row relative frequency table.

Row Relative Frequency Table

		Time Between Visits			
		Week	Month	Year	Total
Type of Pet	**Dog**	11.9%	62.8%	25.3%	100%
	Cat	12.1%	63.0%	24.9%	100%
	Total	12.0%	62.9%	25.1%	100%

The percent of cats that were groomed weekly and the percent of dogs that were groomed weekly are almost equal, about 12%.

The percent of cats were groomed monthly and the percent of dogs that were groomed monthly are almost equal, about 63%.

The percent of cats that were groomed yearly and the percent of dogs that were groomed yearly are almost equal, about 25%.

Based on the groomer's data, there does not appear to be evidence of an association between the type of pet and the time between visits.

1. A store asks each of 100 customers if he or she prefers dogs or cats. You want to know if more women than men prefer dogs.

Frequency Table

Favorite Animal	Gender		
	Men	Women	Total
Cats	20	30	50
Dogs	10	40	50
Total	30	70	100

Row Relative Frequency Table

Favorite Animal	Gender		
	Men	Women	Total
Cats	40%	60%	100%
Dogs	20%	80%	100%
Total	30%	70%	100%

a. Which table will be more helpful in finding that information? Choose the correct answer below.

A. The frequency table is more helpful because you are interested in percents, not frequencies.

B. The frequency table is more helpful because you are interested in frequencies, not percents.

C. The row relative frequency table is more helpful because you are interested in percents, not frequencies.

D. The row relative frequency table is more helpful because you are interested in frequencies, not percents.

b. Do more women than men prefer dogs?

2. You survey 100 students, asking each if he or she plays sports. You want to know if girls are more likely than boys to play sports.

Frequency Table

Plays Sports?	Gender		
	Girls	Boys	Total
Yes	40	32	72
No	10	18	28
Total	50	50	100

Column Relative Frequency Table

Plays Sports?	Gender		
	Girls	Boys	Total
Yes	80%	64%	72%
No	20%	36%	28%
Total	100%	100%	100%

a. Which table will be more helpful in finding that information? Explain your choice.

A. The column relative frequency table is more helpful because you are interested in percents, not frequencies.

B. The column relative frequency table is more helpful because you are interested in frequencies, not percents.

C. The frequency table is more helpful because you are interested in frequencies, not percents.

D. The frequency table is more helpful because you are interested in percents, not frequencies.

b. Which table would be more helpful if you wanted to know if it is more likely than not that students play sports?

3. Think About the Process On a car trip you count the number and types of red and blue cars on the highway. The frequency table shows the results.

Frequency Table

Color	Type of Car		
	2-Door	4-Door	Total
Blue	9	9	18
Red	9	3	12
Total	18	12	30

Column Relative Frequency Table

Color	Type of Car		
	2-Door	4-Door	Total
Blue	50%	75%	60%
Red	50%	25%	40%
Total	100%	100%	100%

Row Relative Frequency Table

Color	Type of Car		
	2-Door	4-Door	Total
Blue	50%	50%	100%
Red	75%	25%	100%
Total	60%	40%	100%

Total Relative Frequency Table

Color	Type of Car		
	2-Door	4-Door	Total
Blue	30%	30%	60%
Red	30%	10%	40%
Total	60%	40%	100%

a. What type of relative frequency table shows the percent of blue cars that have 4 doors?

   A. The row relative frequency table

   B. The total relative frequency table

   C. The column relative frequency table

b. What other percents can you find from the same relative frequency table?

4. Think About the Process Men and women were asked what type of car they own. The frequency table shows the results of the survey. You want to see if a person's gender influences the type of car he or she owns.

Frequency Table

Gender	Type of Car		
	2-Door	4-Door	Total
Men	19	6	25
Women	21	4	25
Total	40	10	50

a. Construct the most useful relative frequency table to detect an association.

Gender	Type of Car		
	2-Door	4-Door	Total
Men	■%	■%	■%
Women	■%	■%	■%
Total	■%	■%	100%

b. Do you want to find the relative frequencies with respect to gender or type of car?

See your complete lesson at MyMathUniverse.com

CCSS: 8.SP.A.4

Part 1

Example Completing Two-Way Tables Using Information From Other Two-Way Tables

Your friend collected data about whether people live in a house or an apartment and what type of vehicle the people drive. Help your friend complete the tables.

Frequency Table

Vehicle Type	Housing Type		
	Apt.	House	Total
Car	■	■	■
Truck	■	■	■
Van	■	■	30
Total	90	■	■

Relative Frequency Table

Vehicle Type	Housing Type		
	Apt.	House	Total
Car	■	30%	■
Truck	5%	■	■
Van	■	5%	15%
Total	■	55%	100%

Solution

The relative frequency table is not a column relative frequency table, because the House column sums to 55%.

The relative frequency table is not a row relative frequency table, because the Van row sums to 15%.

So, the table is a total relative frequency table.

Compare the total for Vans in the two tables. 15% of the population is 30. So, 100% of the total population is 200. Use the total, 200, to find the missing frequencies.

continued on next page >

See your complete lesson at MyMathUniverse.com

Part 1

Solution continued

Frequency Table

		Housing Type		
		Apt.	**House**	**Total**
Vehicle Type	**Car**	■	■	■
	Truck	■	■	■
	Van	■	■	30
	Total	90	■	200

Relative Frequency Table

		Housing Type		
		Apt.	**House**	**Total**
Vehicle Type	**Car**	■	30%	■
	Truck	5%	■	■
	Van	■	5%	15%
	Total	■	55%	100%

Use the total number of people, 200, to find the missing frequencies.

5% of the 200 people live in an Apartment and drive a Truck. 5% of 200 is 10, so the number of the people who fall into the group *Apartment/Truck* is 10.

30% of the 200 people live in a House and drive a Car. 30% of 200 is 60, so the number of people who fall into the group *House/Car* is 60.

5% of the 200 people live in a House and drive a Van. 5% of 200 is 10, so the number of people who fall into the group *House/Van* is 10.

55% of the 200 people live in a House. 55% of 200 is 110, so the number of people who fall into the group *House* is 110.

You know 110 of the people live in a House. Of those, 60 drive a Car, x drive a Truck and 10 drive a Van. The number of people who live in a House and drive a Truck is given by the equation $60 + x + 10 = 110$ where $x = 40$. So the number of the people who fall into the group *House/Truck* is 40.

10 people live in an Apartment and drive a Truck. 40 people live in a House and drive a Truck. The total number of the people who fall into the group *Truck* is 10 + 40, or 50.

There are 200 people in total. 50 of the people drive a Truck and 30 of the people drive a Van. The total number of the people who fall into the group *Car* is 200 − (50 + 30), or 120.

There are 120 people who drive a Car and 60 of those people live in a House.

The number of the people who fall into the group *Car/Apartment* is 120 − 60, or 60.

continued on next page >

Part 1

Solution *continued*

The total number of the people who drive a Van is 30. The number of the people who fall into the group *Van/Apartment* is 30 − 10, or 20.

Frequency Table

		Housing Type		
		Apt.	**House**	**Total**
Vehicle Type	**Car**	60	60	120
	Truck	10	40	50
	Van	20	10	30
	Total	90	110	200

Relative Frequency Table

		Housing Type		
		Apt.	**House**	**Total**
Vehicle Type	**Car**	▪	30%	▪
	Truck	5%	▪	▪
	Van	▪	5%	15%
	Total	▪	55%	100%

Now, use the frequencies to complete the relative frequency table.

60 of the 200 the people live in an Apartment and drive a Car. 60 is 30% of 200, so the percent of people who fall into the group *Apartment/Car* is 30.

20 of the 200 the people live in an Apartment and drive a Van. 20 is 10% of 200, so the percent of people who fall into the group *Apartment/Van* is 10.

90 of the 200 the people live in an Apartment, 90 is 45% of 200, so the percent of people who fall into the group *Apartment* is 45.

40 of the 200 the people live in a House and drive a Truck. 40 is 20% of 200, so the percent of people who fall into the group *House/Truck* is 20.

120 of the 200 the people drive a Car. 120 is 60% of 200, so the percent of people who fall into the group *Car* is 60.

50 of the 200 the people drive a Truck. 50 is 25% of 200, so the percent of people who fall into the group *Truck* is 25.

Relative Frequency Table

		Housing Type		
		Apt.	**House**	**Total**
Vehicle Type	**Car**	30%	30%	60%
	Truck	5%	20%	25%
	Van	10%	5%	15%
	Total	45%	55%	100%

Part 2

Example Comparing Data in Frequency Tables

The tables show shooting statistics for two different players from one practice. Which player do you think is better at making shots? Explain.

Player A

Made Shot?	Type of Shot		
	2-Point	3-Point	Total
Yes	8	17	25
No	12	13	25
Total	20	30	50

Player B

Made Shot?	Type of Shot		
	2-Point	3-Point	Total
Yes	17	6	23
No	23	4	27
Total	40	10	50

Solution

Answers may vary. Sample:

Construct relative frequency tables with respect to the type of shot to show the percent of shots made overall and the percent of each type of shot made. Then compare the two players.

Player A

Made Shot?	Type of Shot		
	2-Point	3-Point	Total
Yes	40%	56.7%	50%
No	60%	43.3%	50%
Total	100%	100%	100%

Player B

Made Shot?	Type of Shot		
	2-Point	3-Point	Total
Yes	42.5%	60%	46%
No	57.5%	40%	54%
Total	100%	100%	100%

When you compare the overall percents of shots made, Player A appears to be better at making shots. Player A made 50% of all attempted shots. Player B made only 46% of all attempted shots.

Solution continued

However, you can also compare the percent of each type of shot that each player made.

Player A made only 40% of the 2-point shots attempted. Player B made 42.5% of the 2-point shots attempted. So Player B made a greater percent of 2-point shots.

Player A made about 56.7% of the 3-point shots attempted. Player B made 60% of the 3-point shots attempted. So Player B made a greater percent of 3-point shots.

Player B is more likely to make a 2-point shot and more likely to make a 3-point shot. So Player B is better at making shots.

1. Todd is starting a trivia team. His weakest categories are history and sports. To decide who he wants to join the team, Todd asks two of his friends trivia questions in each category. The tables show this data.

Tony

| Correct? | Category | | |
	History	Sports	Total
Yes	95	30	125
No	49	6	55
Total	144	36	180

Terri

| Correct? | Category | | |
	History	Sports	Total
Yes	55	83	138
No	27	15	42
Total	82	98	180

a. Which friend looks like the better overall choice? Which friend is more likely to answer a history question correctly? Which friend is more likely to answer a sports question correctly?

b. Explain which friend you think Todd should choose. Indicate what the row relative frequency tables tell you in this situation and explain whether they are useful or not.

2. Max collected data about whether baseball players bat from the left side, the right side, or both sides of home plate and their gender. List the values you would use to complete each table.

Frequency Table

| Bat From? | Gender | | |
	Men	Women	Total
Left	■	■	40
Right	16	■	■
Both	■	■	10
Total	■	63	100

Relative Frequency Table

| Bat From? | Gender | | |
	Men	Women	Total
Left	35%	■	■
Right	■	■	100%
Both	■	30%	■
Total	37%	■	■

3. Sanjay needs a tutor for both math and science. The tables show statistics on whether two different tutors helped students improve their grades in both subjects. Compare the two tutors.

Tutor A

| Improve Grade? | Subject | | |
	Math	Science	Total
Yes	23	79	102
No	6	22	28
Total	29	101	130

Tutor B

| Improve Grade? | Subject | | |
	Math	Science	Total
Yes	48	57	105
No	10	15	25
Total	58	72	130

a. When you look at the overall percent of improvement, which tutor looks better? Which tutor is more likely to improve grades in math? Which tutor is more likely to improve grades in science?

b. Which tutor should Sanjay hire? Explain.

c. Would his decision change if he only needs a tutor for one subject instead of both?

See your complete lesson at MyMathUniverse.com

4. A gas station notes whether people pay with a credit/debit card or cash over three shifts. List the values you would use to complete each table.

Frequency Table

Shift	Payment Method		
	Card	Cash	Total
6 A.M.–12 P.M.	140	■	200
12 P.M.–6 P.M.	■	100	■
6 P.M.–12 A.M.	■	■	360
Total	■	400	■

Frequency Table

Shift	Payment Method		
	Card	Cash	Total
6 A.M.–12 P.M.	■	■	25%
12 P.M.–6 P.M.	■	■	■
6 P.M.–12 A.M.	■	■	■
Total	100%	■	■

5. Think About the Process Meg collected data about what type of pizza topping and crust people prefer.

Frequency Table

Topping	Crust Type		
	Thin	Thick	Total
None	■	■	40
Meat	32	■	■
Other	■	■	40
Total	80	■	160

Relative Frequency Table

Topping	Crust Type		
	Thin	Thick	Total
None	70%	■	■
Meat	■	■	100%
Other	■	50%	■
Total	■	50%	■

a. Is the given relative frequency table a column, row, or total relative frequency table?

b. Complete the tables.

6. Think About the Process Sven watches two different TV channels every day to check the weather. The tables show how accurate the two channels are in predicting if it will rain or not.

Channel X

Correct?	Prediction		
	Rain	No Rain	Total
Yes	85	36	121
No	52	7	59
Total	137	43	180

Channel Y

Correct?	Prediction		
	Rain	No Rain	Total
Yes	54	77	131
No	36	13	49
Total	90	90	180

a. How can you compare the accuracy of the two channels?

A. Construct the total relative frequency table for each channel.

B. For each channel, divide the total in the "No Rain" column by the number of days.

C. For each channel, divide the total in the "Rain" column by the number of days.

D. Construct the row relative frequency table for each channel.

E. Construct the column relative frequency table for each channel.

b. When you look at the overall percent of correct predictions, which channel looks more accurate? Which channel is more accurate when predicting rain? Which channel is more accurate when predicting no rain?

English/Spanish Glossary

. . . . **A** . . . .

Absolute deviation from the mean Absolute deviation measures the distance that the data value is from the mean. You find the absolute deviation by taking the absolute value of the deviation of a data value. Absolute deviations are always nonnegative.

Desviación absoluta de la media La desviación absoluta mide la distancia a la que un valor se encuentra de la media. Para hallar la desviación absoluta, tomas el valor absoluto de la desviación de un valor. Las desviaciones absolutas siempre son no negativas.

Absolute value The absolute value of a number a is the distance between a and zero on a number line. The absolute value of a is written as $|a|$.

Valor absoluto El valor absoluto de un número a es la distancia entre a y cero en la recta numérica. El valor absoluto de a se escribe como $|a|$.

Accuracy The accuracy of an estimate or measurement is the degree to which it agrees with an accepted or actual value of that measurement.

Exactitud La exactitud de una estimación o medición es el grado de concordancia con un valor aceptado o real de esa medición.

Action In a probability situation, an action is a process with an uncertain result.

Acción En una situación de probabilidad, una acción es el proceso con un resultado incierto.

Acute angle An acute angle is an angle with a measure between 0° and 90°.

Ángulo agudo Un ángulo agudo es un ángulo que mide entre 0° y 90°.

Acute triangle An acute triangle is a triangle with three acute angles.

Triángulo acutángulo Un triángulo acutángulo es un triángulo que tiene tres ángulos agudos.

Addend Addends are the numbers that are added together to find a sum.

Sumando Los sumandos son los números que se suman para hallar un total.

English/Spanish Glossary

Additive inverses Two numbers that have a sum of 0.

Inversos de suma Dos números cuya suma es 0.

Adjacent angles Two angles are adjacent angles if they share a vertex and a side, but have no interior points in common.

Ángulos adyacentes Dos ángulos son adyacentes si tienen un vértice y un lado en común, pero no comparten puntos internos.

Algebraic expression An algebraic expression is a mathematical phrase that consists of variables, numbers, and operation symbols.

Expresión algebraica Una expresión algebraica es una frase matemática que consiste en variables, números y símbolos de operaciones.

Analyze To analyze is to think about and understand facts and details about a given set of information. Analyzing can involve providing a written summary supported by factual information, diagrams, charts, tables, or any combination of these.

Analizar Analizar es pensar en los datos y detalles de cierta información y comprenderlos. El análisis puede incluir la presentación de un resumen escrito sustentado por información objetiva, diagramas, tablas o una combinación de esos elementos.

Angle An angle is a figure formed by two rays with a common endpoint.

Ángulo Un ángulo es una figura formada por dos semirrectas que tienen un extremo en común.

Angle of rotation The angle of rotation is the number of degrees a figure is rotated.

Ángulo de rotación El ángulo de rotación es el número de grados que se rota una figura.

Annual salary The amount of money earned at a job in one year.

Salario annual La cantidad de dinero ganó en un trabajo en un año.

Area The area of a figure is the number of square units the figure encloses.

Área El área de una figura es el número de unidades cuadradas que ocupa.

English/Spanish Glossary

Area of a circle The formula for the area of a circle is $A = \pi r^2$, where A represents the area and r represents the radius of the circle.

Área de un círculo La fórmula del área de un círculo es $A = \pi r^2$, donde A representa el área y r representa el radio del círculo.

Area of a parallelogram The formula for the area of a parallelogram is $A = bh$, where A represents the area, b represents a base, and h is the corresponding height.

Área de un paralelogramo La fórmula del área de un paralelogramo es $A = bh$, donde A representa el área, b representa una base y h es la altura correspondiente.

Area of a rectangle The formula for the area of a rectangle is $A = bh$, where A represents the area, b represents the base, and h represents the height of the rectangle.

Área de un rectángulo La fórmula del área de un rectángulo es $A = bh$, donde A representa el área, b representa la base y h representa la altura del rectángulo.

Area of a square The formula for the area of a square is $A = s^2$, where A represents the area and s represents a side length.

Área de un cuadrado La fórmula del área de un cuadrado es $A = s^2$, donde A representa el área y l representa la longitud de un lado.

Area of a trapezoid The formula for the area of a trapezoid is $A = \frac{1}{2}h(b_1 + b_2)$, where A represents the area, b_1 and b_2 represent the bases, and h represents the height between the bases.

El área de un trapezoide La fórmula para el área de un trapezoide es $A = \frac{1}{2}h(b_1 + b_2)$, donde A representa el área, b_1 y b_2 representan las bases, y h representa la altura entre las bases.

Area of a triangle The formula for the area of a triangle is $A = \frac{1}{2}bh$, where A represents the area, b represents the length of a base, and h represents the corresponding height.

Área de un triángulo La fórmula del área de un triángulo es $A = \frac{1}{2}bh$, donde A representa el área, b representa la longitud de una base y h representa la altura correspondiente.

Asset An asset is money you have or property of value that you own.

Ventaja Una ventaja es dinero que tiene o la propiedad de valor que usted posee.

English/Spanish Glossary

Associative Property of Addition For any numbers *a*, *b*, and *c*:
$(a + b) + c = a + (b + c)$

Propiedad asociativa de la suma Para los números cualesquiera *a*, *b* y *c*:
$(a + b) + c = a + (b + c)$

Associative Property of Multiplication For any numbers *a*, *b*, and *c*:
$(a \cdot b) \cdot c = a \cdot (b \cdot c)$

Propiedad asociativa de la multiplicación Para los números cualesquiera *a*, *b* y *c*:
$(a \cdot b) \cdot c = a \cdot (b \cdot c)$

Average of two numbers The average of two numbers is the value that represents the middle of two numbers. It is found by adding the two numbers together and dividing by 2.

Promedio de dos números El promedio de dos números es el valor que está justo en el medio de esos dos números. Se halla sumando los dos números y dividiendo el resultado por 2.

B

Balance The balance in an account is the principal amount plus the interest earned.

Saldo El saldo de una cuenta es el capital más el interés ganado.

Balance of a checking account The balance of a checking account is the amount of money in the checking account.

El equilibrio de una Cuenta Corriente Bancaria El equilibrio de una cuenta corriente bancaria es la cantidad de dinero en la cuenta corriente bancaria.

Balance of a loan The balance of a loan is the remaining unpaid principal.

El equilibrio de un préstamo El equilibrio de un préstamo es el director impagado restante.

Bar diagram A bar diagram is a way to represent part to whole relationships.

Diagrama de barras Un diagrama de barras es una forma de representar una relación de parte a entero.

Base The base is the repeated factor of a number written in exponential form.

Base La base es el factor repetido de un número escrito en forma exponencial.

English/Spanish Glossary

Base area of a cone The base area of a cone is the area of a circle. Base Area = πr^2.

Área de la base de un cono El área de la base de un cono es el área de un círculo. El área de la base = πr^2.

Base of a cone The base of a cone is a circle with radius r.

Base de un cono La base de un cono es un círculo con radio r.

Base of a cylinder A base of a cylinder is one of a pair of parallel circular faces that are the same size.

Base de un cilindro Una base de un cilindro es una de dos caras circulares paralelas que tienen el mismo tamaño.

Base of a parallelogram A base of a parallelogram is any side of the parallelogram.

Base de un paralelogramo La base de un paralelogramo es cualquiera de los lados del paralelogramo.

Base of a prism A base of a prism is one of a pair of parallel polygonal faces that are the same size and shape. A prism is named for the shape of its bases.

Base de un prisma La base de un prisma es una de las dos caras poligonales paralelas que tienen el mismo tamaño y la misma forma. El nombre de un prisma depende de la forma de sus bases.

Base of a pyramid A base of a pyramid is a polygonal face that does not connect to the vertex.

Base de una pirámide La base de una pirámide es una cara poligonal que no se conecta con el vértice.

Base of a triangle The base of a triangle is any side of the triangle.

Base de un triángulo La base de un triángulo es cualquiera de los lados del triángulo.

Benchmark A benchmark is a number you can use as a reference point for other numbers.

Referencia Una referencia es un número que usted puede utilizar como un punto de referencia para otros números.

English/Spanish Glossary

Bias A bias is a tendency toward a particular perspective that is different from the overall perspective of the population.

Sesgo Un sesgo es una tendencia hacia una perspectiva particular que es diferente de la perspectiva general de la población.

Biased sample In a biased sample, the number of subjects in the sample with the trait that you are studying is not proportional to the number of members in the population with that trait. A biased sample does not accurately represent the population.

Muestra sesgada En una muestra sesgada, el número de sujetos de la muestra que tiene la característica que se está estudiando no es proporcional al número de miembros de la población que tienen esa característica. Una muestra sesgada no representa con exactitud la población.

Bivariate categorical data Bivariate categorical data pairs categorical data collected about two variables of the same population.

Datos bivariados por categorías Los datos bivariados por categorías agrupan pares de datos obtenidos acerca de dos variables de la misma población.

Bivariate data Bivariate data is comprised of pairs of linked observations about a population.

Datos bivariados Los datos bivariados se forman a partir de pares de observaciones relacionadas sobre una población.

Box plot A box plot is a statistical graph that shows the distribution of a data set by marking five boundary points where data occur along a number line. Unlike a dot plot or a histogram, a box plot does not show frequency.

Diagrama de cajas Un diagrama de cajas es un diagrama de estadísticas que muestra la distribución de un conjunto de datos al marcar cinco puntos de frontera donde se hallan los datos sobre una recta numérica. A diferencia del diagrama de puntos o el histograma, el diagrama de cajas no muestra la frecuencia.

Budget A budget is a plan for how you will spend your money.

Presupuesto Un presupuesto es un plan para cómo gastará su dinero.

English/Spanish Glossary

C

Categorical data Categorical data consist of data that fall into categories.

Datos por categorías Los datos por categorías son datos que se pueden clasificar en categorías.

Center of a circle The center of a circle is the point inside the circle that is the same distance from all points on the circle. Name a circle by its center.

Centro de un círculo El centro de un círculo es el punto dentro del círculo que está a la misma distancia de todos los puntos del círculo. Un círculo se identifica por su centro.

Center of a regular polygon The center of a regular polygon is the point that is equidistant from its vertices.

Centro de un polígono regular El centro de un polígono regular es el punto equidistante de todos sus vértices.

Center of rotation The center of rotation is a fixed point about which a figure is rotated.

Centro de rotación El centro de rotación es el punto fijo alrededor del cual se rota una figura.

Check register A record that shows all of the transactions for a bank account, including withdrawals, deposits, and transfers. It also shows the balance of the account after each transaction.

Verifique registro Un registro que muestra todas las transacciones para una cuenta bancaria, inclusive retiradas, los depósitos, y las transferencias. También muestra el equilibrio de la cuenta después de cada transacción.

Circle A circle is the set of all points in a plane that are the same distance from a given point, called the center.

Círculo Un círculo es el conjunto de todos los puntos de un plano que están a la misma distancia de un punto dado, llamado centro.

Circle graph A circle graph is a graph that represents a whole divided into parts.

Gráfica circular Una gráfica circular es una gráfica que representa un todo dividido en partes.

English/Spanish Glossary

Circumference of a circle The circumference of a circle is the distance around the circle. The formula for the circumference of a circle is $C = \pi d$, where C represents the circumference and d represents the diameter of the circle.

Circunferencia de un círculo La circunferencia de un círculo es la distancia alrededor del círculo. La fórmula de la circunferencia de un círculo es $C = \pi d$, donde C representa la circunferencia y d representa el diámetro del círculo.

Cluster A cluster is a group of points that lie close together on a scatter plot.

Grupo Un grupo es un conjunto de puntos que están agrupados en un diagrama de dispersión.

Coefficient A coefficient is the number part of a term that contains a variable.

Coeficiente Un coeficiente es la parte numérica de un término que contiene una variable.

Common denominator A common denominator is a number that is the denominator of two or more fractions.

Común denominador Un común denominador es un número que es el denominador de dos o más fracciones.

Common multiple A common multiple is a multiple that two or more numbers share.

Múltiplo común Un múltiplo común es un múltiplo que comparten dos o más números.

Commutative Property of Addition For any numbers a and b: $a + b = b + a$

Propiedad conmutativa de la suma Para los números cualesquiera a y b: $a + b = b + a$

Commutative Property of Multiplication For any numbers a and b: $a \cdot b = b \cdot a$

Propiedad conmutativa de la multiplicación Para los números cualesquiera a y b: $a \cdot b = b \cdot a$

Comparative inference A comparative inference is an inference made by interpreting and comparing two sets of data.

Inferencia comparativa Una inferencia comparativa es una inferencia que se hace al interpretar y comparar dos conjuntos de datos.

English/Spanish Glossary

Compare To compare is to tell or show how two things are alike or different.

Comparar Comparar es describir o mostrar en qué se parecen o en qué se diferencian dos cosas.

Compatible numbers Compatible numbers are numbers that are easy to compute mentally.

Números compatibles Los números compatibles son números fáciles de calcular mentalmente.

Complementary angles Two angles are complementary angles if the sum of their measures is 90°. Complementary angles that are adjacent form a right angle.

Ángulos complementarios Dos ángulos son complementarios si la suma de sus medidas es 90°. Los ángulos complementarios que son adyacentes forman un ángulo recto.

Complex fraction A complex fraction is a fraction $\frac{A}{B}$ where A and/or B are fractions and B is not zero.

Fracción compleja Una fracción compleja es una fracción $\frac{A}{B}$ donde A y/o B son fracciones y B es distinto de cero.

Compose a shape To compose a shape, join two (or more) shapes so that there is no gap or overlap.

Componer una figura Para componer una figura, debes unir dos (o más) figuras de modo que entre ellas no queden espacios ni superposiciones.

Composite figure A composite figure is the combination of two or more figures into one object.

Figura compuesta Una figura compuesta es la combinación de dos o más figuras en un objeto.

Composite number A composite number is a whole number greater than 1 with more than two factors.

Número compuesto Un número compuesto es un número entero mayor que 1 con más de dos factores.

Compound event A compound event is an event associated with a multi-step action. A compound event is composed of events that are the outcomes of the steps of the action.

Evento compuesto Un evento compuesto es un evento que se relaciona con una acción de varios pasos. Un evento compuesto se compone de eventos que son los resultados de los pasos de una acción.

English/Spanish Glossary

Compound interest Compound interest is interest paid on both the principal and the interest earned in previous interest periods. To calculate compound interest, use the formula $B = p(1 + r)^n$, where B is the balance in the account, p is the principal, r is the annual interest rate, and n is the time in years that the account earns interest.

Interés compuesto El interés compuesto es el interés que se paga sobre el capital y el interés obtenido en períodos de interés anteriores. Para calcular el interés compuesto, usa la fórmula $B = c(1 + r)^n$ donde B es el saldo de la cuenta, c es el capital, r es la tasa de interés anual y n es el tiempo en años en que la cuenta obtiene un interés.

Cone A cone is a three-dimensional figure with one circular base and one vertex.

Cono Un cono es una figura tridimensional con una base circular y un vértice.

Congruent figures Two two-dimensional figures are congruent ≅ if the second can be obtained from the first by a sequence of rotations, reflections, and translations.

Figuras congruentes Dos figuras bidimensionales son congruentes ≅ si la segunda puede obtenerse a partir de la primera mediante una secuencia de rotaciones, reflexiones y traslaciones.

Conjecture A conjecture is a statement that you believe to be true but have not yet proved to be true.

Conjetura Una conjetura es un enunciado que crees que es verdadero, pero que todavía no has comprobado que sea verdadero.

Constant A constant is a term that only contains a number.

Constante Una constante es un término que solamente contiene un número.

Constant of proportionality In a proportional relationship, one quantity y is a constant multiple of the other quantity x. The constant multiple is called the constant of proportionality. The constant of proportionality is equal to the ratio $\frac{y}{x}$.

Constante de proporcionalidad En una relación proporcional, una cantidad y es un múltiplo constante de la otra cantidad x. El múltiplo constante se llama constante de proporcionalidad. La constante de proporcionalidad es igual a la razón $\frac{y}{x}$.

English/Spanish Glossary

Construct To construct is to make something, such as an argument, by organizing ideas. Constructing an argument can involve a written response, equations, diagrams, charts, tables, or a combination of these.

Construir Construir es hacer o crear algo, como se construye un argumento al organizar ideas. Para construir un argumento puede usarse una respuesta escrita, ecuaciones, diagramas, tablas o una combinación de esos elementos.

Convenience sampling Convenience sampling is a sampling method in which a researcher chooses members of the population that are convenient and available. Many researchers use this sampling technique because it is fast and inexpensive. It does not require the researcher to keep track of everyone in the population.

Muestra de conveniencia Una muestra de conveniencia es un método de muestreo en el que un investigador escoge miembros de la población que están convenientemente disponibles. Muchos investigadores usan esta técnica de muestreo porque es rápida y no es costosa. No requiere que el investigador lleve un registro de cada miembro de la población.

Cost of attendance The cost of attendance of one year of college is the sum of all of your expenses during the year.

El costo de asistencia El costo de asistencia de un año del colegio es la suma de todos sus gastos durante el año.

Cost of credit The cost of credit for a loan is the difference between the total cost and the principal.

El costo de crédito El costo de crédito para un préstamo es la diferencia entre el coste total y el director.

Converse of the Pythagorean Theorem If the sum of the squares of the lengths of two sides of a triangle equals the square of the length of the third side, then the triangle is a right triangle. If $a^2 + b^2 = c^2$, then the triangle is a right triangle.

Expresión recíproca del Teorema de Pitágoras Si la suma del cuadrado de la longitud de dos lados de un triángulo es igual al cuadrado de la longitud del tercer lado, entonces el triángulo es un triángulo rectángulo. $a^2 + b^2 = c^2$, entonces el triángulo es un triángulo rectángulo.

Conversion factor A conversion factor is a rate that equals 1.

Factor de conversión Un factor de conversión es una tasa que es igual a 1.

English/Spanish Glossary

Coordinate plane A coordinate plane is formed by a horizontal number line called the *x*-axis and a vertical number line called the *y*-axis.

Plano de coordenadas Un plano de coordenadas está formado por una recta numérica horizontal llamada eje de las *x* y una recta numérica vertical llamada eje de las *y*.

Corresponding angles Corresponding angles lie on the same side of a transversal and in corresponding positions.

Ángulos correspondientes Los ángulos correspondientes se ubican al mismo lado de una secante y en posiciones correspondientes.

Counterexample A counterexample is a specific example that shows that a conjecture is false.

Contraejemplo Un contraejemplo es un ejemplo específico que muestra que una conjetura es falsa.

Counting Principle If there are *m* possible outcomes of one action and *n* possible outcomes of a second action, then there are $m \cdot n$ outcomes of the first action followed by the second action.

Principio de conteo Si hay *m* resultados posibles de una acción y *n* resultados posibles de una segunda acción, entonces hay $m \cdot n$ resultados de la primera acción seguida de la segunda acción.

Coupon A coupon is part of a printed or online advertisement entitling the holder to a discount at checkout.

Cupón Un cupón forma parte de un anuncio impreso o en línea que permite al poseedor a un descuento en comprueba.

Credit card A credit card is a card issued by a lender that can be used to borrow money or make purchases on credit.

Tarjeta de crédito Una tarjeta de crédito es una tarjeta publicada por un prestamista que puede ser utilizado para pedir dinero prestado o compras de marca a cuenta.

Credit history A credit history shows how a consumer has managed credit in the past.

Acredite la historia Una historia del crédito muestra cómo un consumidor ha manejado crédito en el pasado.

English/Spanish Glossary

Credit report A report that shows personal information about a consumer and details about the consumer's credit history.

Acredite reporte Un reporte que muestra información personal sobre un consumidor y detalles acerca de la historia del crédito del consumidor.

Critique A critique is a careful judgment in which you give your opinion about the good and bad parts of something, such as how a problem was solved.

Crítica Una crítica es una evaluación cuidadosa en la que das tu opinión acerca de las partes positivas y negativas de algo, como la manera en la que se resolvió un problema.

Cross section A cross section is the intersection of a three-dimensional figure and a plane.

Corte transversal Un corte transversal es la intersección de una figura tridimensional y un plano.

Cube A cube is a rectangular prism whose faces are all squares.

Cubo Un cubo es un prisma rectangular cuyas caras son todas cuadrados.

Cube root The cube root of a number, *n*, is a number whose cube equals *n*.

Raíz cúbica La raíz cúbica de un número, *n*, es un número que elevado al cubo es igual a *n*.

Cubic unit A cubic unit is the volume of a cube that measures 1 unit on each edge.

Unidad cúbica Una unidad cúbica es el volumen de un cubo en el que cada arista mide 1 unidad.

Cylinder A cylinder is a three-dimensional figure with two parallel circular bases that are the same size.

Cilindro Un cilindro es una figura tridimensional con dos bases circulares paralelas que tienen el mismo tamaño.

D

Data Data are pieces of information collected by asking questions, measuring, or making observations about the real world.

Datos Los datos son información reunida mediante preguntas, mediciones u observaciones sobre la vida diaria.

English/Spanish Glossary

Debit card A debit card is a card issued by a bank that is linked to a customer's bank account, normally a checking account. A debit card can normally be used to withdraw money from an ATM or to make a purchase.

Tarjeta de débito Una tarjeta de débito es una tarjeta publicada por un banco que es ligado la cuenta bancaria de un cliente, normalmente una cuenta corriente bancaria. Una tarjeta de débito puede ser utilizada normalmente retirar dinero de una ATM o para hacer una compra.

Decimal A decimal is a number with one or more places to the right of a decimal point.

Decimal Un decimal es un número que tiene uno o más lugares a la derecha del punto decimal.

Decimal places The digits after the decimal point are called decimal places.

Lugares decimales Los dígitos que están después del punto decimal se llaman lugares decimales.

Decompose a shape To decompose a shape, break it up to form other shapes.

Descomponer una figura Para descomponer una figura, debes separarla para formar otras figuras.

Deductive reasoning Deductive reasoning is a process of reasoning logically from given facts to a conclusion.

Razonamiento deductivo El razonamiento deductivo es un proceso de razonamiento lógico que parte de hechos dados hasta llegar a una conclusión.

Denominator The denominator is the number below the fraction bar in a fraction.

Denominador El denominador es el número que está debajo de la barra de fracción en una fracción.

Dependent events Two events are dependent events if the occurrence of the first event affects the probability of the second event.

Eventos dependientes Dos eventos son dependientes si el resultado del primer evento afecta la probabilidad del segundo evento.

Deposit A transaction that adds money to a bank account is a deposit.

Depósito Una transacción que agrega dinero a una cuenta bancaria es un depósito.

English/Spanish Glossary

Dependent variable A dependent variable is a variable whose value changes in response to another (independent) variable.

Variable dependiente Una variable dependiente es una variable cuyo valor cambia en respuesta a otra variable (independiente).

Describe To describe is to explain or tell in detail. A written description can contain facts and other information needed to communicate your answer. A diagram or a graph may also be included.

Describir Describir es explicar o indicar algo en detalle. Una descripción escrita puede incluir hechos y otra información necesaria para comunicar tu respuesta. También puede incluir un diagrama o una gráfica.

Design To design is to make using specific criteria.

Diseñar Diseñar es crear algo a partir de criterios específicos.

Determine To determine is to use the given information and any related facts to find a value or make a decision.

Determinar Determinar es usar la información dada y cualquier otro dato relacionado para hallar un valor o tomar una decisión.

Deviation from the mean Deviation indicates how far away and in which direction a data value is from the mean. Data values that are less than the mean have a negative deviation. Data values that are greater than the mean have a positive deviation.

Desviación de la media La desviación indica a qué distancia y en qué dirección un valor se aleja de la media. Los valores menores que la media tienen una desviación negativa. Los valores mayores que la media tienen una desviación positiva.

Diagonal A diagonal of a figure is a segment that connects two nonconsecutive vertices of the figure.

Diagonal La diagonal de una figura es un segmento que conecta dos vértices no consecutivos de la figura.

Diameter A diameter is a segment that passes through the center of a circle and has both endpoints on the circle. The term diameter can also mean the length of this segment.

Diámetro Un diámetro es un segmento que atraviesa el centro de un círculo y tiene sus dos extremos en el círculo. El término diámetro también puede referirse a la longitud de este segmento.

English/Spanish Glossary

Difference The difference is the answer you get when subtracting two numbers.

Diferencia La diferencia es la respuesta que obtienes cuando restas dos números.

Dilation A dilation is a transformation that moves each point along the ray through the point, starting from a fixed center, and multiplies distances from the center by a common scale factor. If a vertex of a figure is the center of dilation, then the vertex and its image after the dilation are the same point.

Dilatación Una dilatación es una transformación que mueve cada punto a lo largo de la semirrecta a través del punto, a partir de un centro fijo, y multiplica las distancias desde el centro por un factor de escala común. Si un vértice de una figura es el centro de dilatación, entonces el vértice y su imagen después de la dilatación son el mismo punto.

Direct variation A linear relationship that can be represented by an equation in the form $y = kx$, where $x \neq 0$.

Dirija variación Una relación lineal que puede ser representada por una ecuación en la forma $y = kx$, donde x no iguale 0.

Distribution (of a data set) The distribution of a data set describes the way that its data values are spread out over all possible values. This includes describing the frequencies of each data value. The shape of a data display shows the distribution of a data set.

Distribución (de un conjunto de datos) La distribución de un conjunto de datos describe la manera en que sus valores se esparcen sobre todos los valores posibles. Eso incluye la descripción de las frecuencias de cada valor. La forma de una exhibición de datos muestra la distribución de un conjunto de datos.

Distributive Property Multiplying a number by a sum or difference gives the same result as multiplying that number by each term in the sum or difference and then adding or subtracting the corresponding products.
$a \cdot (b + c) = a \cdot b + a \cdot c$ and
$a \cdot (b - c) = a \cdot b - a \cdot c$

Propiedad distributiva Multiplicar un número por una suma o una diferencia da el mismo resultado que multiplicar ese mismo número por cada uno de los términos de la suma o la diferencia y después sumar o restar los productos obtenidos.
$a \cdot (b + c) = a \cdot b + a \cdot c$ and
$a \cdot (b - c) = a \cdot b - a \cdot c$

Dividend The dividend is the number to be divided.

Dividendo El dividendo es el número que se divide.

English/Spanish Glossary

Divisible A number is divisible by another number if there is no remainder after dividing.

Divisible Un número es divisible por otro número si no hay residuo después de dividir.

Divisor The divisor is the number used to divide another number.

Divisor El divisor es el número por el cual se divide otro número.

Dot plot A dot plot is a statistical graph that shows the shape of a data set with stacked dots above each data value on a number line. Each dot represents one data value.

Diagrama de puntos Un diagrama de puntos es una gráfica estadística que muestra la forma de un conjunto de datos con puntos marcados sobre cada valor de una recta numérica. Cada punto representa un valor.

E

Earned wages Earned wages are the income you receive from an employer for doing a job. Earned wages are also called gross pay.

Sueldos ganados Los sueldos ganados son los ingresos que usted recibe de un empleador para hacer un trabajo. Los sueldos ganados también son llamados la paga bruta.

Easy-access loan The term easy-access loan refers to a wide variety of loans with a streamlined application process. Many easy-access loans are short-term loans of relatively small amounts of money. They often have high interest rates.

Préstamo de fácil-acceso El préstamo del fácil-acceso del término se refiere a una gran variedad de préstamos con un proceso simplificado de aplicación. Muchos préstamos del fácil-acceso son préstamos a corto plazo de cantidades relativamente pequeñas de dinero. Ellos a menudo tienen los tipos de interés altos.

Edge of a three-dimensional figure An edge of a three-dimensional figure is a segment formed by the intersection of two faces.

Arista de una figura tridimensional Una arista de una figura tridimensional es un segmento formado por la intersección de dos caras.

English/Spanish Glossary

Enlargement An enlargement is a dilation with a scale factor greater than 1. After an enlargement, the image is bigger than the original figure.

Aumento Un aumento es una dilatación con un factor de escala mayor que 1. Después de un aumento, la imagen es más grande que la figura original.

Equation An equation is a mathematical sentence that includes an equals sign to compare two expressions.

Ecuación Una ecuación es una oración matemática que incluye un signo igual para comparar dos expresiones.

Equilateral triangle An equilateral triangle is a triangle whose sides are all the same length.

Triángulo equilátero Un triángulo equilátero es un triángulo que tiene todos sus lados de la misma longitud.

Equivalent equations Equivalent equations are equations that have exactly the same solutions.

Ecuaciones equivalentes Las ecuaciones equivalentes son ecuaciones que tienen exactamente la misma solución.

Equivalent expressions Equivalent expressions are expressions that always have the same value.

Expresiones equivalentes Las expresiones equivalentes son expresiones que siempre tienen el mismo valor.

Equivalent fractions Equivalent fractions are fractions that name the same number.

Fracciones equivalentes Las fracciones equivalentes son fracciones que representan el mismo número.

Equivalent inequalities Equivalent inequalities are inequalities that have the same solution.

Desigualdades equivalentes Las desigualdades equivalentes son desigualdades que tienen la misma solución.

Equivalent ratios Equivalent ratios are ratios that express the same relationship.

Razones equivalentes Las razones equivalentes son razones que expresan la misma relación.

Estimate To estimate is to find a number that is close to an exact answer.

Estimar Estimar es hallar un número cercano a una respuesta exacta.

English/Spanish Glossary

Evaluate a numerical expression To evaluate a numerical expression is to follow the order of operations.

Evaluar una expresión numérica Evaluar una expresión numérica es seguir el orden de las operaciones.

Evaluate an algebraic expression To evaluate an algebraic expression, replace each variable with a number, and then follow the order of operations.

Evaluar una expresión algebraica Para evaluar una expresión algebraica, reemplaza cada variable con un número y luego sigue el orden de las operaciones.

Event An event is a single outcome or group of outcomes from a sample space.

Evento Un evento es un resultado simple o un grupo de resultados de un espacio muestral.

Expand an algebraic expression To expand an algebraic expression, use the Distributive Property to rewrite a product as a sum or difference of terms.

Desarrollar una expresión algebraica Para desarrollar una expresión algebraica, usa la propiedad distributiva para reescribir el producto como una suma o diferencia de términos.

Expected family contribution The amount of money a student's family is expected to contribute towards the student's cost of attendance for school.

Contribución familiar esperado La cantidad de dinero que la familia de un estudiante es esperada contribuir hacia el estudiante es costado de asistencia para la escuela.

Expense Money that a business or a person needs to spend to pay for or buy something.

Gasto El dinero que un negocio o una persona debe gastar para pagar por o comprar algo.

Experiment To experiment is to try to gather information in several ways.

Experimentar Experimentar es intentar reunir información de varias maneras.

English/Spanish Glossary

Experimental probability You find the experimental probability of an event by repeating an experiment many times and using this ratio: $P(\text{event}) = \dfrac{\text{number of times event occurs}}{\text{total number of trials}}$

Probabilidad experimental Para hallar la probabilidad experimental de un evento, debes repetir un experimento muchas veces y usar esta razón: $P(\text{evento}) = \dfrac{\text{número de veces que sucede el evento}}{\text{número total de pruebas}}$

Explain To explain is to give facts and details that make an idea easier to understand. Explaining can involve a written summary supported by a diagram, chart, table, or a combination of these.

Explicar Explicar es brindar datos y detalles para que una idea sea más fácil de comprender. Para explicar algo se puede usar un resumen escrito sustentado por un diagrama, una tabla o una combinación de esos elementos.

Exponent An exponent is a number that shows how many times a base is used as a factor.

Exponente Un exponente es un número que muestra cuántas veces se usa una base como factor.

Expression An expression is a mathematical phrase that can involve variables, numbers, and operations. See algebraic expression or numerical expression.

Expresión Una expresión es una frase matemática que puede tener variables, números y operaciones. Ver expresión algebraica o expresión numérica.

Exterior angle of a triangle An exterior angle of a triangle is an angle formed by a side and an extension of an adjacent side.

Ángulo externo de un triángulo Un ángulo externo de un triángulo es un ángulo formado por un lado y una extensión de un lado adyacente.

F

Face of a three-dimensional figure A face of a three-dimensional figure is a flat surface shaped like a polygon.

Cara de una figura tridimensional La cara de una figura tridimensional es una superficie plana con forma de polígono.

English/Spanish Glossary

Factor an algebraic expression To factor an algebraic expression, write the expression as a product.

Descomponer una expresión algebraica en factores Para descomponer una expresión algebraica en factores, escribe la expresión como un producto.

Factors Factors are numbers that are multiplied to give a product.

Factores Los factores son los números que se multiplican para obtener un producto.

False equation A false equation has values that do not equal each other on each side of the equals sign.

Ecuación falsa Una ecuación falsa tiene valores a cada lado del signo igual que no son iguales entre sí.

Financial aid Financial aid is any money offered to a student to assist with the cost of attendance.

Ayuda financiera La ayuda financiera es cualquier dinero ofreció a un estudiante para ayudar con el costo de asistencia.

Financial need A student's financial need is the difference between the student's cost of attendance and the student's expected family contribution.

Necesidad financiera Una necesidad financiera del estudiante es la diferencia entre el estudiante es costada de asistencia y la contribución esperado de familia de estudiante.

Find To find is to calculate or determine.

Hallar Hallar es calcular o determinar.

First quartile For an ordered set of data, the first quartile is the median of the lower half of the data set.

Primer cuartil Para un conjunto ordenado de datos, el primer cuartil es la mediana de la mitad inferior del conjunto de datos.

Fixed expenses Fixed expenses are expenses that do not change from one budget period to the next.

Gastos fijos Los gastos fijos son los gastos que no cambian de un período económico al próximo.

English/Spanish Glossary

Fraction A fraction is a number that can be written in the form $\frac{a}{b}$, where a is a whole number and b is a positive whole number. A fraction is formed by a parts of size $\frac{1}{b}$.

Fracción Una fracción es un número que puede expresarse de forma $\frac{a}{b}$, donde a es un entero y b es un número entero positivo. La fracción está formada por a partes de tamaño $\frac{1}{b}$.

Frequency Frequency describes the number of times a specific value occurs in a data set.

Frecuencia La frecuencia describe el número de veces que aparece un valor específico en un conjunto de datos.

Function A function is a rule for taking each input value and producing exactly one output value.

Función Una función es una regla por la cual se toma cada valor de entrada y se produce exactamente un valor de salida.

G

Gap A gap is an area of a graph that contains no data points.

Espacio vacío o brecha Un espacio vacío o brecha es un área de una gráfica que no contiene ningún valor.

Grant A type of monetary award a student can use to pay for his or her education. The student does not need to repay this money.

Grant Un tipo de premio monetario que un estudiante puede utilizar para pagar por su educación. El estudiante no debe devolver este dinero.

Greater than > The greater-than symbol shows a comparison of two numbers with the number of greater value shown first, or on the left.

Mayor que > El símbolo de mayor que muestra una comparación de dos números con el número de mayor valor que aparece primero, o a la izquierda.

Greatest common factor The greatest common factor (GCF) of two or more whole numbers is the greatest number that is a factor of all of the numbers.

Máximo común divisor El máximo común divisor (M.C.D.) de dos o más números enteros no negativos es el número mayor que es un factor de todos los números.

English/Spanish Glossary

H

Height of a cone The height of a cone, h, is the length of a segment perpendicular to the base that joins the vertex and the base.

Altura de un cono La altura de un cono, h, es la longitud de un segmento perpendicular a la base que une el vértice y la base.

Height of a cylinder The height of a cylinder is the length of a perpendicular segment that joins the planes of the bases.

Altura de un cilindro La altura de un cilindro es la longitud de un segmento perpendicular que une los planos de las bases.

Height of a parallelogram A height of a parallelogram is the perpendicular distance between opposite bases.

Altura de un paralelogramo La altura de un paralelogramo es la distancia perpendicular que existe entre las bases opuestas.

Height of a prism The height of a prism is the length of a perpendicular segment that joins the bases.

Altura de un prisma La altura de un prisma es la longitud de un segmento perpendicular que une a las bases.

Height of a pyramid The height of a pyramid is the length of a segment perpendicular to the base that joins the vertex and the base.

Altura de una pirámide La altura de una pirámide es la longitud de un segmento perpendicular a la base que une al vértice con la base.

Height of a triangle The height of a triangle is the length of the perpendicular segment from a vertex to the base opposite that vertex.

Altura de un triángulo La altura de un triángulo es la longitud del segmento perpendicular desde un vértice hasta la base opuesta a ese vértice.

Hexagon A hexagon is a polygon with six sides.

Hexágono Un hexágono es un polígono de seis lados.

English/Spanish Glossary

Histogram A histogram is a statistical graph that shows the shape of a data set with vertical bars above intervals of values on a number line. The intervals are equal in size and do not overlap. The height of each bar shows the frequency of data within that interval.

Histograma Un histograma es una gráfica de estadísticas que muestra la forma de un conjunto de datos con barras verticales encima de intervalos de valores en una recta numérica. Los intervalos tienen el mismo tamaño y no se superponen. La altura de cada barra muestra la frecuencia de los datos dentro de ese intervalo.

Hundredths One hundredth is one part of 100 equal parts of a whole.

Centésima Una centésima es 1 de las 100 partes iguales de un todo.

Hypotenuse In a right triangle, the longest side, which is opposite the right angle, is the hypotenuse.

Hipotenusa En un triángulo rectángulo, el lado más largo, que es opuesto al ángulo recto, es la hipotenusa.

Identify To identify is to match a definition or description to an object or to recognize something and be able to name it.

Identificar Identificar es unir una definición o una descripción con un objeto, o reconocer algo y poder nombrarlo.

Identity Property of Addition The sum of 0 and any number is that number. For any number n, $n + 0 = n$ and $0 + n = n$.

Propiedad de identidad de la suma La suma de 0 y cualquier número es ese número. Para cualquier número n, $n + 0 = n$ and $0 + n = n$.

Identity Property of Multiplication The product of 1 and any number is that number. For any number n, $n \cdot 1 = n$ and $1 \cdot n = n$.

Propiedad de identidad de la multiplicación El producto de 1 y cualquier número es ese número. Para cualquier número n, $n \cdot 1 = n$ and $1 \cdot n = n$.

Illustrate To illustrate is to show or present information, usually as a drawing or a diagram. You can also illustrate a point using a written explanation.

Ilustrar Ilustrar es mostrar o presentar información, generalmente en forma de dibujo o diagrama. También puedes usar una explicación escrita para ilustrar un punto.

English/Spanish Glossary

Image An image is the result of a transformation of a point, line, or figure.

Imagen Una imagen es el resultado de una transformación de un punto, una recta o una figura.

Improper fraction An improper fraction is a fraction in which the numerator is greater than or equal to its denominator.

Fracción impropia Una fracción impropia es una fracción en la cual el numerador es mayor que o igual a su denominador.

Included angle An included angle is an angle that is between two sides.

Ángulo incluido Un ángulo incluido es un ángulo que está entre dos lados.

Included side An included side is a side that is between two angles.

Lado incluido Un lado incluido es un lado que está entre dos ángulos.

Income Money that a business receives. The money that a person earns from working is also called income.

Ingresos El dinero que un negocio recibe. El dinero que una persona gana de trabajar también es llamado los ingresos.

Income tax Income tax is money collected by the government based on how much you earn.

Impuesto de renta El impuesto de renta es dinero completo por el gobierno basado en cuánto gana.

Independent events Two events are independent events if the occurrence of one event does not affect the probability of the other event.

Eventos independientes Dos eventos son eventos independientes cuando el resultado de un evento no altera la probabilidad del otro.

Independent variable An independent variable is a variable whose value determines the value of another (dependent) variable.

Variable independiente Una variable independiente es una variable cuyo valor determina el valor de otra variable (dependiente).

Indicate To indicate is to point out or show.

Indicar Indicar es señalar o mostrar.

English/Spanish Glossary

Indirect measurement Indirect measurement uses proportions and similar triangles to measure distances that would be difficult to measure directly.

Medición indirecta La medición indirecta usa proporciones y triángulos semejantes para medir distancias que serían difíciles de medir de forma directa.

Inequality An inequality is a mathematical sentence that uses $<$, $\leq$, $>$, $\geq$, or $\neq$ to compare two quantities.

Desigualdad Una desigualdad es una oración matemática que usa $<$, $\leq$, $>$, $\geq$, o $\neq$ para comparar dos cantidades.

Inference An inference is a judgment made by interpreting data.

Inferencia Una inferencia es una opinión que se forma al interpretar datos.

Infinitely many solutions A linear equation in one variable has infinitely many solutions if any value of the variable makes the two sides of the equation equal.

Número infinito de soluciones Una ecuación lineal en una variable tiene un número infinito de soluciones si cualquier valor de la variable hace que los dos lados de la ecuación sean iguales.

Initial value The initial value of a linear function is the value of the output when the input is 0.

Valor inicial El valor inicial de una función lineal es el valor de salida cuando el valor de entrada es 0.

Integers Integers are the set of positive whole numbers, their opposites, and 0.

Enteros Los enteros son el conjunto de los números enteros positivos, sus opuestos y 0.

Interest When you deposit money in a bank account, the bank pays you interest for the right to use your money for a period of time.

Interés Cuando depositas dinero en una cuenta bancaria, el banco te paga un interés por el derecho a usar tu dinero por un período de tiempo.

Interest period The length of time on which compound interest is based. The total number of interest periods that you keep the money in the account is represented by the variable n.

Período de interés La cantidad de tiempo sobre la que se calcula el interés compuesto. El número total de períodos de interés que mantienes el dinero en la cuenta se representa con la variable n.

English/Spanish Glossary

Interest rate Interest is calculated based on a percent of the principal. That percent is called the interest rate (r).

Tasa de interés El interés se calcula con base en un porcentaje del capital. Ese porcentaje se llama tasa de interés, (r).

Interest rate for an interest period The interest rate for an interest period is the annual interest rate divided by the number of interest periods per year.

El tipo de interés por un período de interés El tipo de interés por un período de interés es el tipo de interés anual dividido por el número de períodos de interés por año.

Interquartile range The interquartile range (IQR) is the distance between the first and third quartiles of the data set. It represents the spread of the middle 50% of the data values.

Rango intercuartil El rango intercuartil es la distancia entre el primer y el tercer cuartil del conjunto de datos. Representa la ubicación del 50% del medio de los valores.

Interval An interval is a period of time between two points of time or events.

Intervalo Un intervalo es un período de tiempo entre dos puntos en el tiempo o entre dos sucesos.

Invalid inference An invalid inference is false about the population, or does not follow from the available data. A biased sample can lead to invalid inferences.

Inferencia inválida Una inferencia inválida es una inferencia falsa acerca de una población, o no se deduce a partir de los datos disponibles. Una muestra sesgada puede llevar a inferencias inválidas.

Inverse operations Inverse operations are operations that undo each other.

Operaciones inversas Las operaciones inversas son operaciones que se cancelan entre sí.

Inverse Property of Addition Every number has an additive inverse. The sum of a number and its additive inverse is zero.

Propiedad inversa de la suma Todos los números tienen un inverso de suma. La suma de un número y su inverso de suma es cero.

English/Spanish Glossary

Irrational numbers An irrational number is a number that cannot be written in the form $\frac{a}{b}$, where a and b are integers and $b \neq 0$. In decimal form, an irrational number cannot be written as a terminating or repeating decimal.

Números irracionales Un número irracional es un número que no se puede escribir en la forma $\frac{a}{b}$ donde a y b, son enteros y $b \neq 0$. Los números racionales en forma decimal no son finitos y no son periódicos.

Isolate a variable When solving equations, to isolate a variable means to get a variable with a coefficient of 1 alone on one side of an equation. Use the properties of equality and inverse operations to isolate a variable.

Aislar una variable Cuando resuelves ecuaciones, aislar una variable significa poner una variable con un coeficiente de 1 sola a un lado de la ecuación. Usa las propiedades de igualdad y las operaciones inversas para aislar una variable.

Isosceles triangle An isosceles triangle is a triangle with at least two sides that are the same length.

Triángulo isósceles Un triángulo isósceles es un triángulo que tiene al menos dos lados de la misma longitud.

J

Justify To justify is to support your answer with reasons or examples. A justification may include a written response, diagrams, charts, tables, or a combination of these.

Justificar Justificar es apoyar tu respuesta con razones o ejemplos. Una justificación puede incluir una respuesta escrita, diagramas, tablas o una combinación de esos elementos.

L

Lateral area of a cone The lateral area of a cone is the area of its lateral surface. The formula for the lateral area of a cone is L.A. = $\pi r \ell$, where r represents the radius of the base and ℓ represents the slant height of the cone.

Área lateral de un cono El área lateral de un cono es el área de su superficie lateral. La fórmula del área lateral de un cono es A.L. = $\pi r \ell$, donde r representa el radio de la base y ℓ representa la altura inclinada del cono.

English/Spanish Glossary

Lateral area of a cylinder The lateral area of a cylinder is the area of its lateral surface. The formula for the lateral area of a cylinder is L.A. = $2\pi rh$, where r represents the radius of a base and h represents the height of the cylinder.

Área lateral de un cilindro El área lateral de un cilindro es el área de su superficie lateral. La fórmula del área lateral de un cilindro es A.L. = $2\pi rh$, donde r representa el radio de una base y h representa la altura del cilindro.

Lateral area of a prism The lateral area of a prism is the sum of the areas of the lateral faces of the prism. The formula for the lateral area, L.A., of a prism is L.A. = ph, where p represents the perimeter of the base and h represents the height of the prism.

Área lateral de un prisma El área lateral de un prisma es la suma de las áreas de las caras laterales del prisma. La fórmula del área lateral, A.L., de un prisma es A.L. = ph, donde p representa el perímetro de la base y h representa la altura del prisma.

Lateral area of a pyramid The lateral area of a pyramid is the sum of the areas of the lateral faces of the pyramid. The formula for the lateral area, L.A., of a pyramid is L.A. = $\frac{1}{2}p\ell$ where p represents the perimeter of the base and ℓ represents the slant height of the pyramid.

Área lateral de una pirámide El área lateral de una pirámide es la suma de las áreas de las caras laterales de la pirámide. La fórmula del área lateral, A.L., de una pirámide es A.L. = $\frac{1}{2}p\ell$ donde p representa el perímetro de la base y ℓ representa la altura inclinada de la pirámide.

Lateral face of a prism A lateral face of a prism is a face that joins the bases of the prism.

Cara lateral de un prisma La cara lateral de un prisma es la cara que une a las bases del prisma.

Lateral face of a pyramid A lateral face of a pyramid is a triangular face that joins the base and the vertex.

Cara lateral de una pirámide La cara lateral de una pirámide es una cara lateral que une a la base con el vértice.

Lateral surface of a cone The lateral surface of a cone is the curved surface that is not included in the base.

Superficie lateral de un cono La superficie lateral de un cono es la superficie curva que no está incluida en la base.

English/Spanish Glossary

Lateral surface of a cylinder The lateral surface of a cylinder is the curved surface that is not included in the bases.

Superficie lateral de un cilindro La superficie lateral de un cilindro es la superficie curva que no está incluida en las bases.

Least common multiple The least common multiple (LCM) of two or more numbers is the least multiple shared by all of the numbers.

Mínimo común múltiplo El mínimo común múltiplo (MCM) de dos o más números es el múltiplo menor compartido por todos los números.

Leg of a right triangle In a right triangle, the two shortest sides are legs.

Cateto de un triángulo rectángulo En un triángulo rectángulo, los dos lados más cortos son los catetos.

Less than $<$ The less-than symbol shows a comparison of two numbers with the number of lesser value shown first, or on the left.

Menor que $<$ El símbolo de menor que muestra una comparación de dos números con el número de menor valor que aparece primero, o a la izquierda.

Liability A liability is money that you owe.

Obligación Una obligación es dinero que usted debe.

Lifetime income The amount of money earned over a lifetime of working.

Ingresos para toda la vida La cantidad de dinero ganó sobre una vida de trabajar.

Like terms Terms that have identical variable parts are like terms.

Términos semejantes Los términos que tienen partes variables idénticas son términos semejantes.

Line of reflection A line of reflection is a line across which a figure is reflected.

Eje de reflexión Un eje de reflexión es una línea a través de la cual se refleja una figura.

Linear equation An equation is a linear equation if the graph of all of its solutions is a line.

Ecuación lineal Una ecuación es lineal si la gráfica de todas sus soluciones es una línea recta.

English/Spanish Glossary

Linear function A linear function is a function whose graph is a straight line. The rate of change for a linear function is constant.

Función lineal Una función lineal es una función cuya gráfica es una línea recta. La tasa de cambio en una función lineal es constante.

Linear function rule A linear function rule is an equation that describes a linear function.

Regla de la función lineal La ecuación que describe una función lineal es la regla de la función lineal.

Loan A loan is an amount of money borrowed for a period of time with the promise of paying it back.

Préstamo Un préstamo es una cantidad de dinero pedido prestaddo por un espacio de tiempo con la promesa de pagarlo apoya.

Loan length Loan length is the period of time set to repay a loan.

Preste longitud La longitud del préstamo es el conjunto de espacio de tiempo de devolver un préstamo.

Loan term The term of a loan is the period of time set to repay the loan.

Preste término El término de un préstamo es el conjunto de espacio de tiempo de devolver el préstamo.

Locate To locate is to find or identify a value, usually on a number line or coordinate graph.

Ubicar Ubicar es hallar o identificar un valor, generalmente en una recta numérica o en una gráfica de coordenadas.

Loss When a business's expenses are greater than the business's income, there is a loss.

Pérdida Cuando los gastos de un negocio son más que los ingresos del negocio, hay una pérdida.

English/Spanish Glossary

M

Mapping diagram A mapping diagram describes a relation by linking the input values to the corresponding output values using arrows.

Diagrama de correspondencia Un diagrama de correspondencia describe una relación uniendo con flechas los valores de entrada con sus correspondientes valores de salida.

Markdown Markdown is the amount of decrease from the selling price to the sale price. The markdown as a percent decrease of the original selling price is called the percent markdown.

Rebaja La rebaja es la cantidad de disminución de un precio de venta a un precio rebajado. La rebaja como una disminución porcentual del precio de venta original se llama porcentaje de rebaja.

Markup Markup is the amount of increase from the cost to the selling price. The markup as a percent increase of the original cost is called the percent markup.

Margen de ganancia El margen de ganancia es la cantidad de aumento del costo al precio de venta. El margen de ganancia como un aumento porcentual del costo original se llama porcentaje del margen de ganancia.

Mean The mean represents the center of a numerical data set. To find the mean, sum the data values and then divide by the number of values in the data set.

Media La media representa el centro de un conjunto de datos numéricos. Para hallar la media, suma los valores y luego divide por el número de valores del conjunto de datos.

Mean absolute deviation The mean absolute deviation is a measure of variability that describes how much the data values are spread out from the mean of a data set. The mean absolute deviation is the average distance that the data values are spread around the mean.

$$\text{mean absolute deviation} = \frac{\text{sum of the absolute deviations of the data values}}{\text{total number of data values}}$$

Desviación absoluta media La desviación absoluta media es una medida de variabilidad que describe cuánto se alejan los valores de la media de un conjunto de datos. La desviación absoluta media es la distancia promedio que los valores se alejan de la media.

$$\text{desviación absoluta media} = \frac{\text{suma de las desviaciones absolutas de los valores}}{\text{número total de valores}}$$

English/Spanish Glossary

Measure of variability A measure of variability describes the spread of values in a data set. There may be more than one measure of variability for a data set.

Medida de variabilidad Una medida de variabilidad describe la distribución de los valores de un conjunto de datos. Puede haber más de una medida de variabilidad para un conjunto de datos.

Measurement data Measurement data consist of data that are measures.

Datos de mediciones Los datos de mediciones son datos que son medidas.

Measures of center A measure of center is a value that represents the middle of a data set. There may be more than one measure of center for a data set.

Medida de tendencia central Una medida de tendencia central es un valor que representa el centro de un conjunto de datos. Puede haber más de una medida de tendencia central para un conjunto de datos.

Median The median represents the center of a numerical data set. For an odd number of data values, the median is the middle value when the data values are arranged in numerical order. For an even number of data values, the median is the average of the two middle values when the data values are arranged in numerical order.

Mediana La mediana representa el centro de un conjunto de datos numéricos. Para un número impar de valores, la mediana es el valor del medio cuando los valores están organizados en orden numérico. Para un número par de valores, la mediana es el promedio de los dos valores del medio cuando los valores están organizados en orden numérico.

Median-median line The median-median line, or median trend line, is a method of finding a fit line for a scatter plot that suggests a linear association. This method involves dividing the data into three subgroups and using medians to find a summary point for each subgroup. The summary points are used to find the equation of the fit line.

Recta mediana-mediana La recta mediana-mediana es un método que se usa para hallar una línea de ajuste para un diagrama de dispersión que sugiere una asociación lineal. Este método implica dividir los datos en tres subgrupos y usar medianas para hallar un punto medio para cada subgrupo. Los puntos medios se usan para hallar la ecuación de la línea de ajuste.

Million Whole numbers in the millions have 7, 8, or 9 digits.

Millón Los números enteros no negativos que están en los millones tienen 7, 8 ó 9 dígitos.

English/Spanish Glossary

Mixed number A mixed number combines a whole number and a fraction.

Número mixto Un número mixto combina un número entero no negativo con una fracción.

Mode The item, or items, in a data set that occurs most frequently.

Modo El artículo, o los artículos, en un conjunto de datos que ocurre normalmente.

Model To model is to represent a situation using pictures, diagrams, or number sentences.

Demostrar Demostrar es usar ilustraciones, diagramas o enunciados numéricos para representar una situación.

Monetary incentive A monetary incentive is an offer that might encourage customers to buy a product.

Estímulo monetario Un estímulo monetario es una oferta que quizás favorezca a clientes para comprar un producto.

Multiple A multiple of a number is the product of the number and a whole number.

Múltiplo El múltiplo de un número es el producto del número y un número entero no negativo.

N

Natural numbers The natural numbers are the counting numbers.

Números naturales Los números naturales son los números que se usan para contar.

Negative exponent property For every nonzero number a and integer n, $a^{-n} = \frac{1}{a^n}$.

Propiedad del exponente negativo Para todo número distinto de cero a y entero n, $a^{-n} = \frac{1}{a^n}$.

Negative numbers Negative numbers are numbers less than zero.

Números negativos Los números negativos son números menores que cero.

English/Spanish Glossary

Net A net is a two-dimensional pattern that you can fold to form a three-dimensional figure. A net of a figure shows all of the surfaces of that figure in one view.

Modelo plano Un modelo plano es un diseño bidimensional que puedes doblar para formar una figura tridimensional. Un modelo plano de una figura muestra todas las superficies de la figura en una vista.

Net worth Net worth is the total value of all assets minus the total value of all liabilities.

Patrimonio neto El patrimonio neto es el valor total de todas las ventajas menos el valor total de todas las obligaciones.

Net worth statement Net worth is the total value of all assets minus the total value of all liabilities.

Declaración de patrimonio neto El patrimonio neto es el valor total de todas las ventajas menos el valor total de todas las obligaciones.

No solution A linear equation in one variable has no solution if no value of the variable makes the two sides of the equation equal.

Sin solución Una ecuación lineal en una variable no tiene solución si ningún valor de la variable hace que los dos lados de la ecuación sean iguales.

Nonlinear function A nonlinear function is a function that does not have a constant rate of change.

Función no lineal Una función no lineal es una función que no tiene una tasa de cambio constante.

Numerator The numerator is the number above the fraction bar in a fraction.

Numerador El numerador es el número que está arriba de la barra de fracción en una fracción.

Numerical expression A numerical expression is a mathematical phrase that consists of numbers and operation symbols.

Expresión numérica Una expresión numérica es una frase matemática que contiene números y símbolos de operaciones.

English/Spanish Glossary

O

Obtuse angle An obtuse angle is an angle with a measure greater than 90° and less than 180°.

Ángulo obtuso Un ángulo obtuso es un ángulo con una medida mayor que 90° y menor que 180°.

Obtuse triangle An obtuse triangle is a triangle with one obtuse angle.

Triángulo obtusángulo Un triángulo obtusángulo es un triángulo que tiene un ángulo obtuso.

Octagon An octagon is a polygon with eight sides.

Octágono Un octágono es un polígono de ocho lados.

Online payment system An online payment system allows money to be exchanged electronically between buyer and seller, usually using credit card or bank account information.

Sistema en línea de pago Un sistema en línea del pago permite dinero para ser cambiado electrónicamente entre comprador y vendedor, utilizando generalmente información de tarjeta de crédito o cuenta bancaria.

Open sentence An open sentence is an equation with one or more variables.

Enunciado abierto Un enunciado abierto es una ecuación con una o más variables.

Opposites Opposites are two numbers that are the same distance from 0 on a number line, but in opposite directions.

Opuestos Los opuestos son dos números que están a la misma distancia de 0 en la recta numérica, pero en direcciones opuestas.

Order of operations The order of operations is the order in which operations should be performed in an expression. Operations inside parentheses are done first, followed by exponents. Then, multiplication and division are done in order from left to right, and finally addition and subtraction are done in order from left to right.

Orden de las operaciones El orden de las operaciones es el orden en el que se deben resolver las operaciones de una expresión. Las operaciones que están entre paréntesis se resuelven primero, seguidas de los exponentes. Luego, se multiplica y se divide en orden de izquierda a derecha, y finalmente se suma y se resta en orden de izquierda a derecha.

English/Spanish Glossary

Ordered pair An ordered pair identifies the location of a point in the coordinate plane. The *x*-coordinate shows a point's position left or right of the *y*-axis. The *y*-coordinate shows a point's position up or down from the *x*-axis.

Par ordenado Un par ordenado identifica la ubicación de un punto en el plano de coordenadas. La coordenada *x* muestra la posición de un punto a la izquierda o a la derecha del eje de las *y*. La coordenada *y* muestra la posición de un punto arriba o abajo del eje de las *x*.

Origin The origin is the point of intersection of the *x*- and *y*-axes on a coordinate plane.

Origen El origen es el punto de intersección del eje de las *x* y el eje de las *y* en un plano de coordenadas.

Outcome An outcome is a possible result of an action.

Resultado Un resultado es un desenlace posible de una acción.

Outlier An outlier is a piece of data that doesn't seem to fit with the rest of a data set.

Valor extremo Un valor extremo es un valor que parece no ajustarse al resto de los datos de un conjunto.

P

Parallel lines Parallel lines are lines in the same plane that never intersect.

Rectas paralelas Las rectas paralelas son rectas que están en el mismo plano y nunca se intersecan.

Parallelogram A parallelogram is a quadrilateral with both pairs of opposite sides parallel.

Paralelogramo Un paralelogramo es un cuadrilátero en el cual los dos pares de lados opuestos son paralelos.

Partial product A partial product is part of the total product. A product is the sum of the partial products.

Producto parcial Un producto parcial es una parte del producto total. Un producto es la suma de los productos parciales.

English/Spanish Glossary

Pay period Wages for many jobs are paid at regular intervals, such a weekly, biweekly, semimonthly, or monthly. The interval of time is called a pay period.

Pague el período Los sueldos para muchos trabajos son pagados con regularidad, tal semanal, quincenal, quincenal, o mensual. El intervalo de tiempo es llamado un período de la paga.

Payroll deductions Your employer can deduct your income taxes from your wages before you receive your paycheck. The amounts deducted are called payroll deductions.

Deducciones de nómina Su empleador puede descontar sus impuestos de renta de sus sueldos antes que reciba su cheque de pago. Las cantidades descontadas son llamadas nómina deducciones.

Percent A percent is a ratio that compares a number to 100.

Porcentaje Un porcentaje es una razón que compara un número con 100.

Percent bar graph A percent bar graph is a bar graph that shows each category as a percent of the total number of data items.

Gráfico de barras de por ciento Un gráfico de barras del por ciento es un gráfico de barras que muestra cada categoría como un por ciento del número total de artículos de datos.

Percent decrease When a quantity decreases, the percent of change is called a percent decrease. percent decrease =

$$\frac{\text{amount of decrease}}{\text{original quantity}}$$

Disminución porcentual Cuando una cantidad disminuye, el porcentaje de cambio se llama disminución porcentual. disminución porcentual =

$$\frac{\text{cantidad de disminución}}{\text{cantidad original}}$$

Percent equation The percent equation describes the relationship between a part and a whole. You can use the percent equation to solve percent problems. part = percent · whole

Ecuación de porcentaje La ecuación de porcentaje describe la relación entre una parte y un todo. Puedes usar la ecuación de porcentaje para resolver problemas de porcentaje. parte = por ciento · todo

Percent error Percent error describes the accuracy of a measured or estimated value compared to an actual or accepted value.

Error porcentual El error porcentual describe la exactitud de un valor medido o estimado en comparación con un valor real o aceptado.

English/Spanish Glossary

Percent increase When a quantity increases, the percent of change is called a percent increase.

Aumento porcentual Cuando una cantidad aumenta, el porcentaje de cambio se llama aumento porcentual.

Percent of change Percent of change is the percent something increases or decreases from its original measure or amount. You can find the percent of change by using the equation: percent of change $= \dfrac{\text{amount of change}}{\text{original quantity}}$

Porcentaje de cambio El porcentaje de cambio es el porcentaje en que algo aumenta o disminuye en relación a la medida o cantidad original. Puedes hallar el porcentaje de cambio con la siguiente ecuación: porcentaje de cambio $= \dfrac{\text{cantidad de cambio}}{\text{cantidad original}}$

Perfect cube A perfect cube is the cube of an integer.

Cubo perfecto Un cubo perfecto es el cubo de un entero.

Perfect square A perfect square is a number that is the square of an integer.

Cuadrado perfecto Un cuadrado perfecto es un número que es el cuadrado de un entero.

Perimeter Perimeter is the distance around a figure.

Perímetro El perímetro es la distancia alrededor de una figura.

Period A period is a group of 3 digits in a number. Periods are separated by a comma and start from the right of a number.

Período Un período es un grupo de 3 dígitos en un número. Los períodos están separados por una coma y empiezan a la derecha del número.

Periodic savings plan A periodic savings plan is a method of saving that involves making deposits on a regular basis.

Plan de ahorros periódico Un plan de ahorros periódico es un método de guardar que implica depósitos que hace con regularidad.

Perpendicular lines Perpendicular lines intersect to form right angles.

Rectas perpendiculares Las rectas perpendiculares se intersecan para formar ángulos rectos.

English/Spanish Glossary

Pi Pi (π) is the ratio of a circle's circumference, *C*, to its diameter, *d*.

Pi Pi (π) es la razón de la circunferencia de un círculo, *C*, a su diámetro, *d*.

Place value Place value is the value given to an individual digit based on its position within a number.

Valor posicional El valor posicional es el valor asignado a determinado dígito según su posición en un número.

Plane A plane is a flat surface that extends indefinitely in all directions.

Plano Un plano es una superficie plana que se extiende indefinidamente en todas direcciones.

Polygon A polygon is a closed figure formed by three or more line segments that do not cross.

Polígono Un polígono es una figura cerrada compuesta por tres o más segmentos que no se cruzan.

Population A population is the complete set of items being studied.

Población Una población es todo el conjunto de elementos que se estudian.

Positive numbers Positive numbers are numbers greater than zero.

Números positivos Los números positivos son números mayores que cero.

Power A power is a number expressed using an exponent.

Potencia Una potencia es un número expresado con un exponente.

Predict To predict is to make an educated guess based on the analysis of real data.

Predecir Predecir es hacer una estimación informada según el análisis de datos reales.

Prime factorization The prime factorization of a composite number is the expression of the number as a product of its prime factors.

Descomposición en factores primos La descomposición en factores primos de un número compuesto es la expresión del número como un producto de sus factores primos.

English/Spanish Glossary

Prime number A prime number is a whole number greater than 1 with exactly two factors, 1 and the number itself.

Número primo Un número primo es un número entero mayor que 1 con exactamente dos factores, 1 y el número mismo.

Principal The original amount of money deposited or borrowed in an account.

Capital La cantidad original de dinero que se deposita o se pide prestada en una cuenta.

Prism A prism is a three-dimensional figure with two parallel polygonal faces that are the same size and shape.

Prisma Un prisma es una figura tridimensional con dos caras poligonales paralelas que tienen el mismo tamaño y la misma forma.

Probability model A probability model consists of an action, its sample space, and a list of events with their probabilities. The events and probabilities in the list have these characteristics: each outcome in the sample space is in exactly one event, and the sum of all of the probabilities must be 1.

Modelo de probabilidad Un modelo de probabilidad consiste en una acción, su espacio muestral y una lista de eventos con sus probabilidades. Los eventos y las probabilidades de la lista tienen estas características: cada resultado del espacio muestral está exactamente en un evento, y la suma de todas las probabilidades debe ser 1.

Probability of an event The probability of an event is a number from 0 to 1 that measures the likelihood that the event will occur. The closer the probability is to 0, the less likely it is that the event will happen. The closer the probability is to 1, the more likely it is that the event will happen. You can express probability as a fraction, decimal, or percent.

Probabilidad de un evento La probabilidad de un evento es un número de 0 a 1 que mide la probabilidad de que suceda el evento. Cuanto más se acerca la probabilidad a 0, menos probable es que suceda el evento. Cuanto más se acerca la probabilidad a 1, más probable es que suceda el evento. Puedes expresar la probabilidad como una fracción, un decimal o un porcentaje.

Product A product is the value of a multiplication or an expression showing multiplication.

Producto Un producto es el valor de una multiplicación o una expresión que representa la multiplicación.

English/Spanish Glossary

Profit When a business's expenses are less than the business's income, there is a profit.

Ganancia Cuando los gastos de un negocio son menos que los ingresos del negocio, hay una ganancia.

Proof A proof is a logical, deductive argument in which every statement of fact is supported by a reason.

Comprobación Una comprobación es un argumento lógico y deductivo en el que cada enunciado de un hecho está apoyado por una razón.

Proper fraction A proper fraction has a numerator that is less than its denominator.

Fracción propia Una fracción propia tiene un numerador que es menor que su denominador.

Proportion A proportion is an equation stating that two ratios are equal.

Proporción Una proporción es una ecuación que establece que dos razones son iguales.

Proportional relationship Two quantities *x* and *y* have a proportional relationship if *y* is always a constant multiple of *x*. A relationship is proportional if it can be described by equivalent ratios.

Relación de proporción Dos cantidades *x* y *y* tienen una relación de proporción si *y* es siempre un múltiplo constante de *x*. Una relación es de proporción si se puede describir con razones equivalentes.

Pyramid A pyramid is a three-dimensional figure with a base that is a polygon and triangular faces that meet at a vertex. A pyramid is named for the shape of its base.

Pirámide Una pirámide es una figura tridimensional con una base que es un polígono y caras triangulares que se unen en un vértice. El nombre de la pirámide depende de la forma de su base.

English/Spanish Glossary

Pythagorean Theorem In any right triangle, the sum of the squares of the lengths of the legs equals the square of the length of the hypotenuse. If a triangle is a right triangle, then $a^2 + b^2 = c^2$, where a and b represent the lengths of the legs, and c represents the length of the hypotenuse.

Teorema de Pitágoras En cualquier triángulo rectángulo, la suma del cuadrado de la longitud de los catetos es igual al cuadrado de la longitud de la hipotenusa. Si un triángulo es un triángulo rectángulo, entonces $a^2 + b^2 = c^2$, donde a y b representan la longitud de los catetos, y c representa la longitud de la hipotenusa.

Q

Quadrant The x- and y-axes divide the coordinate plane into four regions called quadrants.

Cuadrante Los ejes de las x y de las y dividen el plano de coordenadas en cuatro regiones llamadas cuadrantes.

Quadrilateral A quadrilateral is a polygon with four sides.

Cuadrilátero Un cuadrilátero es un polígono de cuatro lados.

Quarter circle A quarter circle is one fourth of a circle.

Círculo cuarto Un círculo cuarto es la cuarta parte de un círculo.

Quartile The quartiles of a data set divide the data set into four parts with the same number of data values in each part.

Cuartil Los cuartiles de un conjunto de datos dividen el conjunto de datos en cuatro partes que tienen el mismo número de valores cada una.

Quotient The quotient is the answer to a division problem. When there is a remainder, "quotient" sometimes refers to the whole-number portion of the answer.

Cociente El cociente es el resultado de una división. Cuando queda un residuo, "cociente" a veces se refiere a la parte de la solución que es un número entero.

English/Spanish Glossary

Radius A radius of a circle is a segment that has one endpoint at the center and the other endpoint on the circle. The term radius can also mean the length of this segment.

Radio Un radio de un círculo es un segmento que tiene un extremo en el centro y el otro extremo en el círculo. El término radio también puede referirse a la longitud de este segmento.

Radius of a sphere The radius of a sphere, *r*, is a segment that has one endpoint at the center and the other endpoint on the sphere.

Radio de una esfera El radio de una esfera, *r*, es un segmento que tiene un extremo en el centro y el otro extremo en la esfera.

Random sample In a random sample, each member in the population has an equal chance of being selected.

Muestra aleatoria En una muestra aleatoria, cada miembro en la población tiene una oportunidad igual de ser seleccionado.

Range The range is a measure of variability of a numerical data set. The range of a data set is the difference between the greatest and least values in a data set.

Rango El rango es una medida de la variabilidad de un conjunto de datos numéricos. El rango de un conjunto de datos es la diferencia que existe entre el mayor y el menor valor del conjunto.

Rate A rate is a ratio involving two quantities measured in different units.

Tasa Una tasa es una razón que relaciona dos cantidades medidas con unidades diferentes.

Rate of change The rate of change of a linear function is the ratio $\frac{\text{vertical change}}{\text{horizontal change}}$ between any two points on the graph of the function.

Tasa de cambio La tasa de cambio de una función lineal es la razón del $\frac{\text{cambio vertical}}{\text{cambio horizontal}}$ que existe entre dos puntos cualesquiera de la gráfica de la función.

Ratio A ratio is a relationship in which for every *x* units of one quantity there are *y* units of another quantity.

Razón Una razón es una relación en la cual por cada *x* unidades de una cantidad hay *y* unidades de otra cantidad.

English/Spanish Glossary

Rational numbers A rational number is a number that can be written in the form $\frac{a}{b}$ or $-\frac{a}{b}$, where a is a whole number and b is a positive whole number. The rational numbers include the integers.

Números racionales Un número racional es un número que se puede escribir como $\frac{a}{b}$ or $-\frac{a}{b}$, donde a es un número entero no negativo y b es un número entero positivo. Los números racionales incluyen los enteros.

Real numbers The real numbers are the set of rational and irrational numbers.

Números reales Los números reales son el conjunto de los números racionales e irracionales.

Reason To reason is to think through a problem using facts and information.

Razonar Razonar es usar hechos e información para estudiar detenidamente un problema.

Rebate A rebate returns part of the purchase price of an item after the buyer provides proof of purchase through a mail-in or online form.

Reembolso Un reembolso regresa la parte del precio de compra de un artículo después de que el comprador proporcione comprobante de compra por un correo-en o forma en línea.

Recall To recall is to remember a fact quickly.

Recordar Recordar es traer a la memoria un hecho rápidamente.

Reciprocals Two numbers are reciprocals if their product is 1. If a nonzero number is named as a fraction, $\frac{a}{b}$, then its reciprocal is $\frac{b}{a}$.

Recíprocos Dos números son recíprocos si su producto es 1. Si un número distinto de cero se expresa como una fracción, $\frac{a}{b}$, entonces su recíproco es $\frac{b}{a}$.

Rectangle A rectangle is a quadrilateral with four right angles.

Rectángulo Un rectángulo es un cuadrilátero que tiene cuatro ángulos rectos.

Rectangular prism A rectangular prism is a prism with bases in the shape of a rectangle.

Prisma rectangular Un prisma rectangular es un prisma cuyas bases tienen la forma de un rectángulo.

English/Spanish Glossary

Reduction A reduction is a dilation with a scale factor less than 1. After a reduction, the image is smaller than the original figure.

Reducción Una reducción es una dilatación con un factor de escala menor que 1. Después de una reducción, la imagen es más pequeña que la figura original.

Reflection A reflection, or flip, is a transformation that flips a figure across a line of reflection.

Reflexión Una reflexión, o inversión, es una transformación que invierte una figura a través de un eje de reflexión.

Regular polygon A regular polygon is a polygon with all sides of equal length and all angles of equal measure.

Polígono regular Un polígono regular es un polígono que tiene todos los lados de la misma longitud y todos los ángulos de la misma medida.

Relate To relate two different things, find a connection between them.

Relacionar Para relacionar dos cosas diferentes, halla una conexión entre ellas.

Relation Any set of ordered pairs is called a relation.

Relación Todo conjunto de pares ordenados se llama relación.

Relative frequency relative frequency

of an event = $\dfrac{\text{number of times event occurs}}{\text{total number of trials}}$

Frecuencia relativa frecuencia relativa de un evento =

$\dfrac{\text{número de veces que sucede el evento}}{\text{número total de pruebas}}$

Relative frequency table A relative frequency table shows the ratio of the number of data in each category to the total number of data items. The ratio can be expressed as a fraction, decimal, or percent.

Mesa relativa de frecuencia Una mesa relativa de la frecuencia muestra la proporción del número de datos en cada categoría al número total de artículos de datos. La proporción puede ser expresada como una fracción, el decimal, o el por ciento.

Remainder In division, the remainder is the number that is left after the division is complete.

Residuo En una división, el residuo es el número que queda después de terminar la operación.

English/Spanish Glossary

Remote interior angles Remote interior angles are the two nonadjacent interior angles corresponding to each exterior angle of a triangle.

Ángulos internos no adyacentes Los ángulos internos no adyacentes son los dos ángulos internos de un triángulo que se corresponden con el ángulo externo que está más alejado de ellos.

Repeating decimal A repeating decimal has a decimal expansion that repeats the same digit, or block of digits, without end.

Decimal periódico Un decimal periódico tiene una expansión decimal que repite el mismo dígito, o grupo de dígitos, sin fin.

Represent To represent is to stand for or take the place of something else. Symbols, equations, charts, and tables are often used to represent particular situations.

Representar Representar es sustituir u ocupar el lugar de otra cosa. A menudo se usan símbolos, ecuaciones y tablas para representar determinadas situaciones.

Representative sample A representative sample is a sample of a population in which the number of subjects in the sample with the trait that you are studying is proportional to the number of members in the population with that trait. A representative sample accurately represents the population and does not have bias.

Muestra representativa Una muestra representativa es una muestra de una población en la que el número de sujetos de la muestra que tiene la característica que se estudia es proporcional al número de miembros de la población que tienen esa característica. Una muestra representativa representa la población con exactitud y no está sesgada.

Rhombus A rhombus is a parallelogram whose sides are all the same length.

Rombo Un rombo es un paralelogramo que tiene todos sus lados de la misma longitud.

Right angle A right angle is an angle with a measure of 90°.

Ángulo recto Un ángulo recto es un ángulo que mide 90°.

Right cone A right cone is a cone in which the segment representing the height connects the vertex and the center of the base.

Cono recto Un cono recto es un cono en el que el segmento que representa la altura une el vértice y el centro de la base.

English/Spanish Glossary

Right cylinder A right cylinder is a cylinder in which the height joins the centers of the bases.

Cilindro recto Un cilindro recto es un cilindro en el que la altura une los centros de las bases.

Right prism In a right prism, all lateral faces are rectangles.

Prisma recto En un prisma recto, todas las caras laterales son rectángulos.

Right pyramid In a right pyramid, the segment that represents the height intersects the base at its center.

Pirámide recta En una pirámide recta, el segmento que representa la altura interseca la base en el centro.

Right triangle A right triangle is a triangle with one right angle.

Triángulo rectángulo Un triángulo rectángulo es un triángulo que tiene un ángulo recto.

Rigid motion A rigid motion is a transformation that changes only the position of a figure.

Movimiento rígido Un movimiento rígido es una transformación que sólo cambia la posición de una figura.

Rotation A rotation is a rigid motion that turns a figure around a fixed point, called the center of rotation.

Rotación Una rotación es un movimiento rígido que hace girar una figura alrededor de un punto fijo, llamado centro de rotación.

Rounding Rounding a number means replacing the number with a number that tells about how much or how many.

Redondear Redondear un número significa reemplazar ese número por un número que indica más o menos cuánto o cuántos.

S

Sale A sale is a discount offered by a store. A sale does not require the customer to have a coupon.

Venta Una venta es un descuento ofreció por una tienda. Una venta no requiere al cliente a tener un cupón.

English/Spanish Glossary

Sales tax A tax added to the price of goods and services.

Las ventas tasan Un impuesto añadió al precio de bienes y servicios.

Sample of a population A sample of a population is part of the population. A sample is useful when you want to find out about a population but you do not have the resources to study every member of the population.

Muestra de una población Una muestra de una población es una parte de la población. Una muestra es útil cuando quieres saber algo acerca de una población, pero no tienes los recursos para estudiar a cada miembro de esa población.

Sample space The sample space for an action is the set of all possible outcomes of that action.

Espacio muestral El espacio muestral de una acción es el conjunto de todos los resultados posibles de esa acción.

Sampling method A sampling method is the method by which you choose members of a population to sample.

Método de muestreo Un método de muestreo es el método por el cual escoges miembros de una población para muestrear.

Savings Savings is money that a person puts away for use at a later date.

Ahorros Los ahorros son dinero que una persona guarda para el uso en una fecha posterior.

Scale A scale is a ratio that compares a length in a scale drawing to the corresponding length in the actual object.

Escala Una escala es una razón que compara una longitud en un dibujo a escala con la longitud correspondiente en el objeto real.

Scale drawing A scale drawing is an enlarged or reduced drawing of an object that is proportional to the actual object.

Dibujo a escala Un dibujo a escala es un dibujo ampliado o reducido de un objeto que es proporcional al objeto real.

English/Spanish Glossary

Scale factor The scale factor is the ratio of a length in the image to the corresponding length in the original figure.

Factor de escala El factor de escala es la razón de una longitud de la imagen a la longitud correspondiente en la figura original.

Scalene triangle A scalene triangle is a triangle in which no sides have the same length.

Triángulo escaleno Un triángulo escaleno es un triángulo que no tiene lados de la misma longitud.

Scatter plot A scatter plot is a graph that uses points to display the relationship between two different sets of data. Each point can be represented by an ordered pair.

Diagrama de dispersión Un diagrama de dispersión es una gráfica que usa puntos para mostrar la relación entre dos conjuntos de datos diferentes. Cada punto se puede representar con un par ordenado.

Scholarship A type of monetary award a student can use to pay for his or her education. The student does not need to repay this money.

Beca Un tipo de premio monetario que un estudiante puede utilizar para pagar por su educación. El estudiante no debe devolver este dinero.

Scientific notation A number in scientific notation is written as the product of two factors, one greater than or equal to 1 and less than 10, and the other a power of 10.

Notación científica Un número en notación científica está escrito como el producto de dos factores, uno mayor que o igual a 1 y menor que 10, y el otro una potencia de 10.

Segment A segment is part of a line. It consists of two endpoints and all of the points on the line between the endpoints.

Segmento Un segmento es una parte de una recta. Está formado por dos extremos y todos los puntos de la recta que están entre los extremos.

Semicircle A semicircle is one half of a circle.

Semicírculo Un semicírculo es la mitad de un círculo.

English/Spanish Glossary

Similar figures A two-dimensional figure is similar (~) to another two-dimensional figure if you can map one figure to the other by a sequence of rotations, reflections, translations, and dilations.

Figuras semejantes Una figura bidimensional es semejante (~) a otra figura bidimensional si puedes hacer corresponder una figura con otra mediante una secuencia de rotaciones, reflexiones, traslaciones y dilataciones.

Simple interest Simple interest is interest paid only on an original deposit. To calculate simple interest, use the formula $I = prt$ where I is the simple interest, p is the principal, r is the annual interest rate, and t is the number of years that the account earns interest.

Interés simple El interés simple es el interés que se paga sobre un depósito original solamente. Para calcular el interés simple, usa la fórmula $I = crt$ donde I es el interés simple, c es el capital, r es la tasa de interés anual y t es el número de años en que la cuenta obtiene un interés.

Simple random sampling Simple random sampling is a sampling method in which every member of the population has an equal chance of being chosen for the sample.

Muestreo aleatorio simple El muestreo aleatorio simple es un método de muestreo en el que cada miembro de la población tiene la misma probabilidad de ser seleccionado para la muestra.

Simpler form A fraction is in simpler form when it is equivalent to a given fraction and has smaller numbers in the numerator and denominator.

Forma simplificada Una fracción está en su forma simplificada cuando es equivalente a otra fracción dada, pero tiene números más pequeños en el numerador y el denominador.

Simplest form A fraction is in simplest form when the only common factor of the numerator and denominator is one.

Mínima expresión Una fracción está en su mínima expresión cuando el único factor común del numerador y el denominador es 1.

Simplify an algebraic expression To simplify an algebraic expression, combine the like terms of the expression.

Simplificar una expresión algebraica Para simplificar una expresión algebraica, combina los términos semejantes de la expresión.

English/Spanish Glossary

Simulation A simulation is a model of a real-world situation that is used to find probabilities.

Simulación Una simulación es un modelo de una situación de la vida diaria que se usa para hallar probabilidades.

Sketch To sketch a figure, draw a rough outline. When a sketch is asked for, it means that a drawing needs to be included in your response.

Bosquejo Para hacer un bosquejo, dibuja un esquema simple. Si se pide un bosquejo, tu respuesta debe incluir un dibujo.

Slant height of a cone The slant height of a cone, ℓ, is the length of its lateral surface from base to vertex.

Altura inclinada de un cono La altura inclinada de un cono, ℓ, es la longitud de su superficie lateral desde la base hasta el vértice.

Slant height of a pyramid The slant height of a pyramid is the height of a lateral face.

Altura inclinada de una pirámide La altura inclinada de una pirámide es la altura de una cara lateral.

Slope Slope is a ratio that describes steepness.

$$\text{slope} = \frac{\text{vertical change}}{\text{horizontal change}} = \frac{\text{rise}}{\text{run}}$$

Pendiente La pendiente es una razón que describe la inclinación.

$$\text{pendiente} = \frac{\text{cambio vertical}}{\text{cambio horizontal}}$$
$$= \frac{\text{distancia vertical}}{\text{distancia horizontal}}$$

Slope of a line slope =

$$\frac{\text{change in } y\text{-coordinates}}{\text{change in } x\text{-coordinates}} = \frac{\text{rise}}{\text{run}}$$

Pendiente de una recta pendiente =

$$\frac{\text{cambio en las coordenadas } y}{\text{cambio en las coordenadas } x}$$
$$= \frac{\text{distancia vertical}}{\text{distancia horizontal}}$$

Slope-intercept form An equation written in the form $y = mx + b$ is in slope-intercept form. The graph is a line with slope m and y-intercept b.

Forma pendiente-intercepto Una ecuación escrita en la forma $y = mx + b$ está en forma de pendiente-intercepto. La gráfica es una línea recta con pendiente m e intercepto en y b.

English/Spanish Glossary

Solution of a system of linear equations A solution of a system of linear equations is any ordered pair that makes all the equations of that system true.

Solución de un sistema de ecuaciones lineales Una solución de un sistema de ecuaciones lineales es cualquier par ordenado que hace que todas las ecuaciones de ese sistema sean verdaderas.

Solution of an equation A solution of an equation is a value of the variable that makes the equation true.

Solución de una ecuación Una solución de una ecuación es un valor de la variable que hace que la ecuación sea verdadera.

Solution of an inequality The solutions of an inequality are the values of the variable that make the inequality true.

Solución de una desigualdad Las soluciones de una desigualdad son los valores de la variable que hacen que la desigualdad sea verdadera.

Solution set A solution set contains all of the numbers that satisfy an equation or inequality.

Conjunto solución Un conjunto solución contiene todos los números que satisfacen una ecuación o desigualdad.

Solve To solve a given statement, determine the value or values that make the statement true. Several methods and strategies can be used to solve a problem, including estimating, isolating the variable, drawing a graph, or using a table of values.

Resolver Para resolver un enunciado dado, determina el valor o los valores que hacen que ese enunciado sea verdadero. Para resolver un problema se pueden usar varios métodos y estrategias, como estimar, aislar la variable, dibujar una gráfica o usar una tabla de valores.

Sphere A sphere is the set of all points in space that are the same distance from a center point.

Esfera Una esfera es el conjunto de todos los puntos en el espacio que están a la misma distancia de un punto central.

Square A square is a quadrilateral with four right angles and all sides the same length.

Cuadrado Un cuadrado es un cuadrilátero que tiene cuatro ángulos rectos y todos los lados de la misma longitud.

English/Spanish Glossary

Square root A square root of a number is a number that, when multiplied by itself, equals the original number.

Raíz cuadrada La raíz cuadrada de un número es un número que, cuando se multiplica por sí mismo, es igual al número original.

Square unit A square unit is the area of a square that has sides that are 1 unit long.

Unidad cuadrada Una unidad cuadrada es el área de un cuadrado en el que cada lado mide 1 unidad de longitud.

Standard form A number written using digits and place value is in standard form.

Forma estándar Un número escrito con dígitos y valor posicional está escrito en forma estándar.

Statistical question A statistical question is a question that investigates an aspect of the real world and can have variety in the responses.

Pregunta estadística Una pregunta estadística es una pregunta que investiga un aspecto de la vida diaria y puede tener varias respuestas.

Statistics Statistics is the study of collecting, organizing, graphing, and analyzing data to draw conclusions about the real world.

Estadística La estadística es el estudio de la recolección, organización, representación gráfica y análisis de datos para sacar conclusiones sobre la vida diaria.

Stem-and-leaf plot A stem-and-leaf plot is a graph that uses the digits of each number to show the data distribution. Each data item is broken into a stem and into a leaf. The leaf is the last digit of the data value. The stem is the other digit or digits of the data value.

Complot de tallo y hoja Un complot del tallo y la hoja es un gráfico que utiliza los dígitos de cada número para mostrar la distribución de datos. Cada artículo de datos es roto en un tallo y en una hoja. La hoja es el último dígito de los datos valora. El tallo es el otro dígito o los dígitos de los datos valoran.

Stored-value card A stored-value card is a prepaid card electronically coded to be worth a specified amount of money.

Tarjeta de almacenado-valor Una tarjeta del almacenado-valor es una tarjeta pagada por adelantado codificó electrónicamente valer una cantidad especificado de dinero.

English/Spanish Glossary

Straight angle A straight angle is an angle with a measure of 180°.

Ángulo llano Un ángulo llano es un ángulo que mide 180°.

Student loan A student loan provides money to a student to pay for college. The student needs to repay the loan after leaving college. Often the student will need to pay interest on the amount of the loan.

Crédito personal para estudiantes Un crédito personal para estudiantes le proporciona dinero a un estudiante para pagar por el colegio. El estudiante debe devolver el préstamo después de dejar el colegio. A menudo el estudiante deberá pagar interés en la cantidad del préstamo.

Subject Each member in a sample is a subject.

Sujeto Cada miembro de una muestra es un sujeto.

Sum The sum is the answer to an addition problem.

Suma o total La suma o total es el resultado de una operación de suma.

Summarize To summarize an explanation or solution, go over or review the most important points.

Resumir Para resumir una explicación o solución, revisa o repasa los puntos más importantes.

Supplementary angles Two angles are supplementary angles if the sum of their measures is 180°. Supplementary angles that are adjacent form a straight angle.

Ángulos suplementarios Dos ángulos son suplementarios si la suma de sus medidas es 180°. Los ángulos suplementarios que son adyacentes forman un ángulo llano.

Surface area of a cone The surface area of a cone is the sum of the lateral area and the area of the base. The formula for the surface area of a cone is S.A. = L.A. + B.

Área total de un cono El área total de un cono es la suma del área lateral y el área de la base. La fórmula del área total de un cono es A.T. = A.L. + B.

English/Spanish Glossary

Surface area of a cube The surface area of a cube is the sum of the areas of the faces of the cube. The formula for the surface area, S.A., of a cube is S.A. $= 6s^2$, where s represents the length of an edge of the cube.

Área total de un cubo El área total de un cubo es la suma de las áreas de las caras del cubo. La fórmula del área total, A.T., de un cubo es A.T. $= 6s^2$, donde s representa la longitud de una arista del cubo.

Surface area of a cylinder The surface area of a cylinder is the sum of the lateral area and the areas of the two circular bases. The formula for the surface area of a cylinder is S.A. $=$ L.A. $+ 2B$, where L.A. represents the lateral area of the cylinder and B represents the area of a base of the cylinder.

Área total de un cilindro El área total de un cilindro es la suma del área lateral y las áreas de las dos bases circulares. La fórmula del área total de un cilindro es A.T. $=$ A.L. $+ 2B$, donde A.L. representa el área lateral del cilindro y B representa el área de una base del cilindro.

Surface area of a pyramid The surface area of a pyramid is the sum of the areas of the faces of the pyramid. The formula for the surface area, S.A., of a pyramid is S.A. $=$ L.A. $+ B$, where L.A. represents the lateral area of the pyramid and B represents the area of the base of the pyramid.

Área total de una pirámide El área total de una pirámide es la suma de las áreas de las caras de la pirámide. La fórmula del área total, A.T., de una pirámide es A.T. $=$ A.L. $+ B$, donde A.L. representa el área lateral de la pirámide y B representa el área de la base de la pirámide.

Surface area of a sphere The surface area of a sphere is equal to the lateral area of a cylinder that has the same radius, r, and height $2r$. The formula for the surface area of a sphere is S.A. $= 4\pi r^2$, where r represents the radius of the sphere.

Área total de una esfera El área total de una esfera es igual al área lateral de un cilindro que tiene el mismo radio, r, y una altura de $2r$. La fórmula del área total de una esfera es A.T. $= 4\pi r^2$, donde r representa el radio de la esfera.

Surface area of a three-dimensional figure The surface area of a three-dimensional figure is the sum of the areas of its faces. You can find the surface area by finding the area of the net of the three-dimensional figure.

Área total de una figura tridimensional El área total de una figura tridimensional es la suma de las áreas de sus caras. Puedes hallar el área total si hallas el área del modelo plano de la figura tridimensional.

English/Spanish Glossary

System of linear equations A system of linear equations is formed by two or more linear equations that use the same variables.

Sistema de ecuaciones lineales Un sistema de ecuaciones lineales está formado por dos o más ecuaciones lineales que usan las mismas variables.

Systematic sampling Systematic sampling is a sampling method in which you choose every nth member of the population, where n is a predetermined number. A systematic sample is useful when the researcher is able to approach the population in a systematic, or methodical, way.

Muestreo sistemático El muestreo sistemático es un método de muestreo en el que se escoge cada enésimo miembro de la población, donde n es un número predeterminado. Una muestra sistemática es útil cuando el investigador puede enfocarse en la población de manera sistemática o metódica.

T

Taxable wages For federal income tax purposes, your taxable wages are the difference between your earned wages and your withholding allowance. Your employer divides your withholding allowance equally among the pay periods of one year.

Sueldos imponibles Para propósitos federales de impuesto de renta, sus sueldos imponibles son la diferencia entre sus sueldos ganados y su concesión que retienen. Su empleador divide su concesión que retiene igualmente entre los períodos de paga de un año.

Tenths One tenth is one out of ten equal parts of a whole.

Décimas Una décima es 1 de 10 partes iguales de un todo.

Term A term is a number, a variable, or the product of a number and one or more variables.

Término Un término es un número, una variable o el producto de un número y una o más variables.

Terminating decimal A terminating decimal has a decimal expansion that terminates in 0.

Decimal finito Un decimal finito tiene una expansión decimal que termina en 0.

English/Spanish Glossary

Terms of a ratio The terms of a ratio are the quantities *x* and *y* in the ratio.

Términos de una razón Los términos de una razón son la cantidad *x* y la cantidad *y* de la razón.

Theorem A theorem is a conjecture that is proven.

Teorema Un teorema es una conjetura que se ha comprobado.

Theoretical probability When all outcomes of an action are equally likely, $P(\text{event}) = \dfrac{\text{number of favourable outcomes}}{\text{number of possible outcomes}}$.

Probabilidad teórica Cuando todos los resultados de una acción son igualmente probables, $P(\text{evento}) = \dfrac{\text{número de resultados favorables}}{\text{número de resultados posibles}}$.

Third quartile For an ordered set of data, the third quartile is the median of the upper half of the data set.

Tercer cuartil Para un conjunto de datos ordenados, el tercer cuartil es la mediana de la mitad superior del conjunto de datos.

Thousandths One thousandth is one part of 1,000 equal parts of a whole.

Milésimas Una milésima es 1 de 1,000 partes iguales de un todo.

Three-dimensional figure A three-dimensional (3-D) figure is a figure that does not lie in a plane.

Figura tridimensional Una figura tridimensional es una figura que no está en un plano.

Total cost of a loan The total cost of a loan is the total amount spent to repay the loan. Total cost includes the principal and all interest paid over the length of the loan. Total cost also includes any fees charged.

El coste total de un préstamo El coste total de un préstamo es el cantidad total que es gastado para devolver el préstamo. El coste total incluye al director y todo el interés pagó sobre la longitud del préstamo. El coste total también incluye cualquier honorario cargado.

Transaction A banking transaction moves money into or out of a bank account.

Transacción Una transacción bancaria mueve dinero en o fuera de una cuenta bancaria.

English/Spanish Glossary

Transfer A transaction that moves money from one bank account to another is a transfer. The balance of one account increases by the same amount the other account decreases.

Transferencia Una transacción que mueve dinero de una cuenta bancaria a otro es una transferencia. El equilibrio de un aumentos de cuenta por la misma cantidad que la otra cuenta disminuye.

Transformation A transformation is a change in position, shape, or size of a figure. Three types of transformations that change position only are translations, reflections, and rotations.

Transformación Una transformación es un cambio en la posición, la forma o el tamaño de una figura. Tres tipos de transformaciones que cambian sólo la posición son las traslaciones, las reflexiones y las rotaciones.

Translation A translation, or slide, is a rigid motion that moves every point of a figure the same distance and in the same direction.

Traslación Una traslación, o deslizamiento, es un movimiento rígido que mueve cada punto de una figura a la misma distancia y en la misma dirección.

Transversal A transversal is a line that intersects two or more lines at different points.

Transversal o secante Una transversal o secante es una línea que interseca dos o más líneas en distintos puntos.

Trapezoid A trapezoid is a quadrilateral with exactly one pair of parallel sides.

Trapecio Un trapecio es un cuadrilátero que tiene exactamente un par de lados paralelos.

Trend line A trend line is a line on a scatter plot, drawn near the points, that approximates the association between the data sets.

Línea de tendencia Una línea de tendencia es una línea en un diagrama de dispersión, trazada cerca de los puntos, que se aproxima a la relación entre los conjuntos de datos.

Trial In a probability experiment, you carry out or observe an action repeatedly. Each observation of the action is a trial.

Prueba En un experimento de probabilidad, realizas u observas una acción varias veces. Cada observación de la acción es una prueba.

Triangle A triangle is a polygon with three sides.

Triángulo Un triángulo es un polígono de tres lados.

English/Spanish Glossary

Triangular prism A triangular prism is a prism with bases in the shape of a triangle.

Prisma triangular Un prisma triangular es un prisma cuyas bases tienen la forma de un triángulo.

True equation A true equation has equal values on each side of the equals sign.

Ecuación verdadera En una ecuación verdadera, los valores a ambos lados del signo igual son iguales.

Two-way frequency table A two-way frequency table displays the counts of the data in each group.

Tabla de frecuencia con dos variables Una tabla de frecuencia con dos variables muestra el conteo de los datos de cada grupo.

Two-way relative frequency table A two-way relative frequency table shows the ratio of the number of data in each group to the size of the population. The relative frequencies can be calculated with respect to the entire population, the row populations, or the column populations. The relative frequencies can be expressed as fractions, decimals, or percents.

Tabla de frecuencias relativas con dos variables Una tabla de frecuencias relativas con dos variables muestra la razón del número de datos de cada grupo al tamaño de la población. Las frecuencias relativas se pueden calcular respecto de la población entera, las poblaciones de las filas o las poblaciones de las columnas. Las frecuencias relativas se pueden expresar como fracciones, decimales o porcentajes.

Two-way table A two-way table shows bivariate categorical data for a population.

Tabla con dos variables Una tabla con dos variables muestra datos bivariados por categorías de una población.

U

Uniform probability model A uniform probability model is a probability model based on using the theoretical probability of equally likely outcomes.

Modelo de probabilidad uniforme Un modelo de probabilidad uniforme es un modelo de probabilidad que se basa en el uso de la probabilidad teórica de resultados igualmente probables.

English/Spanish Glossary

Unit fraction A unit fraction is a fraction with a numerator of 1 and a denominator that is a whole number greater than 1.

Fracción unitaria Una fracción unitaria es una fracción con un numerador 1 y un denominador que es un número entero mayor que 1.

Unit price A unit price is a unit rate that gives the price of one item.

Precio por unidad El precio por unidad es una tasa por unidad que muestra el precio de un artículo.

Unit rate The rate for one unit of a given quantity is called the unit rate.

Tasa por unidad Se llama tasa por unidad a la tasa que corresponde a 1 unidad de una cantidad dada.

Use To use given information, draw on it to help you determine something else.

Usar Para usar una información dada, apóyate en ella para determinar otra cosa.

V

Valid inference A valid inference is an inference that is true about the population. Valid inferences can be made when they are based on data from a representative sample.

Inferencia válida Una inferencia válida es una inferencia verdadera acerca de una población. Se pueden hacer inferencias válidas si están basadas en los datos de una muestra representativa.

Variability Variability describes how much the items in a data set differ (or vary) from each other. On a data display, variability is shown by how much the data on the horizontal scale are spread out.

Variabilidad La variabilidad describe qué diferencia (o variación) existe entre los elementos de un conjunto de datos. Al exhibir datos, la variabilidad queda representada por la distancia que separa los datos en la escala horizontal.

Variable A variable is a letter that represents an unknown value.

Variable Una variable es una letra que representa un valor desconocido.

Variable expenses Variable expenses are expenses that change from one budget period to the next.

Gastos variables Los gastos variables son los gastos que cambian de un período económico al próximo.

English/Spanish Glossary

Vertex of a cone The vertex of a cone is the point farthest from the base.

Vértice de un cono El vértice de un cono es el punto más alejado de la base.

Vertex of a polygon The vertex of a polygon is any point where two sides of a polygon meet.

Vértice de un polígono El vértice de un polígono es cualquier punto donde se encuentran dos lados de un polígono.

Vertex of a three-dimensional figure A vertex of a three-dimensional figure is a point where three or more edges meet.

Vértice de una figura tridimensional El vértice de una figura tridimensional es un punto donde se unen tres o más aristas.

Vertex of an angle The vertex of an angle is the point of intersection of the rays that make up the sides of the angle.

Vértice de un ángulo El vértice de un ángulo es el punto de intersección de las semirrectas que forman los lados del ángulo.

Vertical angles Vertical angles are formed by two intersecting lines and are opposite each other. Vertical angles have equal measures.

Ángulos opuestos por el vértice Los ángulos opuestos por el vértice están formados por dos rectas secantes y están uno frente a otro. Los ángulos opuestos por el vértice tienen la misma medida.

Vertical-line test The vertical-line test is a method used to determine if a relation is a function or not. If a vertical line passes through a graph more than once, the graph is not the graph of a function.

Prueba de recta vertical La prueba de recta vertical es un método que se usa para determinar si una relación es una función o no. Si una recta vertical atraviesa la gráfica más de una vez, la gráfica no es la gráfica de una función.

Volume Volume is the number of cubic units needed to fill a solid figure.

Volumen El volumen es el número de unidades cúbicas que se necesitan para llenar un cuerpo geométrico.

English/Spanish Glossary

Volume of a cone The volume of a cone is the number of unit cubes, or cubic units, needed to fill the cone. The formula for the volume of a cone is $V = \frac{1}{3}Bh$, where B represents the area of the base and h represents the height of the cone.

Volumen de un cono El volumen de un cono es el número de bloques de unidades, o unidades cúbicas, que se necesitan para llenar el cono. La fórmula del volumen de un cono $V = \frac{1}{3}Bh$, donde B representa el área de la base y h representa la altura del cono.

Volume of a cube The volume of a cube is the number of unit cubes, or cubic units, needed to fill the cube. The formula for the volume V of a cube is $V = s^3$, where s represents the length of an edge of the cube.

Volumen de un cubo El volumen de un cubo es el número de bloques de unidades, o unidades cúbicas, que se necesitan para llenar el cubo. La fórmula del volumen, V, de un cubo es $V = s^3$, donde s representa la longitud de una arista del cubo.

Volume of a cylinder The volume of a cylinder is the number of unit cubes, or cubic units, needed to fill the cylinder. The formula for the volume of a cylinder is $V = \pi r^2 h$, where r represents the radius of a base and h represents the height of the cylinder.

Volumen de un cilindro El volumen de un cilindro es el número de bloques de unidades, o unidades cúbicas, que se necesitan para llenar el cilindro. La fórmula del volumen de un cilindro es $V = \pi r^2 h$, donde r representa el radio de una base y h representa la altura del cilindro.

Volume of a prism The volume of a prism is the number of unit cubes, or cubic units, needed to fill the prism. The formula for the volume V of a prism is $V = Bh$, where B represents the area of a base and h represents the height of the prism.

Volumen de un prisma El volumen de un prisma es el número de bloques de unidades, o unidades cúbicas, que se necesitan para llenar el prisma. La fórmula del volumen, V, de un prisma $V = Bh$, donde B representa el área de una base y h representa la altura del prisma.

Volume of a pyramid The volume of a pyramid is the number of unit cubes needed to fill the pyramid. The formula for the volume V of a pyramid is $V = \frac{1}{3}Bh$, where B represents the area of the base and h represents the height of the pyramid.

Volumen de una pirámide El volumen de una pirámide es el número de bloques de unidades, o unidades cúbicas, que se necesitan para llenar la pirámide. La fórmula del volumen, V, de una pirámide es $V = \frac{1}{3}Bh$, donde B representa el área de la base y h representa la altura de la pirámide.

English/Spanish Glossary

Volume of a sphere The volume of a sphere is the number of unit cubes, or cubic units, needed to fill the sphere. The formula for the volume of a sphere is $V = \frac{4}{3}\pi r^3$.

Volumen de una esfera El volumen de una esfera es el número de bloques de unidades, o unidades cúbicas, que se necesitan para llenar la esfera. La fórmula del volumen de una esfera es $V = \frac{4}{3}\pi r^3$.

W

Whole numbers The whole numbers consist of the number 0 and all of the natural numbers.

Números enteros no negativos Los números enteros no negativos son el número 0 y todos los números naturales.

Withdrawal A transaction that takes money out of a bank account is a withdrawal.

Retirada Una transacción que toma dinero fuera de una cuenta bancaria es una retirada.

Withholding allowance You can exclude a portion of your earned wages, called a withholding allowance, from federal income tax. You can claim one withholding allowance for yourself and one for each person dependent upon your income.

Retener concesión Puede excluir una porción de sus sueldos ganados, llamó una concesión que retiene, del impuesto de renta federal. Puede reclamar una concesión que retiene para usted mismo y para uno para cada dependiente de persona sobre sus ingresos.

Word form of a number The word form of a number is the number written in words.

Número en palabras Un número en palabras es un número escrito con palabras en lugar de dígitos.

Work-Study Work-study is a type of need-based aid that schools might offer to a student. A student must earn work-study money by working certain jobs.

Práctica estudiantil La práctica estudiantil es un tipo de ayuda necesidad-basado que escuelas quizás ofrezcan a un estudiante. Un estudiante debe ganar dinero de práctica estudiantil por ciertos trabajos de trabajo.

English/Spanish Glossary

X

x-axis The x-axis is the horizontal number line that, together with the y-axis, forms the coordinate plane.

Eje de las x El eje de las x es la recta numérica horizontal que, junto con el eje de las y, forma el plano de coordenadas.

x-coordinate The x-coordinate is the first number in an ordered pair. It tells the number of horizontal units a point is from 0.

Coordenada x La coordenada x (abscisa) es el primer número de un par ordenado. Indica cuántas unidades horizontales hay entre un punto y 0.

Y

y-axis The y-axis is the vertical number line that, together with the x-axis, forms the coordinate plane.

Eje de las y El eje de las y es la recta numérica vertical que, junto con el eje de las x, forma el plano de coordenadas.

y-coordinate The y-coordinate is the second number in an ordered pair. It tells the number of vertical units a point is from 0.

Coordenada y La coordenada y (ordenada) es el segundo número de un par ordenado. Indica cuántas unidades verticales hay entre un punto y 0.

y-intercept The y-intercept of a line is the y-coordinate of the point where the line crosses the y-axis.

Intercepto en y El intercepto en y de una recta es la coordenada y del punto por donde la recta cruza el eje de las y.

Z

Zero exponent property For any nonzero number a, $a^0 = 1$.

Propiedad del exponente cero Para cualquier número distinto de cero a, $a^0 = 1$.

Zero Property of Multiplication The product of 0 and any number is 0. For any number n, $n \cdot 0 = 0$ and $0 \cdot n = 0$.

Propiedad del cero en la multiplicación El producto de 0 y cualquier número es 0. Para cualquier número n, $n \cdot 0 = 0$ and $0 \cdot n = 0$.

Formulas

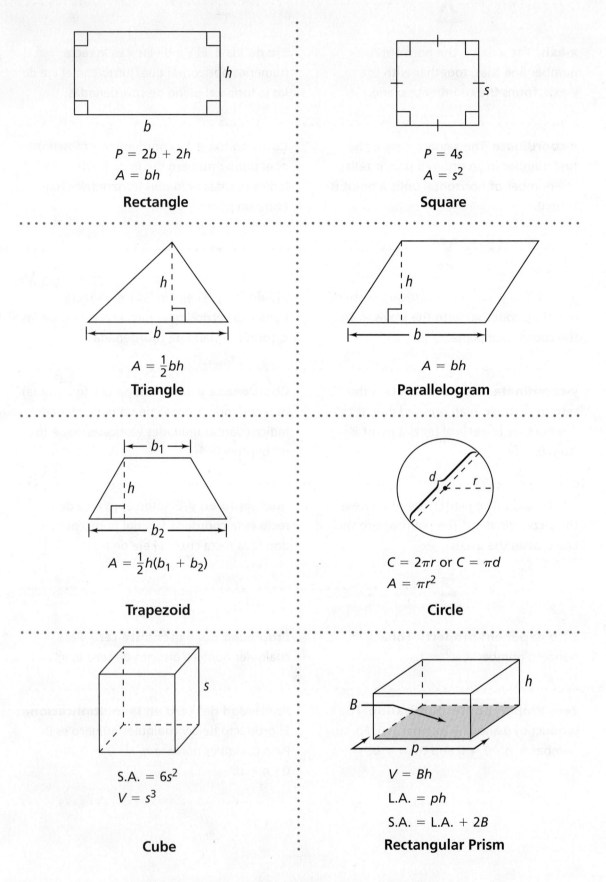

$P = 2b + 2h$
$A = bh$

Rectangle

$P = 4s$
$A = s^2$

Square

$A = \frac{1}{2}bh$

Triangle

$A = bh$

Parallelogram

$A = \frac{1}{2}h(b_1 + b_2)$

Trapezoid

$C = 2\pi r$ or $C = \pi d$
$A = \pi r^2$

Circle

S.A. $= 6s^2$
$V = s^3$

Cube

$V = Bh$
L.A. $= ph$
S.A. $=$ L.A. $+ 2B$

Rectangular Prism

Formulas

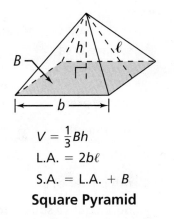

$V = \frac{1}{3}Bh$

L.A. $= 2b\ell$

S.A. $=$ L.A. $+ B$

Square Pyramid

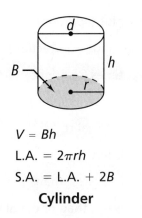

$V = Bh$

L.A. $= 2\pi rh$

S.A. $=$ L.A. $+ 2B$

Cylinder

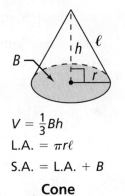

$V = \frac{1}{3}Bh$

L.A. $= \pi r\ell$

S.A. $=$ L.A. $+ B$

Cone

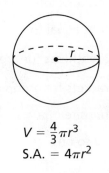

$V = \frac{4}{3}\pi r^3$

S.A. $= 4\pi r^2$

Sphere

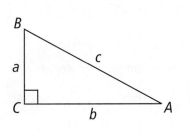

$a^2 + b^2 = c^2$

Pythagorean Theorem

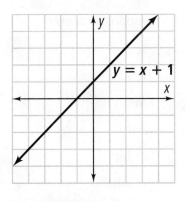

$y = x + 1$

$y = mx + b$, where
$m =$ slope and
$b = y$-intercept

Equation of Line

Math Symbols

$+$	plus (addition)		r	radius
$-$	minus (subtraction)		S.A.	surface area
$\times$, $\cdot$	times (multiplication)		B	area of base
$\div$, $\overline{)}$, $\frac{a}{b}$	divide (division)		L.A.	lateral area
$=$	is equal to		ℓ	slant height
$<$	is less than		V	volume
$>$	is greater than		a^n	nth power of a
$\leq$	is less than or equal to		$\sqrt{x}$	nonnegative square root of x
$\geq$	is greater than or equal to		π	pi, an irrational number approximately equal to 3.14
$\neq$	is not equal to			
$(\ )$	parentheses for grouping		(a, b)	ordered pair with x-coordinate a and y-coordinate b
$[\ ]$	brackets for grouping			
$-a$	opposite of a		$\overline{AB}$	segment AB
$\ldots$	and so on		A'	image of A, A prime
$^\circ$	degrees		$\triangle ABC$	triangle with vertices A, B, and C
$|a|$	absolute value of a			
$\overset{?}{=}$, $\overset{?}{<}$, $\overset{?}{>}$	Is the statement true?		$\rightarrow$	arrow notation
$\approx$	is approximately equal to		$a : b$, $\frac{a}{b}$	ratio of a to b
$\frac{b}{a}$	reciprocal of $\frac{a}{b}$		$\cong$	is congruent to
A	area		$\sim$	is similar to
ℓ	length		$\angle A$	angle with vertex A
w	width		AB	length of segment $\overline{AB}$
h	height		$\overrightarrow{AB}$	ray AB
d	distance		$\angle ABC$	angle formed by $\overrightarrow{BA}$ and $\overrightarrow{BC}$
r	rate		$m\angle ABC$	measure of angle ABC
t	time		$\perp$	is perpendicular to
P	perimeter		$\overleftrightarrow{AB}$	line AB
b	base length		$\parallel$	is parallel to
C	circumference		$\%$	percent
d	diameter		P (event)	probability of an event

Measures

Customary	Metric
Length	**Length**
1 foot (ft) = 12 inches (in.) 1 yard (yd) = 36 in. 1 yd = 3 ft 1 mile (mi) = 5,280 ft 1 mi = 1,760 yd	1 centimeter (cm) = 10 millimeters (mm) 1 meter (m) = 100 cm 1 kilometer (km) = 1,000 m 1 mm = 0.001 m
Area	**Area**
1 square foot (ft^2) = 144 square inches (in.^{2}) 1 square yard (yd^2) = 9 ft^2 1 square mile (mi^2) = 640 acres	1 square centimeter (cm^2) = 100 square millimeters (mm^2) 1 square meter (m^2) = 10,000 cm^2
Volume	**Volume**
1 cubic foot (ft^3) = 1,728 cubic inches (in.^{3}) 1 cubic yard (yd^3) = 27 ft^3	1 cubic centimeter (cm^3) = 1,000 cubic millimeters (mm^3) 1 cubic meter (m^3) = 1,000,000 cm^3
Mass	**Mass**
1 pound (lb) = 16 ounces (oz) 1 ton (t) = 2,000 lb	1 gram (g) = 1,000 milligrams (mg) 1 kilogram (kg) = 1,000 g
Capacity	**Capacity**
1 cup (c) = 8 fluid ounces (fl oz) 1 pint (pt) = 2 c 1 quart (qt) = 2 pt 1 gallon (gal) = 4 qt	1 liter (L) = 1,000 milliliters (mL) 1000 liters = 1 kiloliter (kL)

Customary Units and Metric Units	
Length	1 in. = 2.54 cm 1 mi $\approx$ 1.61 km 1 ft $\approx$ 0.3 m
Capacity	1 qt $\approx$ 0.94 L
Weight and Mass	1 oz $\approx$ 28.3 g 1 lb $\approx$ 0.45 kg

Properties

Unless otherwise stated, the variables a, b, c, m, and n used in these properties can be replaced with any number represented on a number line.

Identity Properties
Addition $\qquad n + 0 = n$ and $0 + n = n$

Multiplication $\quad n \cdot 1 = n$ and $1 \cdot n = n$

Commutative Properties
Addition $\qquad a + b = b + a$

Multiplication $\quad a \cdot b = b \cdot a$

Associative Properties
Addition $\qquad (a + b) + c = a + (b + c)$

Multiplication $\quad (a \cdot b) \cdot c = a \cdot (b \cdot c)$

Inverse Properties
Addition

$a + (-a) = 0$ and $-a + a = 0$

Multiplication

$a \cdot \frac{1}{a} = 1$ and $\frac{1}{a} \cdot a = 1$, $(a \neq 0)$

Distributive Properties
$a(b + c) = ab + ac \qquad (b + c)a = ba + ca$

$a(b - c) = ab - ac \qquad (b - c)a = ba - ca$

Properties of Equality
Addition $\qquad$ If $a = b$,

$\qquad$ then $a + c = b + c$.

Subtraction $\quad$ If $a = b$,

$\qquad$ then $a - c = b - c$.

Multiplication If $a = b$,

$\qquad$ then $a \cdot c = b \cdot c$.

Division $\qquad$ If $a = b$, and $c \neq 0$,

$\qquad$ then $\frac{a}{c} = \frac{b}{c}$.

Substitution $\quad$ If $a = b$, then b can

$\qquad$ replace a in any

$\qquad$ expression.

Zero Property
$a \cdot 0 = 0$ and $0 \cdot a = 0$.

Properties of Inequality
Addition $\qquad$ If $a > b$,

$\qquad$ then $a + c > b + c$.

$\qquad$ If $a < b$,

$\qquad$ then $a + c < b + c$.

Subtraction $\quad$ If $a > b$,

$\qquad$ then $a - c > b - c$.

$\qquad$ If $a < b$,

$\qquad$ then $a - c < b - c$.

Multiplication

If $a > b$ and $c > 0$, then $ac > bc$.

If $a < b$ and $c > 0$, then $ac < bc$.

If $a > b$ and $c < 0$, then $ac < bc$.

If $a < b$ and $c < 0$, then $ac > bc$.

Division

If $a > b$ and $c > 0$, then $\frac{a}{c} > \frac{b}{c}$.

If $a < b$ and $c > 0$, then $\frac{a}{c} < \frac{b}{c}$.

If $a > b$ and $c < 0$, then $\frac{a}{c} < \frac{b}{c}$.

If $a < b$ and $c < 0$, then $\frac{a}{c} > \frac{b}{c}$.

Properties of Exponents
For any nonzero number n and any integers m and n:

Zero Exponent $\qquad a^0 = 1$

Negative Exponent $\quad a^{-n} = \frac{1}{a^n}$

Product of Powers $\quad a^m \cdot a^n = a^{m+n}$

Power of a Product $\quad (ab)^n = a^n b^n$

Quotient of Powers $\quad \frac{a^m}{a^n} = a^{m-n}$

Power of a Quotient $\quad \left(\frac{a}{b}\right)^n = \frac{a^n}{b^n}$

Power of a Power $\qquad (a^m)^n = a^{mn}$